ICED IN

ICED IN

Ten Days Trapped on the Edge of Antarctica

CHRIS TURNEY

CITADEL PRESS
Kensington Publishing Corp.
www.kensingtonbooks.com

CITADEL PRESS BOOKS are published by

Kensington Publishing Corp.
119 West 40th Street
New York, NY 10018

Published in Australia in August 2017 by Penguin Random House Australia, under the title *Unshackled*. Published by Citadel Press in arrangement with the author.

All Kensington titles, imprints, and distributed lines are available at special quantity discounts for bulk purchases for sales promotions, premiums, fund-raising, educational, or institutional use.

Special book excerpts or customized printings can also be created to fit specific needs. For details, write or phone the office of the Kensington sales manager: Kensington Publishing Corp., 119 West 40th Street, New York, NY 10018, attn: Sales Department; phone 1-800-221-2647.

CITADEL PRESS and the Citadel logo are Reg. U.S. Pat. & TM Off.

ISBN-13: 978-0-8065-3852-5
ISBN-10: 0-8065-3852-X

First Citadel hardcover printing: October 2017

10 9 8 7 6 5 4 3 2 1

Printed in the United States of America

Library of Congress CIP data is available.

First electronic edition: October 2017

ISBN-13: 978-0-8065-3854-9
ISBN-10: 0-8065-3854-6

To the extraordinary members of the
Australasian Antarctic Expedition 2013–2014
and the wonderful crews of the *Akademik Shokalskiy*,
the *Xue Long*, the *Aurora Australis,* and the *Astrolabe.*

Thank you.

There seems to be a wide-spread idea that the work of exploration is virtually finished . . . The "race" is over: ergo the work of exploration is done. No more foolish mistake could be made, and none more disastrous in its consequences.
—SIR ERNEST SHACKLETON (1874–1922)

If we teach only the findings and products of science—no matter how useful and inspiring they may be—without communicating its critical method, how can the average person possibly distinguish science from pseudoscience?
—CARL SAGAN (1934–1996)

AUTHOR'S NOTE

All distances are expressed in nautical miles. One nautical mile is equal to 1.151 statute miles or 1.852 kilometers. A "knot" describes the number of nautical miles traveled in an hour. All currency is expressed in Australian dollars unless stated otherwise.

CONTENTS

A Century of Antarctic Exploration

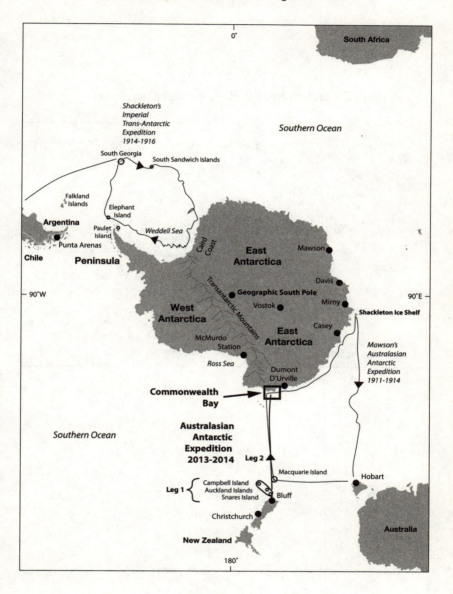

Commonwealth Bay, East Antarctica

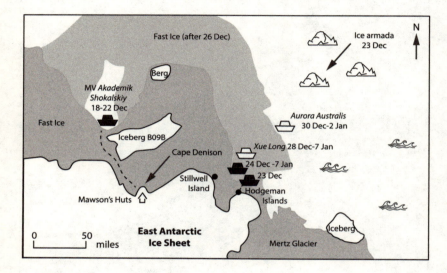

ICED IN

PROLOGUE

We're on our own.

Just thinking the words scares me.

I'm standing alone on a windswept deck looking out over the Antarctic coastline and the wildest landscape I have ever seen. We're over 1,400 miles from civilization, and things don't look good.

Our ship, MV *Akademik Shokalskiy,* has spent the last four weeks fighting the stormiest seas on our planet. For four weeks, I've shared our small vessel with seventy-one other souls, leading a scientific expedition to study this extreme environment. Arriving at the edge of the continent, we successfully crossed thirty-five miles of sea ice to reach a hundred-year-old wooden Antarctic base, a time capsule from the Edwardian age, to complete research the first polar scientists could only have dreamed of. With the science program nearly done, we took the *Shokalskiy* round to the east for one final piece of work. We finished yesterday and, flushed with success, were heading home.

Now we're surrounded by ice . . . lots of ice.

I'm struggling to understand what's happened. Just a few days ago, we sailed these same waters, an area that satellite imagery showed was free of ice. We passed some patches forming on the freezing surface, but nothing to be concerned about. Now we're hemmed in by slabs of ice, some measuring ten feet thick, their immense size signifying they've formed over several winters. The amount of ice smacks of a catastrophic realignment up the coast, somewhere out to the east. Shattered by strong winds or broken up by rising temperatures, the ice has swept out to sea and into our path, too fast for us to dodge.

History is repeating itself. The expeditions of a century ago returned from the Antarctic with tales of adventure, tragedy, heroism . . . and sea ice. Sea ice was the villain of the south; the single greatest reason for lost lives and ships. No vessel was free of the risk, even at the height of summer. And no one experienced it worse than the great explorer Ernest Shackleton, who in 1915 lost his ship, the *Endurance*, to the crushing pressure of pack ice.

I search the horizon through my binoculars, looking for anything that might hint at a route to open water and freedom. The explorers of old like Shackleton learned that ominous dark skies promised open water reflecting on the clouds above, but the nearest "water sky" is two to four miles away. It may as well be a hundred. My freezing breath condenses on the lenses. I rub them clear with my gloves and look again.

Nothing breaks. There's ice as far as the eye can see.

I look at the weathervane overhead. It remains stubbornly fixed on the southeast, and the frenetic spinning of the wind cups shows no let-up on the forty knots we've had all day. Huge slabs of ice jostle for position around the ship. If only the wind would ease off, or better still, change direction, it might loosen the pack and give us a chance to get out of here.

In the frigid wind, I catch a distant laugh from below decks.

It's Christmas Eve 2013. All over the boat, decorations have been put up. Flashing lights adorn the corridors, tinsel hangs around the dining room and banners flutter from the ceilings.

We've even brought two green plastic Christmas trees, already sheltering a pile of presents for tomorrow. There's concern aboard but hopefully we'll be moving again soon.

I lower my binoculars and turn to join the party below.

Six hours later, I wake and sense something is wrong. I lie still for a moment, wondering. Then I realize: the *Shokalskiy*'s quiet. The constant throb of our ship's engines has stopped.

I scramble out of bed and throw on some clothes.

This is bad. This is very, very bad.

I grab my down jacket and leap up the stairs to the ship's bridge. It's half past five in the morning, and most of the expedition team are still in their cabins.

But up on the bridge there's a frenzy of activity. Several Russian crew members, led by the captain, Igor Kiselev, are checking screens and poring over maps. His strained face says it all. It's clear Igor has been up for hours. A native of Vladivostok, white-haired, stocky, and a polar veteran of over thirty years, he is normally bullish. Not this morning. A gruff "Morning" in his strong Russian accent indicates all is not well.

"Chris, we have problem."

"How bad is it?"

"No way out." He sweeps his arm toward the windows and horizon beyond.

I look aghast at the scene before me. The ice has closed up even more. What little water was visible last night has disappeared, replaced by thick, tightly packed blocks of ice that slam into each other, thrusting chaotically into the air.

I look at the navigation monitor, and my stomach knots. The path of the *Shokalskiy* is plotting automatically on the screen. The rudder is blocked and with the engines turned off, our vessel has no steerage; the wind is pushing us, with the pack ice, toward the coast. The rocky outcrops lie just a few nautical miles off the port side. It's like a car crash in slow motion. Unless the wind changes or the ice packs in hard enough between us and the shore, there's nothing we can do to avoid being thrown against the continent. The ship will be smashed to pieces, and we'll have to evacuate everyone on board.

But even more alarmingly, two towering icebergs, each weighing some 80,000 tons, are moving at a great pace off the starboard side. The arrival of icebergs on the scene is a different threat altogether. In contrast to pack ice, which forms in the ocean, icebergs originate from the continent, shed by glaciers and ice sheets, and are far larger. They can extend hundreds of feet into the deep, where they're steered by ocean currents. There they can pick up speeds of two to three knots, ripping through ordinary sea ice and anything else in their path, often in a completely different direction to the prevailing wind. If these icebergs set a trajectory for our 2,300-ton ship, they could be upon us within a couple of hours. There won't be much time for an evacuation; we'll barely have time to get everyone off the stricken vessel before it's crushed to pieces.

And then Igor gives me the bad news: A tower of ice has pierced the ship during the night, ripping a three-foot hole in the hull, threatening one of the water-ballast tanks. The destruction of the *Shokalskiy* has already begun.

I stifle rising panic as Igor pulls out the latest weather charts and spreads them on the table. The tightly packed pressure bars and thick arrows all point to an approaching blizzard and persistent winds from the southeast.

Igor flicks over the page to recent forecasts for the next few days. "No relief."

I reel at the news. We have to get help, and we have to get it fast. I stagger back toward my cabin, numb. This can't be happening.

The trials of past endeavors conjure up the worst possible scenarios in my mind. Shackleton and his men were stuck in the ice for two years. A thousand miles from civilization, they faced isolation, starvation, freezing temperatures, gangrene, wandering icebergs, and the threat of cannibalism. But by sheer positive attitude and superb leadership, the Anglo-Irishman kept his team together and returned everyone home. No matter how bad conditions became, Shackleton never lost a single life.

But there's a difference between him and me, I think, as I open the door to my cabin and see my wife Annette, fifteen-year-old daughter Cara and twelve-year-old son Robert sitting at the table, smiling and laughing, waiting to open their Christmas presents.

Shackleton didn't have his family with him.

PART I
HEADING SOUTH

CHAPTER ONE
The Big Picture

Late January 2013, I was pacing outside my home, the warmth of the Australian summer sun beating down on my face. It was a glorious day, perfect for the beach. Hordes of Sydneysiders had driven the hour down the coast to Austinmer. After parking along the street, young and old struggled by our house under bright mountains of towels, buckets, spades, and inflatables, eager to stake their claim in the sand. Some gave me a glance as they passed by, hearing me speaking loudly into a phone the size of a brick. I couldn't help but wish I were joining them.

I was starting to lose patience. I'd been cut off three times already. The thermometer was hitting over 100°F, and I wanted to get in the sea and cool off.

Things weren't helped by the howling blizzard at the other end of the phone line.

Finally, I got a decent connection. "Chris? Chris? Can you hear me? Annette's had a brilliant idea for our expedition."

I was speaking to my friend and fellow scientist, Chris Fogwill. Chris and I have been mates for years, built on a mutual love of the outdoors. We met in the U.K. when we were appointed to the same university to teach Earth sciences. In years

gone by, we might have been described as geologists or environmental scientists, but it's both these and more. Earth science
takes a complete view of our planet; it pulls together different
disciplines to try to get a better understanding of how our world
works. Earth science isn't just interested in what's below our
feet and why it's there, but looks at how geology, the air, oceans,
ice and life itself are all connected. *How quickly do melting ice
sheets raise sea level? What impact do volcanic eruptions have
on the carbon cycle? If the planet's wind belts get stronger, what
happens to the ocean currents?* Earth science makes links and
answers questions that a single discipline struggles to tackle.

Both Chris and I soon realized we had a shared passion for
using our planet's history to improve predictions of future climate; something that's badly hindered by the century-long
weather-station records that fail to capture the changes we're
likely to face in the twenty-first century. Unfortunately, Nature
rarely provides easy-to-find clues for what happened before scientific observations began. You need to know where to look.
Our short field trips turned into large expeditions as we worked
around the world with friends, digging into peat bogs, probing
lake sediments, coring trees and drilling ice, searching for evidence of past change. As we delved deeper, we started to piece
together a picture of a planet with a tumultuous past that is
rarely, if ever, stable—where wild swings in climate can happen in
a geological blink of an eye. At a time of such massive environmental change that a new geological epoch—the "Anthropocene"
or Human Age—is being considered seriously by world scientists,
such insights are crucial.

In 2010, I was offered the job of a lifetime: an Australian
Laureate Fellowship, one of the most prestigious scientific posi-
tions available. I was granted five years of funding to host a research team at the University of New South Wales to focus on
these wild swings in climate and what they might mean for the
future. It was the position I had always dreamed of. And at

thirty-six years of age, I was one of the youngest to ever be awarded a Laureate. I couldn't say no. I left the U.K. and managed to convince Chris to join me.

Chris is a brilliant scientist. A world leader in glaciology with over ten years' field experience in Antarctica, he can read the landscape like no one else I've worked with. Chris also has an unerring understanding of what gear a team in the field needs and how to use it. No matter what the terrain, Chris will know what and how much kit we have to get and where to get it. What Chris doesn't know isn't worth knowing.

Six weeks before my call to Chris we'd been working in the Antarctic and had returned home just in time for Christmas. But one of our New Zealand colleagues had been expecting his first child and needed someone to take his place on an expedition departing in the New Year. Chris couldn't resist the opportunity. Now he was holed up in a small pyramid tent in the Transantarctic Mountains with three other guys. Tragically, a plane had just disappeared near their field site and all available aircraft were searching in the vain hope they'd find survivors. Chris was patiently waiting for a helicopter pickup, but the weather had taken a turn for the worse: a blizzard was blowing and everyone was grounded. I was forced to shout down the line to be heard above howling winds and flapping tent sheets.

There really is nowhere bigger or more exciting for an Earth scientist than Antarctica. Lurking in the shadows like a disruptive neighbor, it does its own thing, whatever the consequences to anyone else. Antarctica's been implicated in some of the most extreme and abrupt environmental changes our planet has ever experienced. Catastrophic sea-level rise, massive temperature swings and abrupt shifts in tropical rain belts have all been linked to the southern continent. The challenge is getting there to find the clinching evidence.

Most researchers head to the Antarctic on a government ship, but that's easier said than done. Although there are more than thirty research bases across the region, berths on supply ships and aircraft are fiercely fought over for years in advance. If you're lucky—really lucky—you may get two or three of your team on board. If by some miracle you manage to get a large group south for the whole season, forget about them working anywhere that's not near a national base without years of lead time; the cost of operating in the Antarctic is so high, scientists are encouraged to work as close as possible to a research station. The problem is that with a changing planet, the science questions have changed since the first bases were put up over half a century ago. For the last year, we'd been working on an intoxicating solution: Charter our own vessel and take our own team of scientists to a region where big changes are afoot. It was something that hadn't been attempted for decades.

Before government funding became the main source of support for scientists after the Second World War, most researchers were heavily dependent on finding wealthy benefactors and businesses to finance their work. In Antarctica, the hurdles were even greater. It is a vast expanse of unknown with little, if any, prospect of help if things went wrong. As a result, the cost of kitting out, transporting, and supporting a twenty-plus team of scientists, engineers, cooks, medics, and photographers across the perilous Southern Ocean and off the map for a year or more would have run into the equivalent of tens of millions of dollars today. With national governments hesitant to underwrite what would most likely be a costly affair, many explorer-scientists looked to other means. One of the great early twentieth-century pioneers in this regard was the irrepressible Ernest Shackleton, determined to stake his claim in the history books. Blending a heady mix of adventure, exploration, science, and opportunism, Shackleton sold the idea of Antarctica to whoever would listen. It could be whatever you wanted: your name on the map, a territorial claim, a place on the expedition, a scientific study. Any and all were available to those who had money. Shackleton was

the finest leader Antarctica ever saw, inspiring future genera-
tions of scientists and adventurers alike.

If Chris and I were going to attempt anything like Shackleton, we'd have to recreate some of the excitement he generated
a century ago. A return to some of his best-known stomping
grounds was out of the question though. The Ross Sea and geographic South Pole are home to large research bases today, but
they don't have the combination of past and modern environmental changes we were after. We'd looked at other possibilities: Coats Land, Enderby Land, Wilkes Land—remote parts of
the Antarctic that were the target of Shackleton and his contem-
poraries and are largely forgotten or ignored by government op-
erators today. Unfortunately, none seemed to fit the bill. If we
were to raise the estimated $1.5 million needed to bankroll a
six-week expedition to such a remote part of the world, our destination also had to capture the public's imagination. We had to
have the right blend of science, adventure, and history.

With Chris away in the field, Annette and I had been bouncing ideas, and a magical name had come up.

"How about Cape Denison?"

There was a moment's delay as the satellite hook-up relayed
my message.

Cape Denison holds a special place in the history of Antarctic
exploration. A small outcrop of rocks on the East Antarctic coastline, it is forever associated with one of the most spectacular and
often forgotten tales of survival. A century ago, it was the main
base of operations for one of the great explorers of the south,
trained and mentored by Shackleton himself: the Australian scientist Douglas Mawson. His privately funded science team,
with three bases and one research ship, explored a region the
size of the United States between 1911 and 1914. Mawson's
Australasian Antarctic Expedition team had intended to spend
just one year south, but it was not to be. A sudden turn of events
led to tragedy on the ice, the deaths of two men, allegations of

cannibalism, and, with the return of winter sea ice, an extended stay in Antarctica.

Since Mawson's time, scientists had only infrequently visited Cape Denison. After 2010, these visits all but ceased with the arrival of giant iceberg B09B, which lodged itself on the seabed of the adjacent Commonwealth Bay. The appearance of this monster has dramatically altered the coastline by preventing the summer breakout of sea ice formed in the bay, isolating Cape Denison from the rest of the world. How long B09B will remain in place is uncertain, with suggestions ranging from just a few years to centuries. But more important, no one is sure what impact the massive expansion of sea ice is having on the area. Some scientists have argued that the local penguin population may have collapsed because of the greater distance they have to travel for food. Other studies suggest the extra sea ice could have stopped the formation of salty, dense waters that are a fundamental part of the global ocean circulation system. Paradoxically, the shutdown of what's known as Antarctic Bottom Water may also be allowing warm ocean water to reach the edge of the Antarctic continent deep below, melting the fringing ice sheet under the surface with worrying consequences for sea level. Cape Denison is a place where there's a dizzying number of questions any scientist worth their salt would be itching to tackle.

"Oh, my God, that's genius. It completely fits the bill."

Over the next twenty minutes, we excitedly sketched out a science program. As the procession continued past to the beach in the January heat, Chris and I had the making of our enterprise: The Australasian Antarctic Expedition 2013–2014.

Shackleton described the magnetism of Antarctica as being "drawn away from the trodden paths by the 'lure of the little voices,' the mysterious fascination of the unknown." It gets under your skin like nowhere else on Earth. For a scientist, the unknown is a particularly powerful draw. There are so many questions to be answered, so much to learn. At the turn of the twentieth century, Shackleton and Mawson asked what lay south and how this fitted into what was known of more equable climes. After a century of expeditions, the science questions today are no less profound.

With only 2 percent of the continent exposed as rock, the Antarctic holds around 90 percent of our planet's ice and 70 percent of its freshwater. There's so much water that if all the ice melted we would be left with a large landmass in the East Antarctic, an archipelago of mountains where the West and Peninsula were, and global sea levels nearly 200 feet higher, flooding the likes of Dhaka, New York, Sydney, and London. Where, when, and how much of the Antarctic ice sheets will melt in a warmer world is a major focus of research. Offshore, the surrounding Southern Ocean supports hugely productive ecosystems, many of them economically important, including the krill and Patagonian toothfish fisheries. These ecosystems also play a crucial role in soaking up carbon dioxide from the atmosphere and regulating climate. Just how the ocean, atmosphere, and ice interact to influence the world's climate is hugely uncertain. The Antarctic makes up 7 percent of our planet's surface, yet there have never been enough scientists to tackle it.

As a Laureate Fellow, I was determined to make a contribution to the effort. I wanted to learn just how quickly the Antarctic ice sheets could melt. I had recently published a research paper that suggested stronger winds in the mid-latitudes may have changed how the ocean currents circulate around the continent during periods of high global temperatures. One possibility is that past wind shifts may have brought warmer waters up alongside the edge of the ice sheet, raising sea levels more than twenty feet higher than they are today. But did the Antarctic ice sheets collapse in the past? Chris and I had ideas about where we might look to find out.

In the southern summer of 2010, we had flown out from Chile with a private company known as Antarctic Logistics and Expeditions for a four-week season in West Antarctica. We left the small frontier city of Punta Arenas in a balmy 60°F. The sky was overcast, damp, almost oppressive. I was excited but nervous. I had spent several months training for this. As a university student, I'd been in the Territorial Army, including a full month of military exercises alongside U.S. troops under the blistering North Carolina sun at Fort Bragg, but I had never been as fit as I was now. Uncertain of what I might face, I had diligently run six miles a day, climbed once a week, trained for crevasse falls and even learned a multitude of knots. Now it was real. We were going to Antarctica and there wasn't much else I could do apart from keep my wits about me. The aircraft—a converted Soviet transporter that shared more similarities with a rocket than a plane—did not allay my nervousness. We hurtled through the sky at 30,000 feet, the deafening roar from the engines making conversation with Chris or anyone else nigh on impossible. Keen to get my bearings, I made my way up to the front of the cabin. I poured myself a cup of coffee from an urn and, sipping the hot fluid, peered out through the Plexiglas window on the port side of the plane. All I could see through the banks of cloud below were large slabs of sea ice that stretched beyond the horizon. There was no land in sight. It was the farthest I had ever been from civilization.

Four and a half hours after we left Chile we landed in the Ellsworth Mountains. The contrast to damp Punta Arenas couldn't have been greater: blinding sunshine, a frigid 14°F wind, and a vista that took my breath away. The rugged, snow-draped mountains pierced the sky, the deeply gorged valleys proclaiming the sculpting power of ice over millions of years. As we gingerly stepped onto the blue-ice runway, we were greeted by welcoming smiles that were the warmest thing around for a thousand miles.

The Antarctic challenges everything you've learned in the north; every idea you thought you had about the world has to be chucked out and reconsidered. This is an environment where life exists in extraordinarily low temperatures, where snow falls under clear blue skies, and where hurricane-force winds can strike at any moment. The intellectual thrill of discovering and interpreting an entirely new landscape among like-minded expeditioners and adventurers was an exhilarating experience. I immediately became besotted with the place. I never felt so alive; my senses went into overdrive. Everything was new: working, eating, cleaning (sometimes), and sleeping; all in twenty-four hours of brilliant, mesmerising daylight. My appetite became insatiable as I adapted to an environment completely different to anywhere else I had ever been.

Set in a region that drains 22 percent of all ice from the Antarctic continent, the Ellsworth Mountains offered an ideal location to find out what happened to the ice sheets in the past. During our month-long stay, Chris and I climbed mountains, sampled rocks, navigated glaciers and crevasses, dug snow and ice trenches, all to get precious snapshots of how the Antarctic had changed through time. On our return home, we compared our fieldwork results with computer-model simulations of Antarctica's climate and ice sheets over millennia. There had indeed been massive changes in the height of the ice sheet around the Ellsworth Mountains, but we could see that this was only part of the story. The models suggested that some of the greatest changes had been over on the other side of the continent, far out to the east.

But nowhere is more isolated, extreme, and wild than the East Antarctic. With a world-record low temperature of -128.6°F at the Russian base Vostok and precipitation averaging two inches a year, the region has the oxymoronic distinction of being the coldest place on Earth while also being the world's largest desert. The ice sheet here is a behemoth. It doesn't just cover a larger area than the West Antarctic, it's far, far bigger. With an average thickness of 7,300 feet, it's nine times the size of the west in terms of ice volume. Of the 200 feet of global sea level rise locked up in the Antarctic, some 180 feet lies in the east. But because most of the ice sits above sea level, many scientists consider it to have been relatively stable in the past. The thinking is that the ice sheet is so large that without warm ocean waters lapping along the edge of the continent, the East Antarctic should sit there largely unscathed by higher air temperatures; it might actually get larger, a consequence of the increased evaporation from warm surface waters creating more snowfall at high latitudes.

The problem is, as the East Antarctic is so isolated, extreme, and wild, not nearly enough fieldwork has been done there to test these ideas. The most humans have ever managed is to be visitors, and unwelcome ones at that; even today many areas have never been seen by human eyes. As a result, we don't fully understand how the ice sheet has behaved in the past. But we do know now that there are places in the east where ice sits on the seabed, making it vulnerable to a warming ocean. One of the most important is the Wilkes Basin, extending 500 miles inland from Mawson's Cape Denison base. Over an area comparable in size to New Zealand, the Wilkes Basin is covered by 8,000 feet of ice, enough to raise the world's sea level by more than ten feet. If anywhere can drive up the world's sea level, it's the East Antarctic.

Planning for any research expedition has one large and very real elephant in the room: funding. Early on, Chris and I had worked up a detailed budget and estimated we could do a forty-day voyage for around $1.5 million, including the likely charter costs of a ship and fuel. We had a small amount of funding from research grants, but this would hardly be enough to cast off. We had to get a major injection of cash if we were going to take the expedition beyond the planning stage. Unfortunately, it wasn't a good time to raise money in Australia. Many companies were making very public statements about cutting their donations to groups and charities. Hundreds of letters trying to pique interest went unanswered. Only a handful of organizations suggested meeting. Nothing came of them.

A century before, the likes of Shackleton and Mawson sought the stamp of approval from a learned institution. With this support, an expedition could publicly show that the planned venture had merit and use this to raise funds. In Edwardian times, the Royal Geographical Society was as big as it came. A world-leading center of geographic and scientific understanding, the Society's assent carried serious weight. As a Fellow of what's affectionately known as the RGS, I traveled to London to seek its advice.

Today, the RGS is housed in a beautiful, rambling, redbrick mansion just along from the Royal Albert Hall, opposite the Albert Memorial and Kensington Gardens. Walking past the grid-locked traffic and roadworks that seem to be a permanent feature of this part of the city, I signed in and entered a maze of high-ceilinged corridors filled with pictures and memorials commemorating the tragic death in 1912 of Captain Robert Falcon Scott and his teammates in the Antarctic. It was eerily silent, almost mausoleum-like, but in spite of the décor, the Grants Programme staff of the RGS were welcoming. "We're not looking for funding," I assured them, "but your support for what we're trying to do would be a tremendous help." They were enthusiastic, making suggestions about the work, who we might go into partnership with, and what scheme we could best apply for. Four months later the RGS turned us down on a technicality. We didn't have enough U.K.-based students taking part, and they had no other scheme for which we might get approval. I was gobsmacked. If Mawson or Shackleton applied today, they would be rejected. My point of contact at the RGS apologized, embarrassed they no longer had a way to recognize large scientific expeditions, and offered to raise the issue at the next Council meeting. That didn't help us. We needed support, not sympathy.

Fortunately, all was not lost. Just a year earlier, I had published a book called *1912: The Year the World Discovered Antarctica*. Speaking at the Brisbane Writers Festival, I met representatives of Google Australia. They were keen to look at ways I could communicate science on their social media platforms Google+ and YouTube. I was electrified by the idea. Rather than giving talks to small groups, this was a way to reach out to the world: to show how science works and what my team and I were discovering in the field. Soon after, I started posting blogs and short films under the banner "Intrepid Science," and my number of followers soared to tens of thousands.

Two months after the festival, I received an unexpected call from Google's Sydney office.

"Chris, you know your expedition south? Well, we don't want to be pushy but we think we might be able to help. Are you interested?"

Am I? Oh, yes!

The Google representative explained that they ran a school competition every other year called "Doodle4Google," in which schoolchildren are invited to redraw the Google logo inspired by a question or phrase. The successful image is put up online, and the winning school is granted a room full of technology. For 2013, Google wanted to use "If I were an explorer I would . . . ," with an extra twist: the winning Australian and New Zealand teachers would join us on the expedition. It would be a world first for Google. I was to be one of three judges on the entries from both sides of the Tasman.

The competition was to run in the middle of 2013, perfect for marking the centenary of Mawson's expedition. Google immediately started making contact with major companies in Australia about funding the prize. Suddenly we had firms fighting over exclusive rights to the competition. In just a few weeks we had the Commonwealth Bank of Australia offering $500,000. Google had given us the cornerstone investor we so desperately needed to make the expedition a reality.

Leading an expedition to the Antarctic had been my dream ever since I can remember. From an early age, I loved tales of discovery. As a kid, I would bury myself in ripping yarns from history involving explorers, scientists, archaeologists, and inventors; I couldn't get enough of stories where the heroes disappeared from civilization and returned with new discoveries in hand. My favorite was in an old moth-eaten boy's annual: an illustrated account of Sir Ernest Shackleton's failed attempt to cross the Antarctic in 1915. The story of his ship, the *Endurance,* being crushed and the men forced to camp out on the ice for months on end, followed by Shackleton successfully crossing the wild south Atlantic Ocean and raising the alarm, seemed almost too incredible, too fantastic, to be real. One particular image always captured my imagination: a photo of the *Endurance,* lit up against the pitch-darkness of the Antarctic winter, defiant against the pack ice. The danger, the sense of isolation, and the determination to survive struck a deep and profound chord with me. I needed to learn more.

A merchant navy officer by training, Shackleton cut his teeth in the Antarctic during Scott's British National Antarctic *Discovery* Expedition of 1901–1904. Controversially sent home on health grounds, Shackleton went on to lead three of his own expeditions south. The Imperial Trans-Antarctic Expedition of 1914–1917 and the safe return of all his men after encountering the perils of the ice was his crowning achievement in the polar regions. But alongside his brilliant leadership was his remarkable ability to tell a story. Shackleton was famous for capturing the imagination; he electrified the public with tales of adventure and discoveries in a new land. Photographs, film, audio recordings, books, newspaper reports, magazine articles, and public lectures were all used to whisk the audience away to the Antarctic. When Shackleton was in a violent storm, you were clinging on to the ship's tiller with him, when Shackleton was on the edge of starvation, your own stomach gnawed, and when Shackleton laughed at the peculiar idiosyncrasies of the penguins, you were laughing too; all from the safe confines of home. He was so good that other explorers were advised to try to emulate him—though few ever succeeded. After Shackleton, Antarctica was no longer an unknown region to the public: it was suddenly real. This was science communication at its best and it set the standard for future efforts.

Shackleton once remarked, "Sentiment has been the ruling force in every great work that has ever been done, and I shall be sorry when the day comes when science is divorced from sentiment or sentiment from science." The great explorer realized science on its own was not enough. You had to engage the public, to tell a story, to get them excited in the work. A century ago, science and adventure in the Antarctic were very much one and the same thing. You couldn't go off the map and play it safe. To be a scientist in Antarctica, you needed to be an adventurer; if you wanted an adventure, you had to have a scientific justification to get the funding. Shackleton and Mawson sold the Edwardian equivalent of space travel. No wonder the public were so excited. And they paid to make it happen.

Today we live in an age in which society is crying out for scientific solutions to global problems. The urgent need to transition to a carbon-free economy, the need to develop new drugs to combat disease, and the need to improve agricultural yields to meet the appetite of a growing world population are just a few of the many considerable challenges we confront. But in parallel to this increasing demand for science, we face a worrying trend across most of the Western world. From high schools to universities, there's a long-term decline in the number of students of science, technology, engineering, and mathematics—

the so-called STEM subjects—just when we need them most. If we're going to sort out the big issues of tomorrow, we not only need more graduates of STEM, we need a more scientifically literate society, one that can meaningfully debate issues to make informed judgements. It's not about knowing a random number of scientific "facts," it's about understanding how science works. It's about making observations to test ideas and reach the simplest explanation; it's about using critical thinking in all walks of life. The question is, how do you engage without making it boring? As I've taught around the world, I've become convinced that we can do more to excite students and the wider public about science and technology. We need to remember how Shackleton told stories and captured people's imagination.

When I first started teaching at university in the late 1990s, I inherited a course on how to date geological records. Drily called Quaternary Geochronology, the ten-week lecture series was designed to show students how different scientific methods could be used to date the landscape of the last 2.6 million years. The course had been around almost as long. Passed on from staff member to staff member over the years, there were lots of incomprehensible words and mind-bending equations, and virtually no images—very little to excite anyone. I struggled with the delivery and became concerned that I was actually putting the students—and myself for that matter—off science. After a few weeks, I noticed that the only time the students woke up was at the end of each lecture when I gave an example of how a particular technique had been used. I remembered the photograph of Shackleton's ship from my childhood. Start with the story, and then weave in the science. It was a revelation.

The next week, I tried something completely different. I was due to give a lecture on how radioactivity can be used to date rocks. Instead, I decided to go back to basics and look at the modern calendar. I started with the opening scene from the wonderful movie *Monty Python and the Holy Grail* in which King

Arthur and his faithful sidekick Patsy ride through the mist with coconuts. The date: a questionable AD 932. Over the next hour, we looked at how civilizations had wrestled for thousands of years with developing a calendar that described time properly, something we take for granted today but which is very much rooted in science. We looked at the age of King Arthur, how Belgium missed Christmas with the introduction of the modern Gregorian calendar, and why Britain had time riots with fatal consequences—all linked to how our planet orbits the sun. The students were engaged from start to finish.

From then on, I always started with a story. The next year, I re-named the course Dating the Past, and my class numbers doubled.

Scientists need to tell stories—just like Shackleton did.

CHAPTER TWO
A Step into the Unknown

Six months after my beachside call with Chris, I was standing in front of a packed auditorium of 300 expectant faces. An Australian Broadcasting Corporation film crew were up in the wings, their camera lights blazing onto the stage. The glare was so fierce I could barely make out the figures beyond. I was hot. My mouth was parched and my palms were clammy.

How on earth did I get here?

It had been a crazy six months. With the support of Google and the University of New South Wales, the expedition went from an aspiration to reality almost overnight—and with it, the workload went into overdrive. With the launch of the Doodle4Google competition, the university was hosting my public announcement of the Australasian Antarctic Expedition 2013–2014. Personal invitations had been made across Sydney, journalists informed, and the room was packed to capacity. I could hardly believe the response. The idea of a privately funded science expedition in the spirit of Shackleton and Mawson had struck a very big chord with the public. Just a couple of hours before stepping on the stage, I'd received a letter of support from the Australian prime minister, the Honourable Julia Gillard. It was a wonderful shot in the arm, but I was terribly nervous.

I cleared my throat and tried to compose myself.

I looked down at the front row and saw Annette, Cara, and Robert smiling encouragingly back at me. It hadn't been an easy time for the family. Preparing for the expedition had meant I'd been away a lot. And at home I'd spoken of little else; bouncing around ideas about the educational program with Annette, asking the children how best to engage with teenagers and kids. They'd all been brilliantly supportive, working up ideas for the expedition, encouraging me when I felt overwhelmed by the never-ending barrage of tasks. It was a real family effort. I don't deserve them. I really don't.

Right, here goes.

"Well, good evening, ladies and gentlemen . . ."

Cape Denison is as isolated, extreme, and wild as it gets—even by East Antarctic standards. Hit by wind speeds of over 200 miles an hour, "the windiest place on Earth" sits at the foot of the ice sheet, a pinprick of rock hemmed in by sheer ice cliffs at the head of Commonwealth Bay. It is one of a handful of all-too-rare natural harbors along this part of coastline. Getting there is no simple affair. Sitting at 67 degrees south—142 degrees east of Greenwich and 1,400 miles south of New Zealand—Mawson's Antarctic base never became a permanent research station. The practical upshot is there is no airstrip, and few government vessels visit. Some cruise ships are known to dare the Southern Ocean in the summer months, but the remoteness, stormy seas, and ever-present threat of sea ice puts off all but the most adventurous of tourists.

Cape Denison may not be for the fainthearted, but it's a magnet for Earth scientists. The violent winds that roar past it make the offshore region a prodigious producer of sea ice—one of

Antarctica's great "ice factories"—and with it one of the great drivers of our planet's climate. What happens at Cape Denison through the seasons is an exaggerated version of what happens in Antarctica on an enormous scale each year.

With the fall of the winter sun below the horizon, air temperatures plummet, rapidly chilling the ocean and setting off a cascade of dramatic changes across the Antarctic. Pinpricks of ice crystals join to form plate-size sheets, coalescing on the surface into pancake-like shapes that ultimately become floes of ice. The scale at which sea ice is formed is truly spectacular. One month of freezing temperatures, winds, waves and snowfall is enough to create sea ice up to twenty-five inches thick. At the height of winter, it's estimated some twenty-three square miles are produced every minute. By the end of the season, the Antarctic has effectively doubled in size, with nearly 8 million square miles of sea ice. But with the arrival of the summer sun, the system suddenly switches into reverse: warmer temperatures and the seasonal change in winds cause the sea ice to "break out" and flow north, where it melts and returns to the ocean from which it came. Each year the cycle is repeated: vast amounts of sea ice are formed only to melt and then reform twelve months later.

Off Cape Denison, the whole process massively speeds up. The chilling Antarctic winds that blow off the continent year-round freeze the surface of Commonwealth Bay, regardless of whether it's winter or not: the sea ice is formed, blown offshore, a new open area of water known as a polynya is formed, and more seawater is frozen in its place. Instead of once a year, the whole cycle can take just a few days in Commonwealth Bay.

But Cape Denison is special in more ways than one. As sea ice is created offshore, a fundamental process takes place below the surface. The salt in ocean water is effectively squeezed out of the ice—a process described as "brine rejection"—creating a dense mass of water. In most of the Southern Ocean, this cold, super-salty water just diffuses away. In Commonwealth Bay, however, the conditions are perfect for the formation of something known as Antarctic Bottom Water, a key part of the ocean circulation system.

At a basic level, the world's oceans are connected as though by one enormous conveyor belt. At one end of the loop, warm tropical waters popularly known as the Gulf Stream drift up into the North Atlantic where, over the course of a year, the evaporating surface delivers heat downwind equivalent to the output from a million power stations. It's a major reason for the starkly different temperatures experienced along the northern fiftieth parallel; why Europe is over 30°F warmer than Newfoundland and Labrador on the other side of the Atlantic. Eventually, however, this northward-flowing current becomes too cold and salty to stay afloat, and sinks, heading south miles below the surface. Antarctic Bottom Water helps drive the southern, lower limb of this conveyor belt, "recharging" the system with deep water that flows around the continent before splitting off north into the Indian and Pacific oceans to eventually warm and return to the surface, closing the loop.

Sea ice alone isn't enough for the production of Antarctic Bottom Water, however. It needs just the right configuration of coastline and sea floor. And Commonwealth Bay has it all. Each year, the armadas of sea ice formed under the continuous blast of Antarctic winds create the densest water in the world, pouring off the continental shelf to the bottom of the sea floor. It's estimated the polynyas in and around Commonwealth Bay produce a quarter of all Antarctic Bottom Water. This makes it a big player in the world's climate system.

Or it should.

Everything changed with the arrival of iceberg B09B in 2011. The word "berg" doesn't really do it justice—B09B is a monster. Weighing in at an estimated 450 billion tons, this block of ice is sixty miles long and over twelve miles wide. There's enough freshwater in B09B to provide for all of New York's drinking needs for 300 years. And it started out even larger. In 1987, an iceberg the size of Bali broke free from the continent in the Ross Sea. It was one of the largest bergs ever seen. Unlike sea ice, bergs are formed from continental ice, fragments of the ice sheets that cover the Antarctic, created from snowfall that's been buried under intense pressure for thousands of years. At the edge of the continent, the ice either melts or breaks off as flat-topped or "tabular" bergs. If the balance between the lost ice and replacing snowfall falls out of balance, sea levels can either rise or fall, in contrast to sea ice which has no real impact on the world's sea level. Riding the westward-flowing ocean currents, the Ross Sea berg smashed its way along the coast. By the time it reached Commonwealth Bay, the largest remaining part was labeled with the unassuming moniker B09B. Smashing a tongue of ice from the Mertz Glacier that extended sixty-two miles out to sea, the berg grounded itself in Commonwealth Bay. The arrival of this colossus had an immediate and devastating impact on the area. The sea ice that forms in Commonwealth Bay could no longer be swept offshore and became trapped instead. Some scientists have suggested that the arrival of B09B might have collapsed Antarctic Bottom Water production, slowing down the ocean conveyor belt that is so important to the world's climate.

This chain of events could really help scientists understand what's happening elsewhere in Antarctica. Since the 1970s, satellites have provided an almost daily view of what's going on around the Antarctic. Against all expectations, and in spite of a warming world, there seems to be more sea ice surviving the East Antarctic summer each year. It's not by a lot—some years it goes up, some years down—but the trend is unmistakably on the up at the rate of around 1 per cent each decade. It's become so bad in some regions that government ships struggle to reach their bases. One example was at the French base Dumont d'Urville, seventy miles west of Cape Denison, where no open water was seen between March 2012 and November 2015. Air temperatures weren't excessively cold at this time, but the "winter" ice just wouldn't break out. In 2014, it was so bad that supplies had to be driven and helicoptered over the sea ice to keep the science program going.

The East Antarctic is throwing up a wall of ice around its perimeter and no one is quite sure why. One possibility is that the coastal underbelly of the East Antarctic ice sheet is being melted by a warming ocean. If so, the freshwater in the continental ice may be diluting the antifreeze properties of seawater, making it easier to form sea ice on the surface. Worryingly, the largest increase in sea ice appears to be happening just off the Wilkes Basin near Cape Denison—the same part of the East Antarctic that holds enough freshwater to raise global sea levels by a staggering ten feet, and an area that may have collapsed in the past, as some research has suggested. Another idea is that the winds may be playing a role. Sea ice rarely remains where it forms and is moved around by the prevailing air currents. With a change in direction or strength, sea ice can be shuffled into areas that aren't so easily melted in the summer. Of course, both may be happening.

The bottom line is that satellites can only tell us so much. They can show us what's happening on the surface but not under the ice, and they're essentially silent on what happened before the 1970s. If there is going to be more sea ice off the East Antarctic in the near future, an extreme event like the arrival of B09B in Commonwealth Bay, a moment in time when the seascape froze and stayed frozen, may help scientists understand what the future will be like.

There's an old sailor's expression: "Below 40 degrees south there is no law, below 50 degrees south there is no God." Since the sixteenth century, sailors have spoken in awe of the violent westerly winds and seas they experienced fighting their way across the Southern Ocean. With few landmasses to slow them down, the winds found across 40 degrees latitude often reach speeds of twenty-five knots—about 40 percent stronger than their northern hemisphere counterparts—earning them the title the "roaring forties." As shipping pushed farther south, explorers realized that these winds form part of a vast storm belt that includes the "furious fifties" and "screaming sixties," names more reminiscent of terrible rock bands than a major part of our planet's circulation system. The early hunters and traders didn't understand it at the time, but these winds are created by a procession of low-pressure systems carried east by the jet stream, a river of cold air hurtling and twisting round the Antarctic at 30,000 feet. Importantly, something quite profound appears to have been happening in recent decades: The winds seem to be getting even stronger and moving south. To properly understand what's happening at Cape Denison and the wider East Antarctic, our expedition would have to take into account what the winds are doing over the Southern Ocean. They're a crucial part of the bigger picture.

Trying to get a handle on what's happening in the Southern Ocean, however, is easier said than done. Because the region is notoriously wild, it's sparse in scientific data. Most of the records we have today come from satellite observations and sporadic records taken by ships as they hastily beat a path to safer latitudes. Fortunately, scattered across the Southern Ocean are a number of tiny pinpricks of land, the so-called subantarctic islands, many of which are home to weather stations that have been taking careful observations since the mid-twentieth century. In the southwest Pacific, the Australian Macquarie Island lies at the southernmost end of a chain of archipelagos extending down from New Zealand, straddling 48 to 54 degrees south, right under the path of the winds.

If we wanted to understand the changes in westerly winds

and what effect this is having on the Antarctic, the expedition would have to dedicate time to the subantarctics. These islands, precious sanctuaries for wildlife and, covered in vegetation, peat bogs, and lakes, offer the possibility of finding centuries-old plant and animal remains that preserve a record of the changing impact of the roaring forties and furious fifties.

To make the most of our time south, we decided to split the expedition into two legs, to complete a scientific program that would reach all the way to the Antarctic continent. During the first ten days, we aimed to restrict ourselves to the subantarctic islands known as Snares, Auckland, and Campbell, where we'd focus our efforts on changes in the Southern Hemisphere westerlies and in the flora and fauna on these remarkable islands. Returning to New Zealand, the team would then be rotated, followed by a second, four-week voyage to work across the Southern Ocean and on to Cape Denison via Macquarie Island . . . hopefully. By dividing the expedition in two, we had maximum flexibility on who we could take. For the first leg, subantarctic experts; for the second, Antarcticians. There was also a very real fringe benefit: During the first voyage, we could give the ship and all our gear a full shake down. Any problems, and we still had a chance of getting repairs done or gaining replacements before setting out for Cape Denison. We only had one shot at this.

I'll always remember the first time I heard the name Mawson. In 1997, Annette and I had been married one year. I had just completed my doctoral thesis and was incredibly fortunate to be offered a research position in New Zealand. Annette was pregnant with our first child, but we wanted to see as much of the world as possible, young family or not. We moved to the garden city of Christchurch, a city rich in Antarctic history, through which many of the great explorers—Shackleton, Scott, and Sir Edmund Hillary—had passed on their way to the icy continent.

One evening over dinner, a friend mentioned another name: Douglas Mawson.

"Who?" I asked.

"Mawson. Haven't you heard of him? Oh, he's an amazing character. Mawson was a protégé of Shackleton and led the first expedition to the Antarctic from these parts. Just a young guy when he set out. He lost two men on the ice and nearly died. It's an incredible story of survival. Real *Boy's Own Adventure* stuff. Wait a moment, I think I have his story somewhere."

Rummaging through a mountain of books in the lounge room, our friend soon laid his hands on a small paperback.

"Here it is," he declared triumphantly, handing us a well-thumbed copy of *Mawson's Will* by Lennard Bickel. "An absolute classic."

The back cover told a tale of adventure completely unknown to me. Here was an Antarctic explorer new to Annette and me—a towering figure we had never heard of. We weren't the only ones. The more I asked around, the more I realized few had. Mawson may have been a contemporary of Shackleton and Scott, but he wasn't the same household name.

Emigrating to Australia from northern Britain with his family at the tender age of six, Mawson would come to epitomize the spirit of the Empire. By his mid-twenties, he was a towering six-foot figure, athletic and frighteningly intelligent. Fresh out of Sydney University in 1907, he seemed destined to become a field geologist. But fate was to intercede. While mapping outback Australia, Mawson read in the newspapers that his university mentor Edgeworth David, a gentle, wizened-faced professor of geology, was joining Shackleton on the first voyage south led by the Anglo-Irishman: the British Antarctic *Nimrod* Expedition. Mawson excitedly wrote to his mentor, "I should have dearly loved to have gone myself and shall in any case be with you as far as my imagination can carry me." David could take a hint,

and asked Shackleton whether there might be a place for his former student. Mawson was instantly offered a role. He would
one day be a great Antarctic explorer, but for now Mawson was
just plain old "Douglas."

Shackleton's plan was audacious: an all-out assault on the
Antarctic to be the first to reach both the south geographic and
magnetic Poles. Nothing like this had ever been seriously attempted before. From his base on the edge of the Ross Sea, the
distances were vast, the conditions extreme and in the case of
the magnetic Pole, the location not precisely known. While the
geographic Pole marks the southern axis of our planet's rota-
tion, its magnetic sibling had been a scientific enigma for centuries. Thanks to the swirling currents of molten iron within our
planet, the Earth's magnetic field is continuously changing, and
with it the pole's position where the field is vertical to the surface, thwarting the development of accurate navigational charts.
We now know that over the past century the magnetic South
Pole has moved around six miles a year and is currently over the
Southern Ocean. But in Shackleton and Mawson's day, the compass pointed toward the East Antarctic Ice Sheet. When Shackleton and his companions fell just ninety-seven miles short of the
geographic South Pole, Mawson and David were man-hauling a
half-ton sledge of equipment and supplies with Scottish medic
Alistair Mackay, 7,200 feet above sea level. After 103 days, the
three-man team finally reached the edge of the magnetic Pole.
Finding their compass dipping almost (but not quite) vertically,
the men claimed the area for the British Empire, took a quick
photo and with a "Thank God" turned tail and fled back to the
coast. Both parties nearly starved in their efforts but returned to
civilization as heroes. David afterward remarked: "Mawson was
the real leader who was the soul of our expedition to the Magnetic Pole . . . [he is a man] of infinite resource, splendid
physique, astonishing indifference to frost."

Fired by a passion for discovery, Mawson resolved to return

to the Antarctic. Shackleton initially agreed to lead a second effort, but dubious business ventures prevented him taking part.
Undeterred, Mawson decided to lead his own endeavor instead.
After Shackleton's near-miss in 1909, other expeditions were
planning to finish the ninety-seven miles left undone. The British,
Germans, and Japanese—and later the Norwegians—were all
known to be setting a course south, with Scott even promising
Mawson a place on the team that would be first to raise the flag at
the geographic Pole. Mawson just wasn't interested. To him, the
bigger question was what lay to the immediate south of Australia. The region was a complete blank, not just on the map, but
scientifically as well. The region might hold the key to solving
some of the big geological questions of the time and was known
to play a major role in Australia's weather; it was the origin of
the southern blasts that regularly struck Adelaide, Melbourne,
and Sydney with little to no warning. And of course, who knew
what mineral riches waited to be discovered? Apart from a few
pebbles collected a couple of decades earlier, no one had any
real idea what was down there.

Inspired by his former leader, Mawson wanted his expedition
to be sensational. This was not going to be a return to former
discoveries: Mawson was heading off the map into largely uncharted territory. There was no doubt it was an ambitious enterprise. He aimed to set up four research bases—the same number
of Antarctic bases as those run by Australia today—all in a single field season. This was in a part of the world where the only
reports of land had been made by the tough American Captain
Charles Wilkes, who had skirted the edge of what he suspected
was an entirely new continent. It was to be a complete scientific
exploration of the Antarctic region south of Australia.

With a public appeal from Shackleton for the Australian venture, Mawson managed to raise the modern equivalent of over
twenty million dollars in just one year. It was enough to buy and
provision a vessel; employ a team of scientists, engineers, and

ship's crew; and purchase the equipment and supplies to support a scientific expedition in the deep field for fourteen months, all backed up by the first radio link from the Antarctic.

In late 1911, the Australasian Antarctic Expedition headed out from Hobart on board the steamship SY *Aurora*. After nine days fighting the wilds of the Southern Ocean, the *Aurora* reached its first destination, the subantarctic archipelago Macquarie Island, and set down a team with living quarters, supplies, equipment, and a "wireless" station, crucial for keeping contact with the team about to make Antarctica their home. Two weeks later, fully replenished with freshwater, Mawson pushed on south. Recently engaged, the Australian leader regularly wrote to his fiancée, Paquita Delprat, telling her his news and proclaiming his love. Although the letters would not be delivered until the *Aurora* returned home, they helped keep her close.

Angel, I have been thinking such a lot of you these past few days—between the rolling and pitching of the ship— between watch and watch. How grand it would be to fly back to you, even for a few brief minutes. The discomfort . . . drives all my longings into one channel—peace and you.

Reaching the Antarctic coast, the men on the *Aurora* were disappointed to be met by cliffs of ice. Mawson rued his dependence on Wilkes's early claims and couldn't help but vent his spleen to Paquita:

We met heavy impenetrable pack in several directions and failed to break through to the land. Much of this disappointment and trouble I find today are due to an undue reliance I had placed in the accounts of Commander Wilkes who made explorations here in 1840. His accounts are largely erroneous and misleading.

There was nowhere suitable to set up a base. Mawson was forced to push west, and, with summertime fast disappearing, he grudgingly decided he would have to combine two of the bases at the first possible opportunity. When they came upon Cape Denison, Mawson was ecstatic. Greeted by squawking penguins in their hundreds of thousands:

We were soon inside a beautiful, miniature harbour completely land-locked. The sun shone gloriously in a blue sky as we stepped ashore on a charming ice-foot . . . Behind it rose the inland ice, ascending in a regular slope and apparently free of crevasses—an outlet for our sledging parties in the event of the sea not firmly freezing over . . . As a station for scientific investigations, it offered a wider field than the casual observer would have imagined.

Shortly after their arrival, excitement turned to horror when the team was hit by a series of ferocious cold "katabatic" winds that poured off the ice cap. The local topography amplified these gravity-driven dense winds, funneling them straight over Cape Denison. There seemed to be no pattern for when they would strike; the only indication they were imminent was wisps of snow on the upper slopes, warning the men they had just minutes to get to shelter before visibility crashed and the rough waters threatened the *Aurora* and any small boats relaying supplies to shore. Unfortunately, with the imminent arrival of winter pack ice, Mawson had run out of time to find another location. The Australian leader was committed to set up camp immediately if another team was to be dropped off farther along the coast that season. For good or bad, there was no choice—they had to stay. Hurriedly, foundations were blasted out of the rock, the prefabricated wooden huts were put up, the supplies, science gear, sledges and dogs unloaded, and the *Aurora* sent on its way.

Mawson and his seventeen men were left to face the winter to-gether.

The equipment and men struggled in the conditions. They were here to do science, but it was perilous work. Each time the men left the safety of their shelter, they risked their lives. The wind speed averaged thirty-eight knots, equivalent to forty-four miles per hour. In one twelve-hour period, the wind reached a breathtaking eighty-eight miles per hour, hurricane in strength. With swirling snow, the men often complained of losing sight of the hut within a few yards of the doorway. With the boat harbor only seventy paces outside, a loss of direction could easily end in tragedy. The weather station was relatively close, just 200 yards from the hut, set up high on one of the surrounding ridges, but visits could take hours as the men, dressed in the best wind-proof gear Burberry could provide, were often forced to make the journey on all fours, heads down against the elements. Some-times several trips a day were needed to make repairs and keep the gear going in what quickly became known as the "Home of the Blizzard." No one had ever seen anything like it before.

Following our public launch, world interest in the new Aus-tralasian Antarctic Expedition took off. With the involvement of Google, others proffered support. After several meetings, New Zealand outdoor specialists, Macpac, agreed to supply the expe-dition clothing and kit, including tents and sleeping bags, all at a massive discount. Satellite company Inmarsat contributed thou-sands of dollars' worth of access to its network, giving us a pre-cious communication link from the Southern Ocean (or "comms" as it's often referred to in the business). All Terrain Solutions in Brisbane provided free training on the tracked Argo vehicle we needed to make the estimated forty-mile sea ice journey across Commonwealth Bay to reach Cape Denison. No less important, we also received field microscopes, lab equipment, and commercial weather forecasting and state-of-the-art drone mapping, all essential for making the expedition a success.

Alongside these efforts, we looked at other means of funding the expedition. Drawing inspiration from Shackleton and Mawson, we offered berths on the voyage for the public to join the Google-winning teachers on board. This was not a cruise in the traditional sense. We had far more research planned than we could ever hope to achieve with the scientists on board and needed paying volunteers: citizen scientists who would help support the work of the expedition during the voyage. In this regard, we were lucky to have Greg Mortimer join us. Quietly spoken and self-deprecating, Greg is an Australian legend in the mountaineering scene and a pioneer of commercial ventures in the south. We first met Greg in the Ellsworth Mountains. He had visited the Antarctic more than eighty times, climbed remote mountains across the continent, been trapped in sea ice, and returned home still smiling. Greg had decades of experience of Antarctica, and his knowledge of commercial operations and easy-going manner would help make the expedition a reality. Without hesitation, I offered to employ Greg and his company Adventure Associates to advertise for the citizen scientists and act as point of contact on all matters, including health requirements, field clothing, and travel insurance, taking a significant administrative burden off our hands.

With Greg hard at work filling places on the expedition, our attention turned to getting approval for the work program. We couldn't just go where we wanted and do whatever we liked. The Southern Ocean and Antarctic are heavily protected under various national laws and international agreements, including the Antarctic Treaty of 1961, which preserves the continent for science and peace (while also suspending all national claims). Enquiries had to be made, permissions sought, and import permits for all our samples issued. Our offices started to heave with the piles of forms and kit we were amassing. We urgently needed an expedition headquarters—somewhere to handle the meetings, phone calls, and documentation demanded by different authorities while also storing all the ordered equipment now heading our way.

The university was sympathetic and offered us a property. "Eurimbla Avenue," a white, spacious two-storey house, became Chris's and my second home over the next six months. We had the conference room covered with maps and planning schedules the first day we moved in. Within a week, most of the offices in the building were occupied, the air filled with the tapping of keyboards, conversation, and laughter as the details of the expedition were thrashed out. After a fortnight, you would have thought we'd always been there.

Slowly but surely, we made progress toward reaching our target of $1.5 million. Following in the footsteps of Mawson, we had hoped to make our departure from Hobart, but my enquiries fell on deaf ears; an alternative was Christchurch's port at Lyttelton, but it was still reeling from the shocking earthquake that had happened just a couple of years before. In the end, we considered the port of Bluff, near the southern New Zealand city of Invercargill; the only question was the port fees, which threatened to be substantial. I contacted the office of Tim Shadbolt, the local mayor. Tim is a national treasure, a great champion of the region and a professional comedian—Tim's tours of New Zealand instantly sell out—making him one of the most recognised faces in the country. He's also remarkably friendly and agreed to meet me. I flew over, and after some discussion Tim offered to waive the port fees and give us storage space on the dockside. It was an incredibly generous offer that would save us tens of thousands of dollars, so Bluff it was. With the daily program of research activities agreed, we homed in on a departure date of 27 November 2013 and planned our return to

Bluff for 4 January 2014. Thirty-nine days at sea—enough time to do a substantial amount of work.

The University of New South Wales' Dean of Science, Professor Merlin Crossley, helped tremendously. Sponsorship requests, email enquiries, and orders were increasing in number, and no matter how much time I dedicated to the tasks in hand, the list of demands only seemed to grow. Merlin agreed to fund a half-time PA position to support the expedition, and the arrival of Jono Pritchard at Eurimbla was a game-changer for us. Within minutes he had set up the coffee machine and was working through the list of tasks I'd been struggling with. Without Jono, I don't honestly know if the expedition would have ever happened. Joining us, Alvin Stone agreed to be our media contact on shore. We were lucky, and I knew it. With over twenty years in the profession, Alvin is a genius at making science comprehensible to the public. Alongside Alvin, web guru Anthony Ditton designed and administered the public-facing website that would tell the science, adventure, and history of the expedition in glorious images with a real-time map tracking our position. Anthony agreed to join us on the first leg of the expedition to sort out any gremlins, and to continue with the role at home when we carried on to Cape Denison.

But the work didn't stop there. Now in the public eye, we received a tidal wave of requests for interviews and offers to talk to schools and clubs—all opportunities to shout about the science and chase ever-precious funds. Fighting through the mountain of health and safety paperwork and science-permitting applications, Chris was busy sourcing the gear we would need once we left New Zealand. He was on the phone day and night, calling suppliers, arranging the delivery of equipment we needed to support a team in all conditions, chasing the different science groups about what they needed. The logistical planning for such a massive enterprise was extraordinary, and Chris dealt with it profes-

sionally and without complaint. Slowly but surely over the next
four months, more than two tons of scientific gear, supplies,
vehicles, tents and sledges made its way through Eurimbla's
doors, and was carefully inventoried and stored away. As the
rooms filled with gear, so did the anticipation.

By late October, everything was ready to go. For one last
time, equipment was turned on, tents erected and emergency
packs checked over. In the blazing heat of the Sydney sun,
Eurimbla's rooms were emptied and the contents tightly packed
into a container, locked down and sent off to New Zealand. How
we managed to get everything in, I don't know. My mind was
filled with a blur of lists, boxes, fishnets, and traps, and the constant ringing of various phones. The container would be in Bluff
by early November, long before our planned departure at the
end of the month.

Alongside our planning efforts, the biggest job of all was
finding our *Aurora:* a ship to take our expedition to the Antarctic. A century ago, we would have visited the whaling and seal-
ing fleets of the Arctic to secure a vessel. Fortunately, in these
more enlightened times, we've moved on from hunting to
tourism. The downside is that almost all ships working in the region are committed for years in advance. Our expedition was a
one-off, a job of little interest to most. We needed a ship with no
prior commitments—no easy ask in Australian and New Zealand
waters.

With a deep breath, we entered the murky world of international shipping. We contacted anyone who might have a vessel:
companies in the U.K., South Africa, Australia, and New Zealand.
I lost count of the number of calls I made to individuals who were
representing themselves or companies, often with few or no credentials for being able to offer access to a ship. It's a strange
business. During some of the conversations I felt like I was at
real risk of signing up to a Nigerian internet scam. *So you want*

a deposit of $100,000, and you can get us a ship for a bargain price? Right . . .

It was a steep learning curve. The class of vessels, their size, capacity, range, and add-ons were daily questions as Chris and I scoured the world's shipping market. The big stumbling block was a shortage of vessels in the Southern Hemisphere that were both suitable and affordable. Several ships were for sale, but purchasing would have come with horrifying operating costs and the formidable task of finding a suitable captain and crew. Our best option was to hire a vessel with a crew. A small Christchurch-based operator called Heritage Expeditions found the only vessel that seemed to be available: the Russian-registered Академик Шокальский, or, in English, the MV *Akademik Shokalskiy.*

The *Shokalskiy* was just what we needed. Berthed in the north Pacific port of Vladivostok, the 233-foot-long ice-strengthened vessel had been built in 1982, one of a fleet of Soviet ships used to spy on the West in the Arctic. Today, she is operated by the Far Eastern Hydrometeorological Research Institute for friendlier pursuits. In 1998, she was converted to a research and cruise ship, with laboratory space and a lecture room, and capable of carrying fifty-four passengers in relative comfort, with seventeen crew. The *Shokalskiy* had been laid up for the last two seasons, but Heritage assured us she could be brought up to operational standard in no time. With decades of sea-ice experience on board and time spent in Commonwealth Bay before the arrival of B09B, the *Shokalskiy* offered all we wanted. But she didn't come cheap. Including the cost of bringing her down from the north Pacific, the *Shokalskiy* came in at US$31,000 a day. It was that or nothing.

CHAPTER THREE
The Furious Fifties

It's 24 November 2013, and I'm driving out from Invercargill along a quiet, windswept road to the port of Bluff. I'm excited. After months of preparations I'm about to see the vessel that will take us to the Antarctic in three days' time.

At last. A moment to myself.

The rolling green fields hurtle by. I wind down the window and breathe in the damp fresh air. It's been a hectic year.

Alone with my thoughts, I reflect on all that's happened. The dizzying highs and lows of organising an expedition south; research-planning meetings with the teams in New Zealand and Australia; securing the all-important scientific kit and other essential gear; the chasing of permissions; the never-ending stream of naysayers. We've achieved so much, but what has yet to happen hangs heavy on my mind. Uncertainty can be a terribly debilitating thing. I shake my head and cast aside the lingering doubts. We're off in a few days. There's not much else that can be done. There comes a point when you have to let go and trust in the team and all your hard work.

Passing the derelict, weather-beaten Victorian warehouses of Bluff, I drive on to the causeway that leads to the deep-water port. After a brief check of my credentials, I'm waved past security. I can see the *Shokalskiy*'s masts reaching above the dockside buildings. I turn the corner and catch my first glimpse of our ship, its distinctive blue hull and white-topped decks proud among the warehouses and cranes of the port. I've seen lots of photos of the *Shokalskiy* beating a path through Antarctic sea ice. Now here she is, waiting to take our expedition south.

The harborside is bustling with activity. The Heritage guys are frantically getting supplies on board before we officially take over the vessel tomorrow. Three large black inflatable Zodiac boats are being hoisted off the dockside by the ship's rear yellow deck crane and tied down among the lashed fuel drums and crates; they're going to be crucial for getting the team to and from the shore.

I park, and another four-wheel drive filled with gear pulls up beside me. Chris steps out.

"Doesn't she look fantastic?" Chris is grinning from ear to ear.

I nod. I've sometimes wondered whether we'd get this far, but seeing the *Shokalskiy* here makes it all worthwhile.

Close up, I glimpse parts of the bow peeling, the side panels pitted with age. The *Shokalskiy* has been painted, patched up and painted again in her thirty years, yet I can't help but look fondly on her.

She's all ours.

Our Heritage contact Aaron Russ breaks off from the work on the dockside and waves a greeting. Walking over, he introduces the shoulder-high figure accompanying him as Captain Igor, a smiling man of fifty-plus years who shakes our hands in welcome.

"Nice to meet you," Igor says in his heavily accented English. "Please, settle in. I have paperwork, but be free to look round *Shokalskiy*." With an apologetic shrug, he leaves to sort out the mountain of forms required for our departure as Aaron offers to take us round the ship.

Walking up the gangway, it all seems strangely familiar. Chris and I have been studying the ship's plans for months, working out where best to put team members, stores, field gear and laboratory equipment. I know every room before Aaron opens its door. There's one thing that catches me off guard, though: the Russian signs and posters that cover the walls, illustrated with short, abruptly worded English translations.

Silly, really. I should have expected it.

I dump my gear in the forward port-side cabin, just one floor below the ship's bridge on what is known as the boat deck. I'm right next door to the captain's room. With a bed in the corner and a small but functional shower-cum-toilet behind the door, the space is a tribute to the eighties, dominated by orange seating and dark brown melamine walls and table. A bookcase, desk and a couple of cupboards complete what will be my home for the next six weeks. It's clean, functional, and, in spite of the décor, an excellent space for expedition meetings. If I need to get to the bridge I only have to climb one steep flight of stairs. *Perfect.*

The bridge is really the nerve center of a ship. It's where the captain makes most of his decisions; where conditions are assessed, the route is set, reports made, and decisions logged. It's the place to go to find out what's happening. On entering the *Shokalskiy*'s bridge, the first thing that hits you squarely between the eyes is the view: large windows stretch all the way from port to starboard and give a stunning outlook, even over Bluff's harbor. The captain's chair and ship's wheel sit front center, to the side of which a large TV-like screen glows menacingly green as the radar picks out the surrounding buildings. Small flickering monitors report on everything from the ship's route to the weather and call signs of nearby vessels. Printed on a prominent sign at the front of the bridge is the *Shokalskiy*'s call sign, "UBNF," in case someone should unforgivably forget. Banks of control panels fill the space, covered in brightly colored switches, with the Russian labels reminding us this is a Russian ship, run by a Russian crew.

Heading down the central staircase, we drop onto the upper deck, home to the medical room and ship's lounge. This is the main thoroughfare through the ship where the noticeboards will post the daily itineraries and weather reports. The floor below has the labs and kitchen, flanked by the port and starboard dining areas of the main deck. The expedition bunk rooms are on these three levels. The cabins vary in size, with two to four wooden bunks fixed to the walls, all in the same décor as my room. All are tight on space, with bolted cupboards and bookcases for the inevitable rolling at sea. In the expedition manual, we describe it as third-class accommodation but with a five-class heart. That's exactly how it feels.

As we work our way round the *Shokalskiy*, it quickly feels like we've moved into a new home. Although the bridge and cabins are quiet, the rest of the ship is busy. No matter where we go, someone is adapting, modifying, or packing away gear in preparation for departure. Boxes and crates are strewn everywhere, their contents spilling out across the floor. In the fluorescent-lit corridors, Russian crew bustle past, mumbling apologies as they rush to get the ship ready.

In the lounge, Aaron introduces us to the Heritage staff who will be on the voyage. Like everywhere else, the room is littered with half-empty boxes in various stages of unpacking, with books, biscuits, and crates of powdered coffee and Milo (a popular Australasian malt chocolate drink made by mixing with milk or water) piled high on tables and chairs. Nicola and Brad, our young New Zealand chefs, have cooked their way across the Southern Ocean for several years and have recently become engaged. They shake our hands enthusiastically and seem to tower over "Little Nikki," the manager of the ship. Nikki is bright, bubbly, cheerful and no more than five foot tall. It's her first voyage south, but she's grown up at sea, helping her parents run a successful dwarf minke whale-diving operation in Queensland. The Heritage staff are the best in the business and friendly with it. I like them instantly and know we're lucky to have them on board.

Down another flight of stairs at the rear of the ship, what was the second dining area is being converted to a laboratory. This is where most of the work on the voyage will be done, the focus for the research we've planned for the expedition. The melamine tables are nearly finished being covered in wooden panels to create benches. It's a noisy, draughty space, with access to the rear outside deck on one side and the roar of the ship's engine on the other. Diesel fumes linger in the air. Stacks of computer consoles, cables, drying cabinets, coring equipment and tubing lie waiting for a home among the chaos.

"This should work." I turn to Chris. "What do you think?"

He walks into the adjacent room. Two large metal kitchen sinks run along the wall.

"Yeah, great. The computers can stay in the first room, and we'll do the sieving and other wet prep in this space. With the access to the deck through here, we can also prepare any gear for deployment if it's getting too rough outside."

Everything feels like it's falling into place.

Three Russian Orthodox icons look disapprovingly upon us from the laboratory walls. Ignoring their gaze, I pin up two maps: one shows the route from New Zealand to Antarctica, and the other our approach to Cape Denison. Both are covered in colored symbols and dates that set out our scheduled sampling locations. It will be a constant reminder of the task before us. Work is due to start from day one of the expedition.

A lecture room on the lower deck finishes off the tour of the communal spaces. It's here I'll hold the daily briefings to the team.

Like many of the ships of her class, the *Shokalskiy* has plenty of storage space on board. With all our science and field gear, we're going to need it. The rear single-level hold is storing the sledges and the three all-terrain vehicles we have for the expedition; two are on loan from Heritage. The forward hold is narrower and deeper, accessed through a yellow hatch on the front deck. Fortunately, for the heavy gear there's a small crane that can be used to move items between the hold and shore. The air in the hold is heavy with decades of oil, sweat and jute. Climbing down the two flights of steep metal steps, our footsteps echo in the rusting cavernous space. Chris's partner, Eleanor, is already hard at work on the lower level and calls up a greeting. A Ph.D. student, Eleanor is a glaciologist with a keen sense of humor and an expert eye for small details. In spite of the semi-darkness, she's patiently completing the inventory with one of the Russian crew. The space is filling up fast, and all of it will have to be pushed and prodded to fill every nook and cranny. It seems disorganized, but there's method in the madness. All kit has to be checked off, locked down and then double- and triple-checked. We're about to head into the most unpredictable stretch of water on the planet, and we need to know everything has made it on board and is safely packed away. If anything breaks free, it will be a serious hazard.

Back on deck we hear raised voices. Heading aft, we find a group loudly discussing in broken English where to put a twelve-foot stainless-steel arm we've brought with us for the rear deck. This will hold the sonar head for mapping the seabed, and it will be swung out and lowered over the side by the ship's crane. This is Chris's baby. He's spent the last few months working on the design with engineers so it will survive whatever the Southern Ocean throws at it. Unfortunately, it seems the best place to weld the arm to the deck is right on top of one of the fuel tanks.

"Damn!" says Chris, as one of the welding party starts to argue it should go on the port side, too far from the crane to be of use. He rushes over to put the Russian right on where the steel arm needs to be. I leave him to sort out a compromise.

* * *

Seventy-two hours later, I'm standing on the top deck of the *Shokalskiy* as she casts off.

This is a special moment. Two years of planning has come to this. Somehow, we've managed to find a ship and kit-out an expedition, and now we're away on the first leg. Chris is standing nearby, smiling contentedly, the sonar arm just one of many jobs he's sorted out with time to spare. A small army of people are milling about—scientists, students, teachers, and volunteers, all talking and laughing. It's been a crazy few days, but when jobs had to be done, someone always stepped up.

I turn toward a roar and see some of the students happily looking at a group selfie they've taken. It's exactly the atmosphere on board Chris and I wanted. We're fortunate to have them all on the team.

For this expedition, we need great communicators. We're hoping this expedition will be more than just reporting discoveries; we want to engage with people, to show them how science works. Over the last few months, I've been busy posting expedition news, highlighting our science plans, but I'm under no illusion about the amount of work during the forthcoming weeks. I'm going to be too busy leading the expedition. I need help from enthusiastic young researchers who can write blog posts, take photos and make short films of the work we're doing, all to be splashed across the expedition website and our social media network by Anthony. Bastardizing an advert supposedly placed by Shackleton for his *Endurance* expedition, we'd made an international call: *PhD volunteers sought for Antarctic science and adventure.* This advertisement offering places on the expedition led to a deluge of two-minute YouTube applications. The brief was simple: Tell us why you want to join the expedition. The answers ranged from the passionate ("We need to do more to teach children about the world") to the downright desperate ("I just have to go. Right?"). We chose fourteen brilliant Ph.D.

students from the U.S., U.K., Europe, Australia, and New Zealand; fourteen natural storytellers who would return home with experiences they'd treasure and that would guide them in their future careers in science.

I return my gaze forward. The sun is shining and there's hardly a cloud in the sky. I can taste the warm, salty air. I breathe deeply and savor the moment.

It feels good to be leaving Bluff.

We just have the notoriously narrow harbour entrance left to negotiate. We'll then be in the Foveaux Strait, the body of water that separates mainland New Zealand from Stewart Island and out beyond that, the Southern Ocean. Up ahead, a corridor of blue weather-beaten steel columns weaves a path through the messy surf, marking a way through the shallows. A small gray pilot boat leads us out as we cautiously approach the channel. A moment later, the *Shokalskiy* seems to accelerate, and I look over the side. Chaotic waves crash around us. There really is very little leeway on either side.

Suddenly we're out in the open, the angry water replaced by long lazy swells. The ship's horn blasts a farewell.

On the top deck, the increasing roll of the *Shokalskiy* is greeted by cheering.

We're off.

Seven hundred years ago, one of the most courageous ever voyages set out into the Southern Ocean. History, though, has long forgotten the names of the explorers. We don't know who they were or where they left from, but we do know that around the same time New Zealand was discovered by Polynesians, a small group continued a wave of discovery that had begun two centuries before. Whatever their motivation, these brave individuals launched probably nothing larger than a double-hulled canoe into one of the most treacherous stretches of water in the world. In the Southern Ocean, heavy seas are the norm rather than the exception; its storms are the stuff of legend, whipping the surface into a chaotic, foamy mess that threatens any vessel. When ships go down in these waters, they can just disappear— no wreck, no debris, nothing. It's a fearsome place. And yet 700 years ago, a canoe somehow fought through 250 miles of these punishing seas to reach 50 degrees south, where it beached itself on a northern shore of the subantarctic Auckland Islands. No doubt exhausted and relieved at their success, the Polynesians camped, restocked and departed shortly after. Today, all that's left of their extraordinary achievement are a few burnt-out campfires set in among the sand dunes, some small stone tools and a handful of dog-gnawed sea lion bones. Whether they made it back home we will never know. The islands appear to have been forgotten afterward until 1806 when a whaling ship stumbled upon them and staked a British claim.

When the great Antarctic explorer Sir James Ross visited the Auckland Islands on his way south in 1840, he considered "the many advantages this place possesses for a penal settlement." But the dense thicket of "stag-headed vegetation," aggressive sea lions, and wildly changing weather defied attempts at settlement by Europeans. People seldom stayed long, at least intentionally. Those unfortunate enough to be shipwrecked along its shores were forced to eke out an existence hoping for rescue one day, something that was not a foregone conclusion. Today all that remains are a small cemetery and a few scattered bricks and rotten planks among the trees and bushes, testament to the harsh reality of life on the subantarctics.

Although far from ideal for humans, the Auckland Islands are 241 square miles of all-too-rare real estate in the depths of the Southern Ocean. They may suffer a constant barrage of waves, wind, and rain, but the nutrient-rich offshore waters, forested slopes, and shallow east-facing bays make them a precious haven for wildlife. Until recently, seabirds, penguins, seals, and sea lions had flourishing populations, recovering after the mass slaughter of the nineteenth and early twentieth centuries. Mysteriously, though, there's been a collapse in many bird and seal populations. During the 1990s, biologists working on the Auckland Islands noticed that the recovery of New Zealand sea lions—sometimes called Hooker sea lions—was stalling. Alarmingly, numbers shortly after went into free-fall. With around 10,000 individuals left, the species has halved in just twenty years and is officially classified as "critical," the most serious endangered category possible. It's a pattern repeated across the New Zealand subantarctics. On Campbell Island, the small Rockhopper penguins started their decline earlier, with an extraordinary population collapse of 95 percent since the mid-twentieth century and no recovery in sight. With fishing no longer permitted around the islands and hunting long since banned, it's suspicious that different species are hurting at a time when the climate is also changing across the region. A longer, more detailed study might just help us understand what's going on.

The *Shokalskiy*'s voyage to the Auckland Islands is considerably easier than the one taken seven centuries ago. We suffer no major storms or wild seas, and the archipelago appears on the horizon just twenty-four hours after we depart Bluff. A few hours later, we weigh anchor in the sheltered northern waters of Port Ross, near a double bay affectionately called Sarah's Bosom by the British explorers. The New Zealand Department of Conservation are careful over the numbers and timing of visitors to protect the struggling wildlife, so we have the islands to ourselves. To make sure we don't unwittingly introduce any pests, the team are busy brushing, scrubbing, and cleaning every pocket, strap, and crevice in their gear. Tomorrow we aim to go onshore, and the smallest seed could have a devastating impact on this pristine environment.

I leave the sound of laughter and vacuum-cleaning behind

and climb the ladder to the top deck. The moon casts an eerie light over the ship and surrounding slopes, the dense vegetation ending abruptly a couple of hundred feet above. White and gray clouds scud over the windswept peaks. The wind is forecast to strengthen from the west but for now it's surprisingly calm. I can even hear the waves lapping gently against the hull. It's the perfect place to shelter for the night.

I turn on the satellite phone and make sure the antenna is pointing toward the sky.

One moment please, the phone declares.

The handset starts ringing and a moment later I hear Annette: "Hi, love, how's it going?"

It's wonderful to hear her voice.

Annette and I met in our final year at university in the U.K. and fell in love. Within a year, we were engaged. Annette is a brilliant teacher but, amazingly, has always linked her career to mine, often to the detriment of her own. Travel is one of our great shared passions, though. We've lived in many different parts of the world, moving from one academic position to another, driven by a love of experiencing new places and meeting new people. We've had two gorgeous kids; after Cara was born in New Zealand, Robert joined the family a few years later when we were living in Belfast, Northern Ireland.

Over this time, most of our family and friends have struggled to understand my job. It's not nine to five. It demands much more. As an Earth scientist, you have to get into the field and find the sites that will help answer the big science questions. Over the years, the kids have grown up with visits by brilliant, often eccentric characters who drop in en route to some exotic destination. Travel is a necessary part of the job, and I really do enjoy it, but I'd be lying if I said I have no regrets. I've missed a lot of the children growing up, which is something I'll never get back. We made a decision early on that if I was going to support the family with a career in science, Annette would be a stay-at-home mum. On the whole, it's worked out well. Science has looked after us, but it's only been possible because Annette's a wonderful friend, wife, and mother.

"Great, darling, great. We've made it to the Auckland Islands. It's everything I hoped for and more. The place feels like the edge of the known world. The islands just rise out of nothing but are covered in bogs and trees. We've even seen lots of crazy sea lions. It's brilliant to have made it. How are the kids?"

We speak about everything and nothing. Even when I'm away in the depths of fieldwork, I'll ring the family every day. On occasion, I've walked miles to call Annette and the children; I sleep better knowing they're all safe. When I return home, the best I can do is recount stories of where I've been and who I've met. This time, though, it's going to be different. This time, they'll be sharing the adventure with me on the second leg, a chance for me to make up for the last year and to share something special in a part of the world I love. It will be a family experience few have ever undertaken, and the trip of a lifetime. The children are just the right age too. Cara is fifteen years old and Rob twelve, old enough to appreciate where we're going and follow instructions if the need arises.

In the build-up to the expedition, Annette has been working on a major project for the website: "A History of Antarctic Exploration in 30 Objects." Collaborating with museums and art galleries around the world, she has written the equivalent of a book in just two months, helping to raise the profile of the expedition. On the second leg, she'll be working with the scientists to develop lesson plans for schoolchildren back home. Robert is an enthusiastic writer and Cara a keen photographer; rather than any ham-fisted effort I might make to communicate with teenagers and kids, they will be posting blogs and images on the voyage.

I can't wait to see them when we get back to Bluff.

* * *

Four seasons in one day, I mutter to myself.

I'm kneeling on a grassy knoll beside a golden sandy beach. We woke to find the cloud base had fallen overnight. The wind has picked up, and the air is now thick with mist and rain. I keep my head down in front of a small tent sheltering our satellite hook-up from the elements. This rain is like nowhere else on Earth. It just seems to hang in the air, working its way through any weak point in my clothing. I've only been out for a few hours and I'm soaking wet.

I look anxiously behind me. A 200-pound male sea lion is nearby, its snorts and barks directed toward me. My backside is drawing more attention than I'd like, a tempting target for aggressive males during the start of mating season, who are only too keen for an opportunity to show off their prowess. They may be at risk of extinction, but medic and Ph.D. student Ben Fisk stands by with an umbrella ready to tap them on a nose if they get too close. He can't help but look bemused. I'm just nervous.

In the distance, I can hear the purr of one of the outboard motors on a Zodiac inflatable. On board are marine biologists Emma Johnson and broad-shouldered Graeme Clark, zipping across Ross Harbour in scuba gear and dry suits. For a moment, I can just make them out through the fog, and then they're gone. They're about to start a full survey of life on the island's sea floor using a piece of kit called a Baited Remote Underwater Video, or BRUV for short. Basically, it's a metal frame holding a GoPro underwater camera that is pointed toward a tin of tuna on a pole. Left on the seabed for an hour, the camera captures footage of any crabs and fish attracted to the bait. Conditions permitting, Graeme and Emma plan to drop several BRUVs each day and examine the movies back on board, giving them a detailed picture of life below the waves. No one has ever done such a survey of the Aucklands, and the great thing is that the BRUVs cause no damage to the seabed. It's also ridiculously efficient, accomplishing in days what a scuba survey would take weeks to do.

It's nearly time for our first scheduled Hangout on Air. Advertised by Google, over a thousand people have said they'll be joining us from around the world. I'm excited by the possibility. You don't need to be a television broadcaster to go on air anymore. With a camera connected to a computer, I can share ideas and places live through a Google+ account, viewers can ask questions, and as soon as the broadcast is finished, the footage is loaded onto YouTube. Hangouts are perfect for sharing an expedition with the rest of the world, and we've scheduled eight across the next six weeks.

That said, I'm starting to realize why no one has ever tried anything like this before. I promised a Hangout from the Auckland Islands, but the technology is struggling to oblige. The satellite hook-up just isn't happening.

Shit, I hope this works.

Kneeling calmly beside me is Leticia, a bubbly and enthusiastic Google employee. Without Leticia we wouldn't be here. She's supported us from the start, negotiating the funds that helped make the expedition a reality. Google wants to show what's possible with social media, and I don't want to disappoint. Leticia is really keen for this to work, but there's not a trace of concern on her face.

The Inmarsat satellite we're using lies over the tropics, so I try turning the antenna panel a little more to the north. A high-pitched screech suddenly erupts from the device. There are whoops of excitement around me.

That's a relief. I try not to show it on my face. We've practised lots of times before, but Murphy's Law seemed intent on ruining my best efforts.

As part of the Doodle4Google prize, two teachers are with us, Kerrie from New Zealand and Nicole from Australia.

They're both friendly, smiley people who only found out they were on the expedition a few weeks ago. Now they're on a subantarctic island dressed in supposedly waterproof gear readying themselves to answer questions on the wildlife of the Auckland Islands. I hope the rain isn't going to screw up the picture too badly.

The Intrepid Science Google+ page appears on my laptop.

We're connected. Thank Christ for that.

A young sea lion comes up too close, threatening to bite me, and Ben steps in. With a pained bellow, it waddles back to the beach, nursing a sore nose.

Kerrie's and Nicole's students appear on the screen: more than twenty smiling faces from the winning New Zealand and Australian schools, their voices crystal clear.

This is so cool.

"Hi, guys," Nicole greets her class. They wave back.

I've seen the technology at work before, but it still blows me away. We're hundreds of miles from anywhere, we have a colony of barking sea lions behind us and we're talking to the world.

Five days later, I'm scrambling through the undergrowth of Campbell Island with one of my best mates, Jonathan Palmer, just in front of me. I can hear Jonathan cursing under his breath as he struggles to get a grip underfoot. The ground is completely sodden, its surface treacherous. We slip and slide our way through the mud.

"Sssh," Jonathan hisses nervously.

I crouch down. Just minutes ago, we came nose to nose with a sea lion dozing in a grove of *Dracophyllum*, almost perfectly camouflaged against the tree's needle-like leaves. With a roar of surprise and a twitch of its whiskers, the sea lion struggled upright and made its displeasure all too clear. I've never seen

Jonathan move so fast. Turning tail, we fled, the sea lion's bellows and snorts ringing in our ears as it made to give chase. I think we've lost the offended beast, but there could easily be more around. It feels like a scene from the movie *Predator*. We're climbing a small hill, following a well-worn track that looks suspiciously like it's been used by sea lions—they've been known to make their way far up hillsides. Neither of us is in a rush to meet a few hundred pounds of blubber hurtling down the slope.

We step off the track and look around apprehensively.

All clear.

I catch my breath.

We spent four days on the Auckland Islands and soon had our routine down pat. Each evening, I went over the following day's science program with Chris and Greg, then let Igor know our plans. By six the next morning, we'd checked the conditions and confirmed with the bridge what we were doing. Breakfast was at eight, followed by my briefing and then off into the field. If a team needed to stay on shore all day, they picked up lunch from the kitchen, along with sleeping gear and supplies from the stores in case they had to remain longer—a precaution if conditions forced the *Shokalskiy* to make for open water. The biggest loss of time was in shuttling everyone between the ship and shore on the Zodiacs, but we still managed to get eight teams out each day. That's the equivalent of eight days' work for every day in the field. Peaks were climbed, cores of peat and ocean mud taken, the sea floor scanned with sonar, BRUVs dropped to the seabed. We're on track to get the equivalent of a month's fieldwork done in a week—far more than I dared hope. The Hangouts have all worked and the expedition students have been posting lots of great articles and photos online. The science is reaching an audience, and the feedback has been good. Leticia seems genuinely pleased with the international response.

And all this has been achieved in the craziest weather. We've had summer snow quickly followed by storms, blazing sunshine followed by yet more snow and, if we're lucky, a squall.

By 3 December, we'd made it to Campbell Island, a cluster of uninhabited rocks at 52 degrees, a day's sailing south of the Auckland Islands. The climate here is worse than in the Auckland Islands, and that's saying something. On average, only forty days each year are drizzle-free and most of those are gray. Perversely, it's the reason we're here, but that seems of little comfort at the moment. Campbell Island sits right in the path of the westerly winds as they track across the Southern Ocean.

The problem is, as I mentioned earlier, that we have little idea what the climate was doing in these latitudes before the mid-twentieth century. The weather station here has the longest continuous record in the region, but it only goes back to the 1940s. We need to get back a whole heap further if we're to understand the scale of the changes happening today and what might be driving them. This is where *Dracophyllum* comes in. Two species are found on Campbell, making them the most southerly living tree in the southwest Pacific. Their importance for understanding the changing weather is thanks to the genius of Leonardo da Vinci. In the fifteenth century, the Italian polymath realized there was a link between the thickness of tree rings and the growing conditions. Thick rings, he reasoned, must have been when it was a good season for tree growth; narrow rings, terrible. Although we have more sophisticated methods than those available to da Vinci, the principle is still the same. By measuring the ring thickness, we can get a handle on changing climate. *Dracophyllum* is one of nature's weather stations, putting down a ring of growth each year.

Jonathan stops at a tree. It's about ten feet high and must be twenty inches across. He runs his hands up and down its trunk, feeling for rot. Fragments of dark peeling bark fall to the ground. He pauses to consider for a moment.

"This looks like a good one," he suddenly declares, slapping the tree and dropping his rucksack. We glance around. Not a sea lion in sight.

Pulling out a long metal barrel, Jonathan checks the drill bit is at right angles to the trunk and slowly turns the barrel into the tree. There's a sharp squeak as the corer bites and rotates. Soon he's reached the center and is pulling out a delicate straw-like section of wood. Jonathan has worked on trees most of his professional life, and he's been like a man possessed on the sub-antarctics. Drilling into the center of as many trees as we're allowed by the Department of Conservation, Jonathan has taken scores of samples from across the islands. I look at the core he's cradling and try to eyeball the number of rings. The wood will need to be dried out and sanded down before it can be properly measured in the laboratory, but it looks like we have over a hundred years, more than double the length of the weather-station record. I'm thrilled.

Jonathan drops the core into a plastic straw and stows the precious sample carefully away in his pack.

"That's our lot, Chris," he proclaims. "Now let's get out of here before that bloody sea lion turns up."

During our preparations, there was one large hole in the science program I was particularly worried about filling: We didn't have anyone to work on seabirds. It's an area of research I know very little about, and I was loath to cold-call someone I didn't know. Out of the blue, Jonathan dropped by my office.

"Chris, are you still looking for a seabird specialist?" he asked. "If so, I think I have just the person you need. Kerry-Jayne Wilson is brilliant. We used to work together at Lincoln University. She's got more than forty years in the business, and

I know she'll bite your hand off if you offer her a place on the expedition. You'll love her."

A day later, we had our seabird expert. Jonathan was absolutely right. Kerry-Jayne is wild-haired, self-assured, wonderfully upbeat, and the owner of a wickedly dry sense of humor. Without hesitation, she volunteered for both legs of the expedition and hasn't stopped working since. Each day, Kerry-Jayne has led the charge onshore with a group of Ph.D., students who have struggled to keep up. Using a burrow scope made up of a small camera at one end and a monitor at the other, Kerry-Jayne has been getting population counts of different nesting species across the island, adding to data she and others have collected since the 1970s. But it's our last destination on this first leg she's most excited about.

Snares is a small promontory of rocks that time seems to have forgotten; it's something like Campbell Island on steroids. Over the centuries, people have made occasional visits to hunt mutton-birds but never settled, with the practical upshot that there have never been any introduced pests. The result is that a staggering fifty-seven bird species inhabit an area the size of New York's Central Park. Four species of albatrosses, five species of petrels, three species of prions, and six species of penguins, to name but a few. Throw in skuas, cormorants, terns, and gulls, and it's an island that's gone crazy for birds.

It's our final day of work on the first leg. The morning mist is burning off. Snares' jagged, sheer cliffs rise out of the ocean, and the sky is almost dark with the amount of wildlife in the air. I've never seen anything like it. The New Zealand Department of Conservation, which looks after Snares, don't normally allow visitors, but today an exception has been made for a few select teams from the expedition. Kerry-Jayne is at the front of the queue, anxious to be off. With Leticia, Kerrie, and Nicole, I'm hosting a Hangout on Air on the island.

Chris takes us out in a Zodiac. Snares has no natural harbor, but with the light northerly winds, the *Shokalskiy* has found shelter below the cliffs to the south. It's a ten-minute journey across open water to a rocky platform on the eastern side. We leap ashore. A quick wave and Chris disappears to take the rest of the expedition members for a tour of the island's coast. Sea lions watch us suspiciously from a nearby outcrop as we set up next to a large colony of noisy Snares crested penguins, whose distinctive red bills and yellow eyebrows give them a comical professorial look. It's a perfect backdrop for the last Hangout of the first leg, and Leticia is over the moon. Well-practiced by now, we connect effortlessly with the satellite, and a room of smiling faces greets us in return. Professionally, Leticia guides the questions while Nicole and Kerrie merrily share some of their discoveries on the expedition: the wildlife, the changing climate, the history of the islands. The penguins squawk and crow, happily hopping and grooming themselves in the background. The students love it.

I'm just relieved we're finishing the Hangouts on a high.

When we're all done, I stay online. I have one more job to do, something a little different this time: a Hangout in History. It's a new initiative by Google that aims to bring history alive, with actors recreating famous events and pupils asking the questions. The Black Death, Guy Fawkes, Elizabethan England—all are played out with a fantastic grotesqueness that's guaranteed to grab attention. This time, the setting is Elephant Island, 1915. Two months after the *Endurance* has sunk in sea ice, Shackleton's men are stuck on the Antarctic Peninsula and increasingly worried about the "Boss." I'm here to guide the pupils to the great man. I have a script and am primed to drop in clues at the appropriate time. Dressed in heavy clothing, two explorers with clipped English accents emerge on the screen, seated in a tent filled with coils of rope, lamps, and scientific gear. The students appear, wearing Edwardian garb, cheering with excitement. The set-up looks brilliant. We get started, sharing ideas as Shackleton's story unfolds.

All of a sudden, the satellite link drops out. I've been cut off and there's no getting them back.

I hope it's not a sign.

CHAPTER FOUR
There Be Dragons

This is it. This is for real. We're heading for the Antarctic.

It's two o'clock in the afternoon, 8 December, day twelve of the expedition. The *Shokalskiy* only returned to Bluff yesterday and we're already leaving again.

Only two hours ago, immigration officials were on board stamping our passports for departure from New Zealand waters, something we didn't do on the first leg. Now we're off. Gray clouds threaten rain, but most of the team have come up to the top deck to say their good-byes to loved ones at home, milking the last phone reception we'll have for four weeks. There's a palpable sense of excitement in the air as photos are taken and messages sent. Our connection to the world is about to become a whole lot smaller.

I'm nervous. We're heading beyond the subantarctic islands this time. We may have the best possible ship, team, and equipment, but I know my history. Almost all expeditions that set out for Antarctica thought they were well prepared, and few returned with plans fulfilled. All too often, carefully designed science programs went awry because of a change in conditions. Some never returned at all. Shackleton left with high hopes and came back a scarred man; Mawson nearly lost his mind over the loss of two friends. No one sails to the Antarctic without thinking twice. We're going somewhere far beyond immediate help; somewhere that can never be taken for granted. We will have to work hard as a team and trust the conditions favor us if we're to achieve all we're aiming to do.

It's a moment to savor with the family. Few have worked harder to make this expedition happen. And now we're about to share our biggest adventure yet. Cara and Robert are chatting excitedly, taking their last look at land and adjusting to the feel of the ship. They spot my parents, Ian and Cathy, who have traveled from their home in Christchurch to see us off. Next time we see them, the *Shokalskiy* will have traveled more than 3,000 miles across the Southern Ocean. We exchange exaggerated waves with the two small figures on the promontory. Mum and Dad look tiny against the rocks.

I breathe in deeply and catch a last waft of trees, tinged with sea spray. It's a reassuring smell of land, of safety. A trawler passes by, struggling against the current running offshore, its turquoise hull stark against the green promontory of Bluff.

Everything seems very small out here.

I put my thoughts to one side and turn to Annette and give her a hug. "Amazing to be finally off, isn't it?"

She smiles back at me. "Yes, love. I can't believe we're here."

"No regrets?"

"None."

All of a sudden, the siren blares out across the ship's tannoy system. Lifeboat practice.

Everyone on the *Shokalskiy* has an allocated space on one of the two lifeboats. If anything untoward should happen, you need to know where to go. In an emergency situation, the last thing you need is confusion and panic as people struggle to find space on a lifeboat.

Donning our bulky orange life jackets, we make our way to the stern and join the good-natured queue. We're on the port side with the kids, and head toward Nicola the cook at the bottom of the lifeboat ramp. Smiling, she ticks us off the list as we climb into the brightly colored vessel. We sit snugly side by side in the small orange capsule. There's hardly room to breathe, let alone move about. There are twenty-five of us inside, but the lifeboat can carry twice this number. A few whispered conversations break the silence. Minutes later, the last of the team are in and the hatch is slammed shut. The temperature immediately starts to rise. The little light that pierces the dimness comes from a small window above the steering wheel in the stern.

There's a hushed silence as the broad shoulders of Vladimir make their way through the heaving mass to the stern.

"Welcome aboard. I am the second mate and safety officer. We have in this lifeboat some water, some foods and fishing equipment. Now we're starting the engine and check. Please."

Vladimir turns to another Russian crew member, who presses the starter motor. The engine splutters to life. Oars hang from the ceiling in the event that all else fails.

Vladimir declares matter-of-factly: "Our lifeboat in good condition."

Everyone laughs nervously.

We'll only be using the lifeboats if Igor decides the *Shokalskiy* offers absolutely no protection. With wild seas, near-freezing temperatures, and the threat of bergs and sea ice, getting into a lifeboat in the Southern Ocean is only a last resort. With the vessel's sense of claustrophobia, the darkness, and the choking smoke from the engine, the possibility of using it as refuge is not something to dwell on.

The last thirty-six hours has been madness. Even before the *Shokalskiy* docked in Bluff's harbor, we pulled out and checked over all the gear and samples. We kept anything needed for the second leg on board and carefully packaged everything else to return home with the team cycling off. The first leg was a good test of our kit, to find what worked, what didn't, what needed modifying and what we were missing. During the day, replacements were bought in Invercargill; broken gear repaired; water tanks topped up; equipment and supplies restocked and restowed; cabins made ready for our new shipmates. For good or bad, we've done all we can. If we've forgotten anything now we'll have to make do. Everything depends on the team.

I'm sorry we've lost most of the team from the first leg, but I can't help being excited by those who have joined us for the longer voyage. Early on in the planning, we decided against advertising to fill the science roles on the expedition. You have absolutely no idea who will apply. Science attracts people on all parts of the spectrum. Like any walk of life, science has its prima donnas, control freaks, and loners. I've known colleagues who go to work in a dressing-gown, some who bark, some who just stare at their feet. They may be world-class researchers, but that doesn't mean you want to be stuck on a boat with them for weeks on end. Chris and I wanted passionate professionals, who were optimistic and like-minded. And most important, people we could rely on. Confidence in your team is of crucial importance. In a hazardous environment like the Antarctic, you have to trust those to whom you give instructions. Your life might depend on it.

Graeme, Kerry-Jayne, and Eleanor have all worked in the Antarctic before and agreed to remain on board for the second leg, helping us to link the research on the subantarctics with Cape Denison. To replace Emma for the work on the seabed, smiling Argentinian Ziggy Marzinelli has stepped up, a giant of a man with one of the bushiest beards I've ever seen. And for working on penguins and seals, marine biologist Tracey Rogers is joining us with two Ph.D. students Naysa Balcazar-Carbrera and Alicia Guerrero, Chileans with a burning passion for the

Antarctic. Dark haired, with an easy-going manner, Tracey is a world expert on how mammals cope in changing environments, having researched the Antarctic since the 1990s. We're extremely lucky to have Tracey on the team.

In a previous life, Chris was an oceanographer but, with all his responsibilities on the expedition, knew he wouldn't have the time to take on what would be a large part of the research program. We want to make best use of our time at sea and needed someone to take on this role; ideally a rising star in the field, keen to communicate the excitement of what we were doing. With blond curly hair, an irrepressible sense of humor and an exceptional career for someone in his early thirties, Erik van Sebille agreed in his clipped Dutch accent even before I'd finished making the offer in Sydney: "I'll do it, Chris. That sounds so cool."

Others have joined us to complement the science work. As recommended by Greg, I invited Andrew Peacock to be the expedition's chief medical officer. Tall, athletic, and square-jawed, Andrew's been around the world as an expedition doctor and award-winning photographer, and his no-nonsense attitude immediately instils confidence. To support Andrew, we have Mandarin-speaking Ph.D. student and St John's medic Colin Tan, who dazzled us with his YouTube application, and we've also managed to convince Ben Fisk to stay. Ben was only supposed to be on the first leg, but Chris and I were so impressed by his enthusiasm and professionalism we asked him to remain with us for the second. Crucially, the three medics give us plenty of flexibility when we're operating off and around the ship; no one will ever be far from medical support if needed. Alongside these, Australian expeditioner and history lecturer Ben Maddison is joining us. Ben has decades of Antarctic experience, making him a natural choice for supporting the logistics on and about the ice, while his boyish charm will be a great help organizing the lecture program for the volunteers on the voyage.

Last night we held the expedition briefing for the second leg in a room at the front of the Kelvin Hotel in central Invercargill. Forty-eight scientists, volunteers, and media crammed into a space meant for half that number. It was a surprisingly warm summer evening, and with almost no ventilation the room was stifling. I started the evening with an introduction to the expedition: what we hoped to achieve, who the science team were, the roles of everyone on board, and how things had gone so far. Greg followed. Softly spoken, he described the logistics for departure: where everyone would be picked up and when, and how the baggage would get to the *Shokalskiy*. As Greg spoke, I scanned the room and put names to faces. The selection of volunteers was the part of the preparations I had least control over.

Antarctic expeditioners can be an even crazier bunch than scientists. You meet all sorts, from inspirational individuals who have achieved remarkable personal feats of physical and mental endurance—triumphs I can never hope to emulate—to those desperate to return home with frostbite scars as some weird, screwed-up way of showing how macho they are. When Greg advertised berths for sale on the expedition, Chris and I weren't sure who we'd get. We wanted enthusiastic volunteers who would work alongside the scientists on board—people willing to get up at any hour to help drop equipment off a rolling deck into the Southern Ocean, people who wouldn't think twice about taking ocean measurements from a couple of feet of sea ice. Perhaps because we were up-front about it being a science expedition, we didn't get anyone who was a testosterone-pumped psycho. Instead we were oversubscribed with educators, IT experts, wine-makers, and psychiatrists.

There's a full mix of ages and life experiences in the room. Cara and Robert are the youngest on the team. Elizabeth, a retired teacher, may be the oldest at seventy-six, but she has an extraordinary amount of energy and is feisty with it. We have Janet, a Green senator-elect for the Australian federal parliament, making copious notes. Kerry-Lee, a Chinese banker, is seated in the front row concentrating on all that's being said. I met Terry and Rob in Adelaide during one of the many talks I've given around Australia and New Zealand; with day jobs in advertising and computer management, both have broad grins on their faces in anticipation of the trip. None of them have been to the East Antarctic before.

We also have three journalists. Over the years, I've been interviewed by *The Guardian* on its weekly science podcast. The success of this series is in no small part thanks to its host Alok Jha, a personable and witty man with the most extraordinary mop of dark hair, which seemingly has a life of its own, including a cult following on Twitter as @AloksHair. Regardless of the topic, Alok has a remarkable ability to distil the most complex ideas into beautiful prose that makes you care about science, which is something I'm deeply envious of. Last year Alok mentioned he'd love to go to Antarctica, and I couldn't resist asking if he'd like to join the expedition. With offices in London, New York and Sydney, *The Guardian* were supportive and, after several calls and meetings, offered international coverage in both print and online, with a dedicated web page "Antarctica live" to follow the progress of the expedition. In fact, they were so enthusiastic they asked if cameraman Laurence Topsham could come along as well. A gentle giant of a man—he towers above me, and I'm 6' 2"—Laurence had recently returned from the Arctic and was keen to get south. During our planning, Alok also introduced me to Andrew Luck-Baker, a radio producer, sound man, and interviewer with the BBC. Andrew offered to do four radio shows for the World Service, broadcasting while we're in the Antarctic. It was a complete no-brainer. I offered all three of them berths on the *Shokalskiy* with internet access for filing their reports home. If we wanted to show science in action and tell the world about our discoveries, we couldn't have hoped for better.

*   *   *

We ride out into the Southern Ocean on the back of a high-pressure system, the wind a steady ten knots from the south-west. The conditions don't bode well. Our sea crossing looks like it's going to be rougher than the first leg and a lot more unpleasant. We're sailing along the edge of the Campbell Plateau, a vast submarine tableland extending off New Zealand. When we visited the Auckland and Campbell islands we were lucky. Sailors speak with the greatest respect of these waters, and rightly so. The Campbell Plateau is notorious for its wild, stormy seas, caused by the exceptionally steep relief of the seabed near our position. The easterly flowing currents in these parts have traveled thousands of miles, uninterrupted by any landmass, and with an average depth of nearly three miles, across some of the deepest oceans on the planet. When these waters meet the start of the Campbell Plateau, the effect can be devastating on the surface. Over a mere forty miles, this huge body of water suddenly finds itself forced up and over a sheer cliff of rock and mud into shallows only a third of a mile deep. The upshot is that even a moderate breeze can create a scene from *The Tempest*. By the time we're out in open water we have a twenty-knot wind, and the *Shokalskiy* is swaying . . . a lot. What was a gentle pitch leaving Bluff has turned into a roller-coaster, with a ten-foot swell swinging the vessel 20 degrees from one side to the other; it's the hangover of a storm that recently passed away to the south.

We have three days before our first stop at subantarctic Macquarie Island. Three precious days at sea to settle in, catch our breath and find our sea legs. Inside the *Shokalskiy*, I'm learning to anticipate the ever-changing angles. For the unwary, one moment you're walking along the corridor, the next you're being unceremoniously slammed into the wall. The rails along the walls have become my best friend as I hang on tight, carefully choosing when to commit to the next big stride down the corridor. I'm one of the lucky few; the constant rolling has had a more immediate effect on others. Within a day of departing Bluff, all but the strongest of stomachs are in bed. Greg warned the team of this, with the promise that for all but the worst cases, everyone would have their sea legs in a couple of days. It's providing little comfort.

Within a few hours of leaving Bluff, Alok catches me in the corridor outside the dining room. He looks in pain. "You never said it would be this bad."

Before I can respond to Alok's complaint, he dashes to his cabin, the door slamming behind him, and I don't see him or many of the others again for the first day.

Annette and Cara are two of the worst sufferers. I never anticipated just how ill they might be.

"Why didn't you tell me you suffered so much from seasickness?" I ask Annette as she lies in our bunk, trying to remain as still as possible. Although our cabin is relatively spacious, its position at the top of the *Shokalskiy* means it's lurching more than most.

"I didn't think it would be this bad," she replies. That's just like Annette, never wanting to make a fuss. Cara feels terrible and a little teary. She and Robert are in their own cabin on the main deck. The room may be two floors down, but it's not making much difference. Cara hasn't the strength to get out of bed, so I go and find her a bucket, then stroke her hair to try to comfort her. It's rotten being sea-sick. You feel ill, tired, thirsty, and heady, all at the same time. There's little relief apart from drugs, rest, lots of rest and more drugs. Sea-sickness feels like it will never end. You just want to curl up and die, anything to stop the pain.

I go to the medical room on the upper deck and find Andrew at his desk, surrounded by cabinets filled with dressings and ointments. Like all medical areas, the place smells of bleach. True to form, Andrew is completely untouched by the constant rolling and has spent most of the day dispensing sea-sickness pills like they're going out of fashion. It's not the most riveting of jobs, but it does mean he, Ben, and Colin have managed to meet almost everyone on the team within the first twenty-four hours. I ask Andrew whether he can check on Cara and Annette.

"Sure, mate," he says happily in his broad Australian accent. Within half an hour, the patients have been reassured, plied with drugs and are passed out asleep.

"Thanks, Andrew, it's crap seeing them like this."

"No worries, Chris. They'll be right in a couple of days," he says, and heads off to finish his rounds.

Robert is far more buoyant. "Dad, I'm feeling all right," he tells me proudly. "It's just Mum and Cara, isn't it?"

Minutes later, though, he feels queasy and runs down to his cabin to hide for the rest of the day.

Bless him.

We'll be off the Campbell Plateau soon. It will be a lot calmer then.

The following day, I wake to find the winds have eased off and we've reached deeper water. I can tell this even before I get upstairs—the steps to the bridge don't feel like a bucking bronco. The effect on everyone is instantaneous; it's as if they've been wakened from a long sleep. Suddenly the lounge and corridors are filled with life. People are moving around, chatting good-naturedly and getting to know one another, familiarizing themselves with the layout of their new surroundings. Annette and Cara aren't at their brightest, but at least they're up. Robert has made a full recovery and is bouncing around, full of the joys of spring, no doubt helped a little by knowing his poor sister is still suffering.

Other smiling faces appear. Names become personalities. There's nineteen-year-old Taylor studying media at university; Sean, who wants to be a professional expeditioner; Pat, who's just graduated with a degree in science and commerce. Kerry, a smiling bundle of energy, is an expeditioner in her own right; she was part of the first Australian 2007 kayaking team—and one of the first two women—to make the pioneering 1,200-mile crossing between New Zealand and Australia. Mary is a bubbly woman who is a human resources coach in her day job; Joanne, a smiling, generous educator who works for the New South Wales government. Psychiatrist and keen wildlife photographer Muru and his pharmacist son Vik are taking their first Antarctic voyage together. "I promise I won't be analysing anyone, Chris," Muru assures me. And out on deck, I find Estelle walking the ship; quiet and athletic, keen to keep fit when she's not working with the scientists on board.

Our first destination is Macquarie Island, 2 degrees south of Campbell. "Macca," as it's popularly known, is a World Heritage site and famed for its stunning natural environment. Sitting on the boundary of the Indo-Australian and Pacific tectonic plates, it's a magnet for scientists and tourists. When Mawson's captain, John King Davis—affectionately known to his crew as "Gloomy Davis"—first surveyed the shallow waters around Macquarie with the *Aurora*, he speculated he might have found a long-hoped-for drowned land bridge between Australia and Antarctica. This bridge was widely thought at the time to be the explanation for the similar wildlife observed across the southern continents. With the discovery of plate tectonics, we now know that by a geological quirk, a section of the sea floor was squeezed to the surface 700,000 years ago, creating the narrow twenty-one-mile island. The result is that Macca is the only place in the world where you can study what's happening three miles below your feet without having to compete with temperatures over 350°F and pressure a thousand times that of the surface. While the geology is unique, the big attraction is undoubtedly its stunning wildlife. The island is just north of where polar and subtropical ocean waters meet, making the offshore waters incredibly rich in nutri-

ents and capable of supporting vast colonies of king penguins—
second only to emperors in size. Throw in rockhopper penguins,
elephant seals and albatrosses, and you have a nature-lover's
dream.

Arranging our visit to Macquarie wasn't easy. Putting aside
the fact that the island is battered by westerly winds and surrounded by one of the most inhospitable seas in the world, its
Tasmanian administrators are fiercely protective of their charge.
With an Australian Antarctic Division research station at the
northern end of the island, the approval process can be most
charitably described as protracted. A visit demands negotiating
a minefield of departments, committees, and never-ending requests for details that threaten to suck the life out of any research program. After months of emails and phone calls, all we
have to show for our efforts is a permit to visit the tourist
areas—under strict supervision—and approval for a very limited amount of scientific work. And to top it all, permission arrived just five days before we departed. In some ways, it's
strangely reassuring. Mawson only received his approval six
days before leaving Hobart. Some things never change.

The problem is, I'm not sure we're even going to get to Macquarie. There's a beautiful clear sky overhead, but clouds are
forming in the distance, and the sea surface is looking decidedly
messy. White-crested waves are breaking around me, stark
against the granite-gray sea. I search the horizon with my binoculars and can just make out the island. We're getting close,
maybe within ten miles or so. *An hour, perhaps?*

A large wave crashes over the bow.

Maybe longer. This isn't a good scenario for landing at an island with no natural harbor.

I head to the bridge to find out what's happening. Compared
to the windy deck, it feels wonderfully warm. Down below I
find Kerry-Jayne at her post, up front on the port side. Since we
left Bluff, Kerry-Jayne has been taking seabird observations

every hour. She's also been patiently training some of the volunteers to help her identify key species as they sweep across the bow of the *Shokalskiy*. Volunteers stand by, binoculars at the ready for anything that Kerry-Jayne might miss. It's just one of the many tasks they're helping the science team with. When the ten minutes are up, Kerry-Jayne will head outside to the stern of the ship and check the numbers tally with the previous observations; she's only stopping for meals and sleep, all the way to Commonwealth Bay.

There's a cry of delight from everyone on the bridge when Macquarie looms from the clouds on the horizon.

"We're nearly there, Chris!" Mary calls from the window. "I can't believe we're nearly there."

It's reassuring to see land. Whether we make it onto shore or not is another matter.

"It's a sight for sore eyes, isn't it, Mary? All that vacuuming will be worth it."

Just like when we went to the New Zealand subantarctic islands, our visit has to be carefully prepared for. Most of last night was spent in the lounge and on deck emptying pockets, scrubbing boots and vacuum-cleaning jackets and bags, inside and out. It was all done with good humor, but the fear of introducing a pest meant everyone had to be checked and double-checked. Velcro straps proved to be particularly bad; grass seeds have a knack for refusing to budge.

Igor is busy giving instructions to third mate Dmitri as he brings the *Shokalskiy* in toward the island. I don't disturb him. On the ship, we've split the responsibilities for the expedition in three. I handle the science program and give the briefings. Chris is in charge of the logistics and making sure all the equipment is ready for the day's work. Greg, our point of contact with the *Shokalskiy*'s captain and crew, coordinates with the Heritage staff on board; when we get to the ice, he'll be in charge of operations. This division of work helps reduce confusion with the ship's crew and minimizes any duplication of effort. There's inevitably some overlap, but it builds on everyone's strengths and seems to be working well.

"How's it looking, Greg?" I ask.

"Not good, Chris. It's pretty choppy out there. We can't get the Zodiacs off the ship and land them safely on the beach. The wind's just too strong at the moment. Over the past twenty-four hours, it's been coming in from the north. It's edging round to the northwest, but not nearly enough to calm things down."

We're drawing up alongside the eastern side of the island now. It's a beautiful view. Even though we've only been at sea for three days, the vibrant green slopes are a welcome sight. There's so much life. Albatrosses, petrels, and shearwaters sweep around our ship, weaving between the waves, skimming just above the surface. King penguins play in the water, diving one moment, looking up at us the next. A couple of orcas—more popularly known by their less politically correct name "killer whales"—swim by, their distinctive narrow fins breaking the surface. Picking up one of the binoculars on the bridge, I look out to the long, low isthmus at the northern end of the island and make out the Australian Antarctic Division research station. The buildings, power generators and a satellite communication dome sit just below Wireless Hill, where Mawson's relay station sent expedition messages and weather observations back to Australia a century ago. I can even discern the dark line of fuel tanks with "Macquarie Island" spelled out on them in white paint. It's frustratingly close. Unfortunately, the cliffs and beaches are obscured by crashing waves. Even if we could get a team into the Zodiacs, landing on the coast isn't going to be safe. We don't want to end up smashed on the beach.

We've planned for two days at Macquarie, and if we need to stay longer we will lose precious time at Cape Denison. The weekly Australian Antarctic Division sea ice reports and other imagery we've been receiving via our satellite hook-up shows a route through to the northern edge of Commonwealth Bay, but we can't assume it will remain open. We'll need to be flexible when we're in the ice, and I'm loath to fall behind our schedule before we've really started.

Suddenly, the radio on the bridge comes to life. "You're bobbing around like a cork, over," calls the Macquarie Base Commander cheerily.

"Thanks, Macquarie," Greg replied. "It feels like it."

The *Shokalskiy* is rocking almost as much as when we were on the Campbell Plateau, and it's threatening to get worse. We look at the weather forecast with Igor. The winds don't seem likely to change enough for at least another twenty-four hours. I make the call. "Let's leave it, Greg. We'll do Macquarie on the way back."

He nods in agreement. Macca will have to wait for our return. The weather isn't looking good for the next few days, and we could be waiting around a long time before getting onshore. Persevering could have a big knock-on effect farther south.

"On your way back, feel free to pop in," the Base Commander says breezily as we bring up the anchor to leave.

I walk out on the main deck and look over the starboard side. It's ten o'clock at night, a day since we left Macquarie Island. We're at 58 degrees south. The temperature may have dropped to a chilly 40°F but it's a beautiful evening: the clouds have lifted, the sun is shining, and the ocean is almost gentle. We're getting close to the Antarctic as defined by the Treaty. The air temperature certainly feels like it.

The disappointment of bypassing Macquarie yesterday has quickly passed, helped in no small part by the energy of Erik and Chris. As soon as we reached open water, they set about getting an ambitious thirty-six-hour oceanographic experiment underway. During the last few days, Erik has been busy emailing the land-based team members, interrogating the latest satellite imagery, to find out where the cold, nutrient-rich polar waters of the Antarctic clash and mix with the warmer northern waters, a crucial driver of the ocean conveyor belt that helps maintain the world's climate. This convergence of different waters should be close to Macquarie Island, but it rarely stays in any one place for long, as it meanders across the Southern Ocean. Although the ocean surface might look the same, somewhere up ahead there's a sharp temperature difference of several degrees over just a few miles, a phenomenon the satellites can pick up and guide us to.

The problem is that no one really knows just how much mixing takes place across the Antarctic Convergence. To try to answer this question, we've brought all manner of gear for dropping a hundred miles either side of this important ocean front, some of which bears a strong resemblance to children's toys. A key piece of kit is the Argo floats, confusingly bearing the same name as our all-terrain vehicles. These torpedo-shaped devices are designed to drift freely between the surface and a depth of 1.5 miles, measuring temperature and salinity as they go. Every few days for four years or so, they'll return to the surface and transmit their collected data to a satellite as part of an international program to monitor the world's oceans. Alongside the Argos we'll be deploying drifter buoys, made up of a plastic float tethered to what's lovingly known as a "holey-sock," a forty-five-foot column of fabric similar in appearance to a kid's play tunnel but with holes in the sides to minimize turbulence in the water. The holey-sock hangs below the surface to act as a sail in the ocean currents, giving an accurate measure of surface water drift and relaying its position home via satellite. We'll download this precious data on our return home over the coming months. To complement all this, we'll also be using temperature probes known as Expendable Bathythermographs (or XBTs for short) that will be fired into the ocean from a launcher that looks like a toy gun. As the probe drops to the sea floor, it relays the temperature back along a spool of uncoiling copper wire connected to a computer on board.

All this doesn't come cheap. The Argos alone cost somewhere around US$15,000 each, and the drifters US$1,800. Fortunately, the American National Oceanic and Atmospheric Administration have helped out. If all goes well, we should get the first accurate picture of mixing across the Convergence, a real coup for the expedition. I briefly considered doing the experiment on our return, but Erik is keen to get on with the work.

"Let's get it done, Chris. We know where the front is, and the weather's good for dropping the gear off the rear deck. We might not be so lucky on the way back."

I couldn't really argue with that.

There's a strict schedule for when and where the deployments have to take place if we're to get the information Erik wants. We only have one shot at getting it right, and to do so we need bodies. Erik has given a lecture about the planned work that has fired up the whole ship, taking people's minds off Macquarie. Almost everyone has signed up to the various time slots posted on the noticeboard.

As I walk toward the rear lower deck to start my shift, Erik is busy finishing off with the previous group completing their four-hour shift. Chris has been coordinating the deployments during the day and is now having a well-earned sleep.

Erik cheerily calls out a welcome to me. He's excited. I peer into the lab and look down the list of deployments. Over the thirty hours that have run so far, something has been put over the side every fifteen minutes. We've dropped around $80,000 of kit into the Southern Ocean.

"Great effort, guys," I say, impressed at how much has been done. Smiling but weary, people stagger off to bed.

Joined by Tracey, Colin, and Janet, we work under Erik's careful direction over the next four hours. In the lab off the rear

deck, Erik checks the coordinates on the computer and esti-
mates the time we'll be on station. The VHF is turned to Channel 73 and a quick call up to the bridge confirms the location.
Ten minutes later we drop our first Argo float over the side. A
quarter of an hour later, Erik is counting down for us to drop a
pair of floats off the back of the *Shokalskiy*: *ten, nine, eight . . .
three, two, one. Go!* Timing is key. To work out just how much
mixing is going on in the surface waters, the drifters have to hit
the surface at precisely the same time. Another fifteen minutes
pass, and we take it in turns to fire the XBTs into the surging
water below. On the hour, we drag a long funnel net behind the
back of the ship and trawl for plankton and other living organisms in the ocean surface. And then fifteen minutes after that we
do it all again. It's long, hard work and we have to keep our wits
about us. By one in the morning, the sun has finally set and we
turn on the deck's halogen lights, piercing the darkness. An al-
batross briefly sweeps into view, its ten-foot wingspan lit up
against the gray mass beyond, and then it's gone. We work in silence apart from the hum of the ship's engine and the breaking
waves, concentrating on the job at hand. I can see my breath in
the air. It really is getting cold. Large swells roll past, sometimes breaking over the deck. We're wearing life vests, but our
wet feet are a reminder that we're only inches from near-freezing waters. If anyone fell in they would only have minutes before succumbing to the cold; it's highly unlikely we'd be able to
get them out in time.

"We've just finished a trawl," I call out to Erik. "How about
I go and get hot drinks for everyone?"

There's an enthusiastic murmur of agreement, and I dash up
to the lounge. Shortly after, I'm precariously balancing a tray of
steaming mugs of tea and coffee down the steps to the waiting
team. It's not a complete success, but most of the contents are
delivered. The effect is almost instantaneous. Within moments the
team are cupping their drinks contentedly, chatting and laughing,

sharing stories from the increasingly distant lives we had before the *Shokalskiy*.

Erik is smiling. "Chris, come and check this out."

He leads me through the open door of the lab into the wet room at the back, its bright lights almost blinding me. A laptop is set up on the side table, reds, greens, and blues filling the screen. It's a plot of the temperatures we've measured. When the first teams started over thirty hours ago, the surface was a relatively warm 41°F. We're now in the blue. The sea surface is down to 34°F.

"It's so cool, Chris. We've crossed the Convergence. We're in the Antarctic!"

I wake at 6.30. I lie still for a moment and sigh. I'm knackered. I stare at the ceiling tiles and listen. All I can hear is Annette's soft breathing next to me and the hum of the ship's engine. There are no voices or movement outside. The last of the deployments should have finished at 4.00 A.M., so everyone must be getting some rest. It's going to be a lazy day. We'll need to take it easy after all the hard work everyone's put in.

I get out of bed, put on my down jacket and insulated boots, and stagger up the stairs to the bridge. It's as silent as the *Mary Celeste*. No one is around except Vladimir, the second mate, who is at the wheel.

"Morning, Vlad. How are things?"

"Not good." He grimaces. "Autopilot broken. Only manual, and in this." He points disgustedly at the thick fog outside the window.

The autopilot will be fixed when the crew stir in the morning. In the meantime, Vlad is going to have to stay at the wheel. I leave him muttering and check the expedition weather station display I've set up in the bridge. The air temperature has dropped again. It's only 34°F. I'm glad I put on warm clothing.

It's eerily quiet on the top deck. I can only see a few hundred feet, and the poor visibility adds to the sense of isolation. We're making solid progress at a steady ten knots, but there's not much to see. Using both of the ship's 1,147-kilowatt diesel engines might speed things up a bit, but the extra fuel used is not always worth it. In rough conditions, it soon becomes a game of diminishing returns. Sometimes it's better to keep on one engine, save the fuel and keep the course. We've estimated the voyage to the edge of Commonwealth Bay should take around ten days, but if we run into thick sea ice, it could be a lot longer finding a way through.

I open up my heavy-duty plastic case and set up the comms system on one of the benches. I turn the panel antenna north toward the satellite, pointing just above the horizon. Fortunately, we're not rolling much this morning, and with any luck I should be able to get a stable connection quickly. A moment later, the high-pitched screech tells me I have a connection. I load up the latest science blog and movie onto our social-media accounts, and download the sea-ice images and weather forecast. No real change in sight. The only thing of interest is a low-pressure system out to the west that seems to be drawing warm northerly air down over us, only to be chilled by the cold ocean waters. It certainly explains the terrible visibility. It looks like we're set to have fog for the next couple of days.

Thud.

I wake, disoriented. It's not a noise I've heard before.

Thud.

I sit up quickly and rub the heavy condensation off the inside of the porthole. The falling snow grabs my attention, but then I notice a slab of white passing by on the starboard side.

We've reached the edge of the sea ice.

I throw on my clothes and rush downstairs to the main deck. It's seven in the morning and most of the team are already up, enjoying the view from the bow in awed silence. Thick fog continues to surround us, granting only a few hundred yards of visibility. Through the gloom, floes of white and blue approach and casually drift by. Sitting low in turquoise water, the passing ice comes in fantastic shapes and sizes: many flat, disc-like, others honeycombed fragments, rotten from melt as they drift inexorably north into warmer waters. I look at my GPS. We're at 63 degrees south, a whole degree of latitude north of where Mawson and his men first sighted sea ice a century ago, almost to the day.

Traveling at just a few knots between the floes, the motion of the sea is noticeably gentler. The chaotic high seas have been replaced by tranquil, millpond-like conditions. The few waves are shadows of their cousins farther north, and they pass lazily by, leaving little impression on the surface. There's hardly a breath of wind. Coin-sized flakes of snow drop lightly on the deck. It's deathly silent, broken only by muted exclamations of excitement as someone sees a solitary emperor penguin standing to attention in the falling snow on a nearby floe, barely giving us a second glance as we pass by. Robert and Cara are wearing their down jackets for the first time on the voyage, making snowballs on the deck and taking photos with Taylor, Sean, and Pat. There's a shriek of laughter. It's good to see Cara smiling again.

After days of rolling on the high seas, we've crossed an invisible boundary and entered somewhere otherworldly, almost spiritual; it's a place I'm struggling to capture in words. Mawson's meteorologist and expeditioner Cecil Madigan made a valiant effort when he first entered the pack ice: "My poor pen cannot describe it, its quietness, its perfect whiteness with the marvelous cobalt blue in the hollows, and green where it can be seen through the water." We may be a hundred years apart, but I suddenly find myself standing silently beside Madigan, humbled by the majesty of this world. There's little else I can do.

CHAPTER FIVE
Off the Map

Sailing through sea ice is like living through a bombardment. One moment all is calm; the next, the peace is shattered by a protracted crushing and grinding sound that reverberates throughout the vessel. You can't predict when it will happen; there's no warning of the gut-wrenching screech as the ship rams the next floe blocking our path to Cape Denison. At times like this, the *Shokalskiy* seems almost vulnerable, and it's a reminder that only a few inches of steel lie between us and the freezing Southern Ocean waters. It's a nerve-jarring experience.

Igor and his team are careful, selecting which ice floes to negotiate while keeping an eye on what lies beyond. A nudge here, a diversion there. If the ice refuses to yield, a slight acceleration. For a moment, we seem to hang in the air, and then suddenly we're falling, accompanied by a whoosh of water as the force of the ship cleaves the floe, opening up a channel for the *Shokalskiy* to carry on her way. It's a tried and tested method that's been used since the times of Mawson and Shackleton. Choosing the right floe, however, is important. The *Shokalskiy* can comfortably tackle ice several inches above the surface. The rule of thumb is that at least four-fifths of an ice floe or berg is submerged below the surface. So for every foot of ice on the surface another four lie submerged, an important statistic when you're taking a vessel deep into the pack ice, hundreds of miles from the nearest living soul. It's a predicament that's terrified sailors at these latitudes for centuries.

In 1841, the British naval explorer James Ross was in an international race to reach the magnetic South Pole. Taking a different route from his French and American competitors, Ross chose to direct his two heavily strengthened wooden ships poleward from their stay on the Auckland Islands into a sea filled with ice and the unknown. The thick sea ice conditions threatened to trap a team for whom any help would be too little, too late. The constant "hard thumping" and fear of impending disaster had an impact on Ross's health, and his thick black hair went white with worry. Against the expectations of most on board, his small flotilla broke through to find open water and the discovery that the magnetic Pole lay inland. Ross's legacy was enormous: The Ross Sea would prove to be a launch pad for future endeavours, including Shackleton's very own *Nimrod* expedition. But after two seasons fighting Antarctic sea ice, Ross swore he would never go south again, not for "any money and a pension to boot."

Today, sea ice continues to be a major hazard to Antarctic shipping. Government and commercial ships can still get trapped sailing these waters. In 2003, the Italian Antarctic supply vessel, the *Italica*, was beset by ice in the Ross Sea and had to be broken out by a privately chartered Russian icebreaker, the *Kapitan Khlebnikov*. Even this season, ships are struggling to deliver supplies and personnel. A couple of days ago, news reached us that the Australian icebreaker, the *Aurora Australis,* had been delayed reaching Hobart after being trapped for three weeks off its East Antarctic base at Casey—and this with weekly sea ice reports for the area. No matter where you are, Antarctic waters remain some of the most treacherous in the world.

The *Shokalskiy* may be an ice-strengthened vessel, but she isn't invincible. No vessel is.

In Igor's capable hands, the ice we're meeting is proving little impediment to progress. Over the last twenty-four hours, we've averaged four knots and traveled nearly a hundred miles. I'm surprised at how much progress we've made. The *Shokalskiy* may be weaving and bashing its way through, but we continue to maintain a southerly bearing.

The rolling swell of just a few days ago is already a distant memory. With each floe we strike, each shake of the ship, there is less concern on board, fewer anxious faces at mealtimes and briefings. Our world has now become sea and ice, a world completely divorced from the one we once knew. It's a world where new skills have to be learned if we are to make the most out of the ten days we plan for these waters.

Safety is paramount in the south. No matter what the task or urgency, safety always comes first. Yesterday, Greg took advantage of our new environment to familiarize everyone with traveling and working safely around sea ice: to check before you step; to dress warmly and wear a life vest; to follow instructions on the ice; and always—"And I do mean always"—be prepared for a change in the conditions. We'll only be operating off the *Shokalskiy* when conditions are suitable and the forecast shows we have a large-enough weather window, but you can't take anything for granted in the Antarctic. The Zodiacs are going to be our main means of transport along the edge of Commonwealth Bay, so it's important the whole team feels comfortable using them. This morning we're fortunate. The sun has burned off what was left of the fog and there's hardly a breath of wind. The surface is like a millpond. It's as close to a controlled environment as possible, perfect for a practice run among the floes. We may be in the middle of the Southern Ocean, but for a few hours at least we've found ourselves in a sheltered bay of ice islands.

Igor reverses the thrust of the ship and brings the *Shokalskiy* to a halt in a stretch of open water.

On the upper deck, the hum of the engine is almost drowned out by excited chatter. It's the first time anyone has been off the ship since Bluff, and the deck is a heaving mass of bright down jackets, windproof trousers, gloves, hats, and sunglasses. The sky is deep blue and the water sparkles in the light. In the distance, several brilliantly white table-topped bergs finish off a picture-postcard scene. It's a glorious day. We couldn't have hoped for better.

Off the rear deck, instructions are shouted in Russian as the Zodiacs are lifted one at a time by the crane and dropped gently into the water. Greg and Chris take the first two inflatables, each armed with a VHF radio in case of any problems. Over the ship's tannoy, Nikki outlines the plans for the afternoon, reminding the team of the key points from Greg's training yesterday. "And don't forget to turn your name tag when you leave the ship."

The name tag system is critical for operations off the ship. At the top of the stairs on the upper deck there's a conspicuously large wooden panel covered in lurid green and yellow plastic tags, one for each member of the expedition. When leaving the *Shokalskiy*, the named side of the tag is meant to be turned over, signifying you're off the ship—a quick and easy way to find out where everyone is without a precious loss of time searching for individuals.

Ready to go, Nikki stands at the top of the gangway to check everyone off as they head down to the waiting Zodiacs.

Warm clothing? Yes.

Life jacket on and clipped in? Yes.

Name tag turned? Oh bugger, no.

Back you go.

With a sheepish grin, the guilty party walks back past the good-natured queue, followed by howls of laughter and hollering.

You only forget once on a voyage.

Today it's all about getting familiar with ice travel using the Zodiacs, in order to travel confidently from ship to floe. Nikki is driving the inflatable I've joined and chats away happily to those on board. In no time at all, everyone is perched happily on the tubes, stepping on and off the snow-covered ice as if they've been doing it for years. As soon as we're on the water it's clear this doesn't just have to be a training exercise. The area is positively brimming with life. Every other floe has two-feet tall Adélie penguins parading in full view, their trademark black-and-white dinner jackets easy to spot among the natural ice sculptures. These inquisitive creatures are more than 160 miles from their nesting sites on the continent, here to feed on the krill so abundant in these waters during summer. A few penguins watch our approach and, alarmed, trip, stumble and glide away on their stomachs as cameras click furiously. Someone quips: "I wish my students showed as much interest as Adélies." Muru and Vik laugh good-naturedly next to me. It's an old joke but a good one.

After two hours, Greg is satisfied with everyone's progress and calls the inflatables back to the *Shokalskiy*. We need to push on while the conditions are good. The latest satellite images show that the opening in the sea ice we spotted at Macquarie has now closed. Once the Zodiacs are safely stowed away, we're going to have to find another way into Commonwealth Bay.

As I climb the ship's gangway, Robert runs up clutching his iPhone. "Dad, check this out. I filmed it!" he calls out from under his layers of insulated clothing and goggles.

We rest our heads against one another and look down. On the screen, a sleek, gray-colored whale comes to the surface of the water, followed by an impressive blast of air and condensation from its blowhole. It's a shot in a million.

"Well done, Robs, that's fantastic! I can't believe you managed such a good picture."

"I was so lucky," he buzzed. "Everyone else was struggling to get their cameras out. I was just there and took it with this." Robert gives the phone a shake, with the biggest grin I've ever seen.

I'm so proud. This is just what Annette and I wanted: a moment that will stay with him forever.

"What kind of whale do you think it is, Dad?"

"I'm honestly not sure. Let's ask Tracey. And we could also try Nikki. They might know." It may be a dwarf minke, the very same species Nikki grew up with in Queensland. Each summer they head south to feed on the krill, but at 65 degrees south we're at the limit of their range. "Let's load the movie onto YouTube later. If Tracey or Nikki don't know, someone else out there might have an idea. How about you write a blog entry? It'll be great for people to read what you've done today."

There are mercifully few places on the planet where the landscape changes before your very eyes, where the scenery is constantly on the move, where features on the horizon disappear without a moment's notice and well-trodden paths vanish without trace. It's an unsettling concept. We have a deep-seated human need to understand our environment, to know our bearings and the way home. Unfortunately, it's not always possible in the Antarctic.

Sea ice is anything but easy to navigate. The ceaseless tussle between wind, waves, and ocean currents means it's constantly on the move, pushed and pulled in all directions, opening up stretches of water in some areas, driving it together in others. Shackleton once described it like a "gigantic and interminable jigsaw devised by nature. The parts of the puzzle in loose pack have floated slightly apart and become disarranged; at numerous places they have pressed together again . . . until it becomes 'close pack,' when the whole of the jigsaw puzzle becomes jammed." It's a jigsaw puzzle that's always changing; a maze where paths suddenly shut and maybe, just maybe, open up elsewhere.

In the Antarctic, you need all the help you can get to deal with Shackleton's jigsaw. We decided to get the best satellite communications we could afford, allowing us to download the latest imagery as it became available. Most cruise ships and private expeditions are forced to call colleagues at home. *What does the sea ice look like? Can you see a way through?* Our satellite system is worth every cent, allowing us to see what lies over the horizon and respond immediately; this is information the *Shokalskiy* wouldn't have otherwise. The only problem is, satellite images have a limited shelf life. As soon as they're taken, the clock is ticking: The ice continues its onward march and in extreme circumstances can be different in just a few hours.

Since the Zodiac training, frustration has threatened to set in. We've prodded and probed the ice. We've searched for openings; we've tried bashing through; we've followed leads of water. Each time we've only found impenetrable pack ahead. Each time Igor has called us up to the bridge, pointed out the thick multi-year ice lying ahead, and with a shrug said: "No way through." Each time we've been forced to beat a hasty retreat. There's nothing we can do but try elsewhere. I'm seriously starting to wonder whether we're going to get through. After all the planning, after all the hard work by everyone, is it possible we won't get any farther? We do have alternatives—other places we might try to reach the continent—but these won't help us answer the questions about iceberg B09B. Anywhere else will inevitably be a poor second choice, and there's no guarantee the sea ice there will be any easier to navigate.

Tonight, I'm hoping we might have better news. I head up to the top deck. With most of the team in bed, the ship is strangely quiet. The evening feels oppressive, and it's not just my mood. At these latitudes, the sun remains low on the horizon, but there's little warmth in its rays. The twenty-knot wind is biting and thick cloud has rolled in from the south. Just before I came up, the weather station was recording 30°F. With windchill, it feels more like 18°F.

Bloody freezing.

I set up the comms and wait for a connection, lost in thought.

Suddenly a friendly voice speaks up behind me. "Evening, sir." It's Terry, one of the volunteers.

Terry is wildly supportive of the expedition. A frustrated scientist, he was one of the first to sign up, keen to get involved in whatever needed to be done. In his orange windproof jacket and gray woolly hat pulled down hard over his head, I can just make out a beaming face and frosted stubble.

"Evening, Terry. Lovely weather." I stomp my feet, trying to get some warmth into my body.

"Certainly is. Just came out to see what's happening before bed. Mind if I keep you company?" He slaps his gloved hands together several times against the cold.

"I'd be glad of it. Just trying to get the latest sea-ice images. Shouldn't be too long."

The sudden high-pitched scream tells me we've locked onto the satellite. Taking my gloves off, I quickly tap the keyboard to hook up the laptop on the WiFi and go online. I don't want to hang around long—in this temperature the batteries will quickly drain.

A moment later a map of Antarctica appears on the screen, surrounded by pixelated colors.

"Any good?" asks Terry, looking over my shoulder.

I zoom in on our position. *Maybe.* The vivid colors show the concentration of sea ice. Purple for 100 percent ice cover, green for half, deep blue for open water. Posted online for free by the

University of Bremen, it gives a good overview of the conditions during the last twenty-four hours.

"Looks like something might be opening up north of Commonwealth Bay, Terry, but I'll need to confirm."

I don't dare to hope. I download the image and switch to my Gmail account for the latest sea-ice report promised from Tasmania. For $1,000 a day we're getting visible light images—effectively photos—sourced from the American satellite known as MODIS (which is far easier to say than its full title: the Moderate Resolution Imaging Spectroradiometer). Unlike the Bremen sea-ice data which has a resolution of 4 miles, MODIS can see down to 0.6 miles. Enough to be sure.

There is a gap.

Two days later, we've broken into open water and the most spectacular view I've ever seen: an armada of icebergs, stretching as far as the eye can see. We're in the company of giants. Hundred-foot-high blocks of ice, their sheer cliff sides towering above the *Shokalskiy*, are leisurely making their way north from the continent that has been their home for tens of thousands of years. The banks of cloud have gone, swept away by a lull in the low-pressure systems passing overhead. Under the bright sunshine and intense blue sky, the statue-like bergs are dazzling white. It's unbelievably quiet. Shackleton captured the moment perfectly on his *Nimrod* expedition when he wrote: "A stillness, weird and uncanny, seemed to have fallen upon everything when we entered the silent water streets of this vast unpeopled white city." It's just us, the bergs and open water.

The great British scientist Edmund Halley, best known by his namesake comet, was the first to describe an encounter with Antarctic icebergs back in 1700, when he sailed into the south Atlantic to map the Earth's magnetic field. Spotting what he first thought was "land with chaulky cliffs and the topp all covered with snow," the adventurous Brit was forced to retreat when these "islands of ice" threatened to trap his vessel. Igor wisely steers a wide berth.

I go to find Chris. He's on the rear deck. The hold is open and there's gear everywhere. The two Bens and Colin are putting together the large sledges with help from some of the volunteers. The three Argo vehicles have been brought up for a check-over. Chris turns the ignition on one. The engine splutters and promptly dies.

"How are they looking?" I call out.

Chris glances up from under the hood and makes a face. "Okay-ish. Our tracked Argo is good, but I've just taken a look at the vehicles from Heritage. They're meant to have been fully serviced, but it's a bit rough."

He leans back over the Argo's steering wheel and tries the ignition again. It eventually comes to life. "They start, just, but I'm glad we have our own. I'm not sure how far we'll be able to push these other two." Chris looks away, frustrated.

This isn't good news. Chris has worked hard to get us to Mawson's Huts. We can't be sure what to expect: whether the ice surface will be smooth or badly broken up or even have areas of open water. We have the quad bikes, but they're really only meant for support. The eight-wheeled Argos are key. Capable of crossing almost any terrain, these vehicles are even amphibious—an important consideration if we break through the sea ice. And now it looks like we may have a problem.

Chris thumbs toward Serge, a white-haired engineer standing nearby in his oil-stained blue overalls. Always smiling, Serge has been exchanging ideas and modifying gear with Chris during the voyage south, in loud broken English and lots of sign language. They seem to understand each other. "Serge here is confident they'll do the job," Chris says, and shrugs.

Serge nods his head toward the Argo and puts his arm around Chris's shoulders. "All good, good," he says, beaming.

Chris breaks into a smile. "They'll be fine," he mimics and shakes his head in mock despair.

Serge roars with laughter.

The *Shokalskiy* picks up more speed, and I peer over the side.
There's nothing between us and B09B.

We really are going to make it.

One hundred years ago, the arrival of summer at Cape Denison brought a new set of challenges to the men on Mawson's
Australasian Antarctic Expedition. After a winter spent making
scientific measurements in hurricane-force winds, they were
eager to explore further afield. Tents, sleeping bags, food supplies and fuel were all carefully prepared and distributed; science equipment, sledges and clothing were made ready for a
journey into the unknown. By early November the winds had
eased off a little—though they never really stopped—and five
sledging parties set out. Of these, Mawson led what he called
the "Far Eastern Party." Their mission: to travel over the Antarctic Plateau and reach the edge of Scott's operations in the Ross
Sea, taking weather observations and mapping as they went. To
cover the ground quickly, the men used dogs to drag the sledges,
the only team on the expedition to do so. After penning the fate-
ful words to his fiancée Paquita, "It is unlikely that any harm
will happen to us," Mawson set out with Xavier Mertz, a Swiss
champion ski runner, and Belgrave Ninnis, a young British
Royal Fusilier officer. Five weeks into their journey, disaster
struck.

On 14 December 1912, the team hit a crevasse-ridden area,
one of the deadliest types of terrain in Antarctica. Close to melting point, ice will flow with gravity—albeit slowly—where any
stress in its structure can cause the surface to split wide open. In
extreme circumstances, crevasses the width of a football field
have been known to form, their sheer sides sometimes dropping
hundreds of feet. Unfortunately, a crevasse in itself is only half
the hazard. What makes them extraordinarily dangerous is that
their wedge-shaped openings can be covered by drifting snow,

creating the false impression of a solid surface. They're an oc-
cupational hazard in Antarctica that's ideally avoided. Unfortunately for Mawson, Mertz and Ninnis, this wasn't an option.

Deciding the safest way to negotiate this dangerous ground
was in single file, Mertz led the way with Ninnis at the rear; just
in case of any problems up front, the British officer was charged
with looking after the best dogs and most of the supplies. The
last thing they wanted was to lose their most essential gear and
supplies down a crevasse. Progress was inevitably slow as they
found a way through, the three men acutely aware of how vulnerable they were. Shortly after noon, Mertz looked back and signaled to Mawson anxiously. The Australian turned and saw . . .
nothing. No Ninnis, no dogs, no sledge or supplies. Instead, an
ugly dark gash, eleven feet across, had appeared in the ice. Sick-
eningly, two sledge tracks led up to the far side but only one
continued beyond. A snow bridge had collapsed to reveal a
chasm that disappeared into darkness far below. They cried out
to their friend, but only the whines of a fatally wounded dog
came back in reply.

They were in a terrible situation. Not only had they lost Ninnis, but they were now more than 300 miles from base with, as
Mawson ruefully reflected, a "bare one and a half week's man-
food." They were thirty-five days out from Cape Denison and
weren't expected back for another month. No one was going to
start looking for them. The two explorers turned their backs on
the icy grave and started their desperate attempt to reach Cape
Denison.

With their tent lost in the crevasse, the two men salvaged a
broken sledge discarded on the way out and, with a spare tent
cover, lashed together a makeshift shelter. Cups were fashioned
from used tins of food and spoons made from the wood they had
at hand. They were fortunate to have a field stove with fuel, but
to supplement their meager supplies the men were forced to eat
their way through the remaining dogs.

As they struggled back, both men were surprised to find how quickly they succumbed to exhaustion. It was a horrific journey. Along with the gnawing pangs of hunger, their diaries worriedly commented on peeling skin, loss of hair, dizzy spells and dysentery. Of the two men, Mertz deteriorated more quickly, with frequent bouts of depression and lethargy. Vitamins hadn't yet been discovered, but we now know that dog's livers have exceptionally high levels of vitamin A, almost certainly the cause of the symptoms they suffered from. They had no idea but the dogs were slowly killing them. Tragically, the last line in Mertz's diary reads: "The dog meat does not seem to agree with me because yesterday I was feeling a little bit queasy." In a final bout of madness, the poor man bit off one of his fingers and died shortly after.

The loss of his companion hit Mawson hard. With the arrival of yet another storm, the Australian was forced to stay by Mertz's grave for three days. He was over a hundred miles from another living soul with barely enough food to cover the distance back to base. Years later, there was speculation that Mawson resorted to cannibalising Mertz, a claim he strenuously denied. Understandably, though, he does appear to have fallen into despair. Two days later, he pulled himself together. Remembering the lines by his favorite poet Robert Service, "Buck up, do your damnedest and fight, It's the plugging away that will win you the day," he resolved to continue. If Mawson could reach a prominent high point, a search party might at least find his body and diaries. Alone he set off across the icy surface.

Mawson was in a terrible physical state and feared he might collapse. From the start his "feet felt lumpy and sore." In too much pain to continue, the loneliest man in the world stopped to investigate and taking off his boots, was horrified to find the soles of his feet had come away, exposing the raw skin below. Shocked, Mawson carefully smeared his feet with lanolin—a cream found in sheep's wool that's believed to be good for skin—and strapped the soles back on, a routine he would repeat every morning. Remarkably, in spite of all this, Mawson continued to record the weather each day; he was determined to return home with some science to show for all that had befallen them.

Mawson maintained his trudge across the snow and ice toward Cape Denison, his journey from hell far from done. While traveling over what he later named the Mertz Glacier, Mawson suddenly felt the ground give way and found himself "dangling fourteen feet below on end of rope in crevasse—sledge creeping to mouth." Expecting the sledge to follow him into the crevasse at any moment, he "thought of the food left uneaten in the sledge—and, as the sledge stopped without coming down, I thought of Providence again giving me a chance."

Determined to live, Mawson hauled himself back to the surface, struggling to avoid disturbing the sledge his very life was hanging from. Just when he reached the top, the snow lid collapsed and Mawson fell back the full length of the rope, spinning breathlessly above the dark chasm, the sound of falling snow and ice echoing far below him. Briefly contemplating slipping from his harness but fearing a slow and painful death, he resolved to try "one last tremendous effort." Incredibly, after four and a half hours in the crevasse, the Australian reached the surface, and this time stayed there. Determined not to find himself in the same situation again, Mawson made a rope ladder on which to climb out of any future crevasses, saving himself during several later falls.

Two weeks after his agreed date of return and 24 miles out from Cape Denison, Mawson stumbled upon a small snow cairn that had been built by a search party. In it he found supplies and a note with the news that everyone else had returned safely and the *Aurora* was still in Commonwealth Bay. Incredibly, the cairn had been built that very morning. Unfortunately for Mawson, he couldn't see anyone on the horizon and was too weak to catch up.

Disappointed, but with renewed hope, Mawson pushed on
and three days later reached Aladdin's Cave, a small ice cham-
ber the expedition had dug into the glacier overlooking Cape
Denison. Inside Mawson found a cornucopia of supplies, including oranges and a pineapple. "It was wonderful once more
to be in the land of such things!" Against all the odds, he was
nearly there.

Fate once again interceded. With Mawson readying for the
2.5-mile descent to Cape Denison, a blizzard suddenly struck
and would blow for a week. Waiting impatiently, the Australian
gorged on fruit to build up his strength and improvised a set of
crampons using scraps of wood, rope and nails. When the winds
eased five days later, Mawson decided to make a break for it. He
staggered down the glacier and soon saw men working around
the hut. But when Mawson looked out to sea his heart dropped.
On the horizon was smoke: The expedition ship had sailed that
very morning. John King Davis had delayed the *Aurora* as long
as he dared, but in the end he had no choice. With winter fast approaching, Davis was racing against the clock; he had to beat
the sea ice and get round to the other expedition members left
precariously on the Shackleton Ice Shelf the year before, 1,500
miles out to the west. Just in case, Davis had left five volunteers,
with the promise to return the following year. Spotting Mawson,
the men rushed to meet him, but had no idea who stood before
them. "My God! Which one are you?"

Mawson was a shell of the man who had been so strong and
proud three months earlier. He had defied death, but at what
cost? Mentally and physically shattered, Mawson had lost two
friends and was now stuck in the Antarctic for another year. He
was aching to get home to Paquita, but he needed time to recover and build up his strength for the voyage. Months later,
Mawson continued to find himself hanging around the other
men, "not so much to talk to them," as Paquita later recounted,
"as just to be with them." After all that had befallen him, Maw-

son needed to be close to other human beings, to know he was no longer alone.

If we're going to follow in the path of Mawson, we'll have to be careful.

It's four-thirty in the morning. I groan. It's time to get up.

The outside light pierces the darkness of the cabin, casting shadows across the room. I get up slowly and dress, trying not to disturb Annette. She moans in protest. I kiss her lightly on the head.

"Don't wake, love," I urge. "Get some rest. I'll be back tomorrow."

That's the plan, at least.

We reached the edge of the Antarctic continent two days ago. Two days to come to terms with the enormity of the challenge before us. More than 30 miles of sea ice lies to the south, locked fast to the continent, filling what was Commonwealth Bay, behind which Cape Denison and the imposing East Antarctic Ice Sheet disappear into the clouds. But there's one thing, and one thing only, that fills the horizon: the vast monolith that is iceberg B09B. I've seen the pictures, I've lived and breathed the reports, but none of them have really prepared me for its sheer size. It's a monster, plain and simple. No wonder the whole place is so screwed up.

Since we arrived, Chris has been reconnoitering the area in an Argos, trying to find a way across this "fast ice," past B09B to Cape Denison. Each time, he's come back dismayed. "The surface is just too broken up, Chris. As soon as you get anywhere near the big berg or even the smaller ones, everything gets messed up." They all seem to have large areas of broken mushy ice at their base, churned up by constant rocking back and forth on the seabed. These areas are no-go zones, effectively blocking our way, even in the Argos, which are working well—justifying Serge's confidence. In the end, we've decided we

need to get as much distance as possible between us and the
bergs if we're going to reach Mawson's Huts. Looking out to
the west, Chris reckons the surface might be easier to travel
over. If we hug what was the narrow coastal fringe along the
edge of the ice sheet, we might stand a better chance of getting
around. The MODIS satellite images seem to support this, but
with 0.6-mile resolution, it's a little like looking through the
bottom of a milk bottle—you can vaguely make out what's on
the other side, but you're not absolutely sure. The alternative is
to sail round to what's known as the Hodgeman Islands on the
eastern side and drive the Argos in from there, but that's a day's
sailing from here.

It's not surprising people have failed to get to Cape Denison
during the last couple of years. And it could remain like this for
many more. If we want to get in and find the answers we're
searching for, now is the time. Chris and I had gone over the
plan many times before, but we went over it again late last
night. For the attempt, we'll take two Argos and mark waypoints in our GPSs as we go. Communication between the vehicles will be done using hand signals, VHF radios, and satellite
phones. We've also scheduled two calls with the *Shokalskiy* at
1200 and 2000 to check in and keep everyone up to date on our
progress. The weather station and forecasts show a low-pressure
system has just passed away to the north, with the promise of
fine, stable weather over the next couple of days. It may be perfect conditions for an attempt on Cape Denison, but I've slept
fitfully, tossing and turning as I go over every aspect of our plan
for the umpteenth time. We'll never get the science answers we
want if we don't give it a go. It's time to try.

I close the door to our cabin with one last glance back at
Annette's sleeping figure and head downstairs. The *Shokalskiy*
is deathly quiet.

While we've been moored alongside the fast ice, the rest of
the team have been using the time to get on with the science pro-

gram. Taking the sledges and quad bikes, Erik has been exploring the northern edge of the ice to look at the ocean below. Enthusiastically supported by Kerry, Mary, and Terry, Erik has
dropped probes through the ice to measure the temperature and
saltiness of the water hundreds of feet below; many at the same
locations as expeditions in the past, including Mawson's original effort. Amazingly, Erik's team is finding the water is close to
freezing and exceptionally salty far below the surface. Against
expectations, the data seems to show the production of Antarctic
Bottom Water has bounced back after the Mertz Glacier was
smashed apart by B09B. With the change in sea-ice cover, it just
looks like where it's being formed has shifted over to a new location where the wind can work its magic. It doesn't seem the
southern limb of the ocean conveyor belt is at risk of collapsing
anytime soon. It's a great result for the expedition.

Meanwhile, we've continued broadcasting science using
Hangouts on Air. Yesterday, Kerry-Jayne agreed to be interviewed by me about life at the edge of the sea ice, but we saw
far more than we bargained for. Halfway through the broadcast,
a group of Adélie penguins suddenly ran away from the water's
edge in blind panic. Provoking cries of "Oh my God!" from the
onlookers, the threatening shape of an orca broke the surface
some sixty feet away. They're known to rush ice floes to tip prey
into the water, but thankfully this one headed away from us toward two unsuspecting penguins on another floe. It must be the
first time a hunt has been beamed live from Antarctica. I'm not
sure we'll ever be able to beat this.

I shoulder open the upper deck door and step outside. It's
still, very still. Small waves are gently lapping against the hull,
and the ship's engine is humming away in the background. In
the distance the skyline is a mixture of blues and pinks as the
early-morning sun struggles to rise above the East Antarctic.
There's meager warmth in the light. It's a bitter 14°F with windchill.

Goddamn, it's cold.

I involuntarily rub my gloved hands together to try to shake some warmth into my body. It's so cold, even the Adélies seem to have disappeared.

As I make my way to the rear deck, I see a small group has gathered, talking in hushed tones, clouds of breath vapor hanging in the air. Six of us are making the attempt today: Chris and Eleanor to take geological samples from the edge of the ice sheet, Ben Fisk for medical support in the field, Ian and Jon from the Mawson's Huts Foundation to complete repairs on the historic building, and myself. The group is a jumble of blue, orange, and yellow, Ian and Jon wearing their distinctive Australian Government-issue down jackets, all finished off with an eclectic assortment of hats, gloves, scarves and glasses. Greg is also up with Laurence, who has come to film our departure. The only one who isn't kitted up is Serge, who is wearing his usual blue overalls, apparently oblivious to the cold. Operating the ship's crane, Serge picks up the two Argos and our trailer and lightly drops them over the side onto the neighboring sea ice. Thanks to Chris's hard work, the Argos are packed up and ready to go. And just in case anything goes wrong, each vehicle has an emergency duffel bag with supplies, shelter and fuel to survive unsupported for two weeks—something Chris has organized for every team operating onshore. If the *Shokalskiy* urgently needs to leave, we'll be all right.

"You okay, mate?" Chris asks as I jump off the ladder onto the sea ice.

"I'm fine, Chris. Just trying to think of anything we might have forgotten."

In truth, I'm going over the hurdles we might face. Our route involves a traverse of thirty-five miles of uncharted sea ice, negotiating jumbled surfaces and tidal cracks along the way. Speaking it out loud doesn't help anyone, though. There's nothing more we can do to prepare. While we're gone, I've left Tracey to take the volunteers out in the Zodiacs to help her search for seals along the sea-ice edge. If we fail to reach Cape Denison, at least some science will be getting done.

We're as ready as we'll ever be.

The surface frost cracks loudly as I walk toward the two parked vehicles. Chris, Eleanor, and I are taking the Argo with tracks, Ben, Ian, and Jon, the older wheeled vehicle.

Chris leans in over the dashboard of our Argo and turns the key. It starts up straight away.

"That's a good sign," I shout to Chris over the roar of the engine, and he smiles back.

"How about I start driving and you take over in a couple of hours?" he asks.

"Sounds good." I get into the front seat, and Eleanor sits behind us on the gear.

The two Argos are ready to go, and we pull away jerkily. I look behind to see Greg waving and Laurence filming. "See you tomorrow," I shout, waving back.

I hope.

The dome of the ice sheet rises twenty miles away to the south. To our left, B09B and a flotilla of smaller tabletop-shaped bergs lie trapped, frozen in time, their deep blues contrasting sharply against the white of the surrounding fast ice. Our plan is to head directly toward the ice sheet and keep the bergs on our left. Within a few miles of the base of the ice sheet we'll turn sharply southeast, hug what was coastline just a few years ago and hopefully find a way through. If we get a clear run, we could be at Cape Denison in four to six hours; if not, we'll be back at the *Shokalskiy* in time for breakfast.

Chris pulls away slowly and soon has us up to a speed of fourteen miles per hour. It's a world away from the dusty Brisbane training course on which we learned to drive the Argos just a few months ago. As the vehicle picks up speed over the ice, a frigid blast of air almost takes my breath away. I immediately pull up the windscreen to shelter us from the worst of the wind and tuck my scarf in more closely around my nose and ears.

When I look behind, I see the second Argo following closely. I give a thumbs-up, and Ben enthusiastically responds. The *Shokalskiy* has disappeared somewhere under a bank of dark gray water sky. Out to the west, a brightening horizon promises clearer, warmer conditions later.

"All good, Chris," I shout.

He nods. It's hard to hear anything above the engine, and Chris is concentrating on looking ahead. The light is bad, which makes the contrast terrible. At any moment, we could hit a bank of snow, drop down a gully, or, worse still, break through the sea ice. I stand to look ahead for any broken ground or dozing seals. The seals are a sure sign a tidal crack lies ahead, a break in the ice that's allowed them onto the surface. I gasp for breath as the cold wind bites into my face, but it's a welcome relief from being shaken apart. With no suspension to speak of, the Argos may be safe but they're not comfortable.

All clear. So far.

As passengers, Eleanor and I continue to scan the horizon, looking for any change in the conditions ahead. Sometimes we'll see a snow patch up ahead, but with a tap on the arm Chris is alerted and it's easily bypassed. Occasionally we see a seal in the distance, but the cracks in the ice are small and negotiated at a lower speed. Slowly but surely the bergs pass away on our left and just over an hour after leaving the *Shokalskiy* we change direction and head southeast. It seems hard to believe that a few feet below us the ocean is over a mile deep.

Probably best not to think about it.

After two hours, we decide to take a short break. We've made excellent progress, but the next part of the route is going to be the more challenging. Hugging the edge of the ice sheet, we have no idea what lies ahead. This close to the continent there's a good chance the fast ice might be seriously disturbed at the surface, broken up by the enormous pressures being exerted on all sides. We stop to check everyone is okay, and after a welcome hot drink we push on.

It's my turn to drive.

I cautiously start the Argo, refamiliarizing myself with the controls. If we're going to get through, it'll be decided shortly. With a clear stretch of fast ice, I get the vehicle up to its top speed of twenty-two miles per hour. In places, large snow patches are wind-blown into fantastic shapes and steep sides. These sastrugi, as they're called, threaten to tip the Argo if taken too quickly, and require careful navigation. A couple of times the wheeled Argo gets bogged in snow, but our tracked vehicle has no trouble pulling out.

As we continue southeast, I become aware that the bergs are gradually getting closer. Soon they're less than a mile away to our left, and the route ahead is becoming decidedly less clear. Seeing no obvious way forward, I turn a corner. My heart sinks. The surface is choked with chaotically strewn ice blocks. The bergs are close in to shore, screwing up the surface. Ridge upon ridge of ice extends far into the distance, heaved up by the pressure. Our tracked Argo might make it, but the wheeled vehicle? No way.

We can't get through this.

Chris turns to see what the hold-up is. "Oh, shit. This is the same stuff I've had the last couple of days."

I scan the way ahead, trying to see somewhere, anywhere, we might be able to find a way through.

I hear a hopeful voice from behind. "I think I saw a way through back there, Chris."

I look around and see Ian standing in his vehicle pointing back. Turning our vehicles in a clumsy wide arc, we retrace our path out and, sure enough, it looks like there may be a route tucked in close to the edge of the ice sheet.

How on earth did I miss that?

The wall of white from the bergs and ice sheet had fooled me into thinking there was no way forward. I'd swung east where there seemed to be some color in the sky. It was an easy mistake.

Checking the other Argo is with us, I slowly approach the berg that appeared to block our path, hoping against hope that we'll be able to continue our journey. It would be gut-wrenching to be forced back after we'd made it this far. I turn the corner and a wave of relief passes through me: a vast plain of fast ice comes into view, stretching far off to the horizon. There's not a berg in sight. With relief, I turn the throttle and accelerate.

It's a humbling experience being out here. We're exploring somewhere no one has ever traveled before, to see something that no one has ever looked upon before. Shackleton described a similar experience on his *Nimrod* expedition when he wrote: "It falls to the lot of few men to view land not previously seen by human eyes, and it was with feelings of keen curiousity, not un-mingled with awe, that we watched the new mountains rise from the great unknown that lay ahead of us." Until now, I had never really understood what he meant. We're the first people to ever make this journey. We're seeing a new landscape unfold before our very eyes, just like the Shackletons of old. For the first time, I know we're going to make it to Cape Denison.

Lost in thought, I suddenly hear Eleanor call out next to me: "Isn't that rock ahead?"

CHAPTER SIX
In Adélie Land

The old weather-beaten pine buildings stand proud against the Antarctic ice. The pitted and heavily patched timbers of Mawson's Huts have held firm against a hundred years of violent weather.

The strange thing is, there's hardly a breath of wind.

This is crazy. We're supposed to be in the windiest place in the world and there's not even enough to fly a kite.

I look around to get my bearings. Beyond the Huts, the steep slope of the ice sheet rises toward the Antarctic plateau, 7,000 feet above where I stand; somewhere up there Mawson found shelter in Aladdin's Cave after his epic walk for survival. On either side, two light-gray, rounded, rocky promontories run parallel to one another; Memorial Hill on the western side with a large cross dedicated to Ninnis and Mertz, and an automatic weather station atop the ridge to the east, in the very same location the original expedition made their observations from a century ago. Thick, drifting snow covers large parts of the building and entrance, but among the surrounding boulders is a profusion of Edwardian rubbish, a cornucopia of discarded items: rusting tins, tools, springs, coils, batteries, brightly colored broken glass bottles, all heaped together by group as if some obsessed collector has been hard at work. Scattered around, the shattered frames of outbuildings and piles of wood protrude from the snow. Away to my left, poles and tangled wire lie thrown to the ground, the remains of the first radio mast in Antarctica.

The whole place is seriously messed up. I'm not supposed to be able to walk on water and yet here I can. I jump and land on the sea ice with a thud. No movement. Nothing. The ice here must be several feet thick. I may as well be standing on solid ground. I look out to where there should be sea. Nothing but ice as far as the eye can see.

When Mawson and his men were here for two years, they described the deafening noise from 200,000 Adélie penguins living around the Huts. Now it's eerily silent. The rocky outcrops are covered in foul-smelling guano, but the rookeries are almost completely deserted. We suspected things were going to be bad, but nothing's prepared me for this. Thousands of neatly arranged circles of rocks have no occupants. Instead, the place is littered with the frozen remains of young birds. The few penguins on nests look back listlessly, completely unconcerned at our presence, struggling to nurse their precious eggs in a desperate attempt to keep their colony going. It's a world away from the thriving penguins we saw at the sea-ice edge.

Cape Denison is dying.

We'd arrived a few hours ago. Once we saw the distant outcrop of rock, we knew we were going to make it. In a scene reminiscent of *Wagons West*, both Argos sped up, and within an hour we'd arrived at Mawson's Huts. It feels surreal to be here. After two years of dreaming and planning, we drove across thirty-five miles of fast sea ice and just pulled up. We might be tired, but it was almost easy in the end, in no small part thanks to Chris. All his planning worked brilliantly. Unfortunately, there was little time to celebrate.

Our immediate priority was shelter. The last thing we needed was to be caught in the open by one of Cape Denison's famous blizzards. Fortunately, it's not just Mawson's Huts that offer protection. Tucked away behind the old base is a small modern building known as the Sorensen Hut. Tied down with stainless steel cabling, the faceless accommodation block and laboratories have been built and added to over the years for summer work by the Mawson's Huts Foundation. After half an hour of shovelling the drift from the entrance, we managed to prise open the door. Inside, we found a solitary guest: Stay the Dog, patiently sitting on a table, passport round its neck, absently gazing out of the window at a handful of Adélie penguins waddling past. Starting life as a Guide Dog fundraiser on the streets of Hobart, this battered three-legged fiberglass canine is the unofficial mascot of Australian expeditioners in the Antarctic. After its living counterparts were removed from the continent in 1994 as part of the Antarctic Treaty, Stay became the only dog left behind, and has been lovingly dognapped from base to base ever since. We're under strict instructions from the Australian Antarctic Division team on Macquarie Island to deliver Stay on our return. I'm happy to oblige. They'll definitely let us return now.

Leaving Ian and Jon to dig out Mawson's Hut, Chris and Eleanor immediately set to work collecting rock samples from the ridges of rubble that straddle Cape Denison. Known as "moraines," they're an important focus for understanding what's happened in the Wilkes Basin. When ice flows over a landscape, freezing, grinding, and pulverising anything in its path, chunks of rocks can be plucked from the "surface" and carried away. With enough time, these rocks will make their way to the edge of the ice sheet, where they build up to form impressive ramparts, relics of a once larger ice sheet. With so much water locked up in this part of Antarctica, even small changes in the size of the ice sheet may significantly affect the world's sea level. The big question is when.

Chris and Eleanor are going to use a technique known as cosmogenic dating to find an answer. It's a method that's probably the closest thing in science to alchemy, and has only been developed in the last few decades, long after Mawson and his men left Cape Denison. It takes advantage of the fact that the surface of our planet is constantly being bombarded by high-energy particles called cosmic rays that originate far out in space. These have little effect on rocky fragments being transported deep in the ice, but once at the surface, the rubble is exposed to the full might of cosmic rays, and dramatic changes in their chemical makeup take place; oxygen, for example, can morph into the element beryllium, while silicon may turn into a rare form of aluminum. The amounts are vanishingly small, but by collecting the rocks discarded on the surface, we can measure the build-up of these exotic elements. If we know the rate at which cosmic rays strike the planet, we can calculate an age. It's a powerful tool for dating the past that hasn't been used at Cape Denison or anywhere else along this 1,500-mile stretch of Antarctic coastline. We'd previously tried to get government support to do this work, but national logistics were too stretched to help, so Chris is keen to get as many samples as possible.

With Chris and Eleanor off in one of the Argos, Ben and I set to work on the automatic weather station behind Mawson's Huts. The place is a graveyard for weather stations. The record-breaking winds here have pummeled station after station over the years. The present incumbent stopped transmitting data in 2011, and the University of Wisconsin team responsible for its operation are keen for us to try to get it working again. My mind is only half on the job, though. Cape Denison is suspiciously calm. I'm looking for any wisps of snow on the upper slopes; something to show the katabatics are about to sweep down upon us. I keep glancing up, expecting to call Ben down from the top of the station tower at any moment. If the winds start up, we'll only have a couple of minutes to get to shelter before they strike.

There's not a breath of wind, let alone the howling blizzards we anticipated. I came expecting a narrow weather window for us to work within, some of it possibly on all fours, just as in Mawson's day. Instead, the air is remarkably still and getting ridiculously warm. The gray banks of cloud have cleared, and we're now in brilliant sunshine. I take out my hand-held weather meter: 39°F. I'm actually in danger of overheating.

Probably best push on before the weather does crap out.

I take off a layer of clothing and turn my attention back to a box filled with a confusing array of wires, fuses, and data loggers. With Ben checking the connections between the solar panels and transmitter above, I continue my tests. A red flashing light keeps flickering on and off, taunting me. *Nothing.* I check the skyline again. *All clear.* I try swapping some of the components with the spares we've been sent. Still no response. In the end, I decide to replace the storage card; if the problem is with transmitting the signal back to civilization, the least we can do is take the data with us and hope the next visitors have better luck. Cape Denison looks like it's defeated yet another weather station.

I call up the tower. "Ben, let's reboot the system and I'll ring the U.S. on the satellite phone. Maybe it needs a bit more time. Let's go and give Ian and Jon a hand."

"Sure, Chris, whatever you say," he replies good naturedly, and climbs down.

We pack up the gear and lock everything away just in case we're unable to get back. If the weather does suddenly deteriorate, we don't want to leave anything out to be blown away and smashed. We walk over to Mawson's Hut, where the two conservationists are busy hacking away at the snow and ice around the entrance.

"G'day, Chris, g'day, Ben." Ian wipes sweat from his forehead. "Come to give us a hand?"

After a couple of hours, the door is finally cleared. Inside it's like a tomb, deathly quiet, the barest of light penetrating what was originally the workroom and radio station. I stumble through the dark to the main living area, a cavernous space bathed in light from the roof windows. There's an overpowering smell of age. A table and heavily rusted stove sit along the side wall; tins of flour, hunks of dried-out dark meat, and empty bottles of stout and whisky are scattered around the kitchen area. Wooden bunks edge the room, the black-painted initials of their occupants still clear; an occasional book or stack of magazines lie on the shelves above them. Even with all the hoarfrost inside the hut, it's easy to imagine the room filled with the laughter of eighteen men, reminiscing about the day's events and loved ones back home. I linger for a moment in "Hyde Corner," where the popular Mertz and Ninnis resided. It's heartbreaking to think the two friends slept here, dreaming of their return home after one final trip out. When news of their deaths reached the base, the surviving men sobbed themselves to sleep.

Mawson had his own cubicle, set apart from the rest of the men. With no natural light, my eyes take a moment to see through the gloom, empty save for a bed, chair, and a few oddments. Even with a hundred years of separation I can feel the isolation: Mawson perched on the side of the bed in this lonely space, left to his anguished thoughts, wracking his brain, trying to rationalize what happened on the ice; the other men outside uncertain of what to say or do. I can't help but feel I'm trespassing.

As I step back into the main living space, Ian grabs my attention. "Look in the corner, Chris," he says with a conspiratorial smile.

He points to what looks like a small cupboard on the other side of the hut. It's Frank Hurley's darkroom. In this tiny space, the photographic genius produced his astounding images of the expedition.

Peering round the door I see a short pencil inscription on the wall: *Near enough is not good enough.*

No matter what Antarctica threw at him, Hurley remained a perfectionist.

At eight o'clock, we sit outside Mawson's Huts and cook up a small meal on our stoves. It's been a good day. Chris and Eleanor have sampled the moraines across Cape Denison, Ben and I have done all we can with the weather station, and Ian and Jon are hard at work making repairs to Mawson's Huts. The whole area is bathed in a golden glow. It's deliciously warm. I can't believe we're here. Twelve hours ago, we weren't even sure we were going to make it.

I make the scheduled call. "Greg? Hi, it's Chris."

"Chris, how are you?"

"Fine, mate. Look, things have gone really well here. I'd like to get another team into Cape Denison. What's the forecast like?"

There's a moment's pause. I hear sheets of paper being ruffled in the background.

"It should be possible. Looking good for at least another thirty-six hours."

Brilliant. We're here to work, and the weather is being kind. I've decided to leave Ian and Jon; they insist another twenty-four hours would be invaluable for their conservation work. If we rotate the science teams we can get things done on both fronts.

I outline the people I want sent out as soon as we get back to the ship: Graeme and Ziggy to drill through the sea ice and find out what's happening on the seabed, Kerry-Jayne to do a bird survey, particularly a census on the penguins to find out just how many of these poor birds remain in the colony, and Alok so he can make a report in *The Guardian*. We've also had a request from the Australian Antarctic Division to measure the thickness of the sea ice for future flights into Cape Denison, which Graeme and Ziggy can do while they're probing the ice; the Division had hoped to fly in a ski plane during our visit but this doesn't look like it's going to happen now. We'll bring Ian and Jon out on the return of this convoy, leaving one berth for a volunteer. If the weather remains good, we'll arrange another convoy out, probably led by Chris and me after we've had some rest. I'm keen to return. Drilling the glacier for ice offers the chance to develop an ancient record of climate; it should help us find out how stable this part of the ice sheet has been in the past.

Greg suggests a ballot would be the fairest option for the volunteer's slot. I agree and leave him to sort the details.

I sign off: "Great. Thanks, Greg. We'll be back by 7 A.M."

"Bye," comes the cheery reply.

Now we just have to get back.

Which Argo to take? The older vehicle from Heritage is struggling to provide any heating. Our new Argo has a full window shield and delivers warmed air into the driving space.

Ben and Chris toss a coin for the privilege.

"Oh, bugger," moans Chris. Ben and I will be driving the new Argo. Poor Chris and Eleanor will be having the colder journey back to the *Shokalskiy*.

Our immediate problem is the temperature. It's been far too warm today. Water has poured off the ice sheet and formed a large lake below the huts, blocking our exit. These are weird conditions. We may be only visiting for a day, but Mawson was here two years and never reported anything like this. We have to wait until midnight for the sun to dip in the sky in the hope the fall in temperature will reduce the thaw. The melting has slowed noticeably but even so there's an impressive torrent escaping the lake. If we get it wrong, the Argos will be turned over by the force of water. It takes us half an hour of careful navigation to work our way safely through the maze of pressure ridges. All of a sudden, we're through and out onto open fast ice back to the *Shokalskiy*.

We drive away from Cape Denison in blazing midnight sunshine, a plain of ice ahead, the whites and blues of the East Antarctic rising away to the left. I turn to see Ian and Jon waving farewell. The sun's rays are falling on their tiny outpost, bathing the slopes in a gentle red light, the outcrops of rock soon lost against the surrounding ice sheet. It's hard to believe this is the same place described by Mawson in *Home of the Blizzard*. More like *Home of the Calm*. Cape Denison is the very opposite to what I expected. Remote and isolated, yes, but also very beautiful.

The temperature plummets, and we're soon traveling in 14°F. The surface becomes covered in hoarfrost as the melt from the day refreezes, giving the vehicles more grip, allowing us to pick up speed. Chris and Eleanor pull ahead; the wheeled vehicle is more likely to get stuck, so it's prudent to keep them up front. Sitting on the top speed, we follow the waypoints marked in my GPS. We now know where we're heading and hope we can cut a couple of hours off our return journey. I occasionally catch Stay out of the corner of my eye and do a double take. It seems odd taking a fiberglass dog out for a drive. No matter how much I try, she soon catches me unaware and I have to look again. Two men and a dog driving across Antarctica. You couldn't make it up.

As the sun disappears behind the ice sheet, a full moon floats above the horizon. The sky fills with a pastel pink. After twenty-four hours on the go, tiredness is starting to set in, and the icescape is fast assuming a surreal, fantastic appearance. By three in the morning, B09B has become a vast city wall; the small bergs, buildings. Off to our right, I can even make out a pyramid, fiercely lit in red and pink. If it wasn't so bloody cold, you'd think we were crossing a desert.

But Stay isn't the only wildlife about. As we drive across the flat open surface to the *Shokalskiy*, I make out a dark figure approaching. I can't decide whether it's real or my imagination.

"Ben, what's that?" I shout out over the engine's roar.

He looks in the direction of my pointing arm. "Is it a person?"

At least I know I'm not the only one seeing things.

As we get closer, the poorly formed image materializes into an Adélie penguin traveling with dogged perseverance. Clearly in a hurry, this solitary bird completely ignores us as we pass, scuttling by as quickly as its small legs can carry it. I can't help but smile. I'm suddenly aware penguin tracks crisscross the ground in all directions, some heading toward the *Shokalskiy*, others farther around to the east; none seem to lead to Cape Denison. Shortly after, convoys of penguins start to appear. It's clearly the hour for commuting Adélies.

Chris's voice suddenly comes over the VHF from the other Argo: "Chris, can you hear me?"

"Hi, mate. Yes, all okay?"

"Sort of. Eleanor's freezing in this piece of junk. Okay if we stop to warm up and maybe swap vehicles?"

I signal to Ben and we come to a halt. Poor Eleanor is frozen to the core, her face blasted red by the cold, her lips almost shivering.

"It's okay, Chris, I'm fine," she says when she sees the look of concern on my face. "I just need to warm up a bit."

We pour hot drinks from our thermos flasks and pass round some chocolate. The effect is almost immediate, and within minutes Eleanor is laughing and smiling again. We all feel the benefit. Just to be sure, I swap my place with Eleanor and make for the older Argo. Nearby, half a dozen penguins have joined us for a break, watching us out of idle curiosity, standing in a line that would make any parade ground proud. Getting ready to leave, I'm checking the strapped-down kit on the back of our Argo when an almighty racket breaks my concentration. Startled, I turn to see beating wings accompanied by manic squawks as two penguins attempt to tear strips off one another. Then, just as quickly as it began, the protagonists stop and return to the line as if nothing happened. Moments later they're all off to who knows where, apparently unconcerned by the fracas. Grinning, we start up the Argos and drive away in the opposite direction.

An hour later, we reach the sea ice edge, exhausted, to find that while we've been away, the *Shokalskiy* has pushed off from the side. We made better time than expected and no one is here to meet us. We need someone to come out, but multiple calls to the bridge go unanswered. We're stuck on the ice with no immediate prospect of warmth from the few rays of light breaking the horizon. Eleanor is feeling the cold again. To be honest, we all are; after a four-hour journey crossing sea ice, we're freezing. With windchill, it's a bitter -3°F. The constant blast of frigid air has swept away any benefit we might have felt from our all-too-brief break. I've never felt so cold in all my life. Chris immediately sets about putting up a tent.

After an hour of jumping on the spot and eating a hot snack from the stove, I finally manage to get through to the bridge. Vlad, the second mate, answers.

"Vlad, is that you? Can we get a lift?"

"No problem, Chris. We'll be with you in ten minutes. Let us just get Zodiac in water."

There's no explanation for the unanswered calls.

Chris joins me at the sea ice edge. "Thank Christ for that. I thought we were going to be stuck here all day. Eleanor's okay, but I'll be glad when we're back on board."

We pack up the tent and gather together the ninety pounds of rocks Chris and Eleanor collected at Cape Denison.

After what seems an age, a Zodiac finally pushes off from the ship, a handful of Adélie penguins looking on. As the inflatable approaches, I can see the smiling bearded face of Ziggy standing above the outboard engine.

"How are you?" he asks, waving in greeting.

My frustration and exhaustion suddenly disappear.

We're almost back.

"We made it, Ziggy. We actually made it!"

"That's great news, Chris," he shouts in his soft Argentinian accent. "I'll pull in by you. The guys on board are getting ready to head out."

As soon as Ziggy pulls up by the sea ice edge, Ben jumps in and we hurriedly pass him the samples. I'm keen for everyone to warm up and share the news with the rest of the team, particularly Annette and the kids. Time is of the essence, though. If we want to get another team out to Cape Denison, we have to move quickly.

As the inflatable draws alongside the *Shokalskiy,* I see Greg beaming at the top of the gangway. Clutching Stay the Dog I climb toward him, flushed with success.

Grabbing me by the neck, Greg looks me in the eyes. "Well done, mate, well bloody done," he said. "You did it!"

I nod dumbly. After all the work, all the doubters, the last twenty-four hours have made it all worthwhile. We reached Cape Denison, gathered a rich trove of scientific samples and made it back safely.

"Now get inside and warm up. We'll get your gear on board. The next team are just having breakfast and making ready to head out. Be good to talk before they leave."

I smile an acknowledgment and put Stay inside, flip my name tag and walk wearily to my room. The ship is silent; most of the team are sensibly still asleep. It's only just gone five in the morning.

Quietly opening my cabin door, I peer inside and see the curtains are drawn, just as I left it.

"Annette?" I whisper. "Are you awake, darling?"

"Hello, love," returns a tired figure, sitting up in our bed.

I knew Annette would be awake. I gingerly step over the kit littering the floor and hug her.

"The whole ship roared with excitement when Greg announced you'd made it," she says. "I'm so proud."

Annette's whole face is smiles. I love her so very much.

"And the kids are okay?" I ask.

"They're great. During the day, Tracey took the Zodiacs out to find leopard seals, and we went with her. I got some great material for a lesson plan, and the kids loved it."

"I'm so glad," I reply, pleased to hear everything was fine. "I've left the Mawson Hut Foundation guys there for at least another day. If the weather craps out, they can shelter in the hut. The next group are preparing downstairs. I need to go through the route with Graeme and Ziggy. Greg also wants a chat, so I'd better go."

I give Annette a kiss and leave her to wake up properly over a cup of tea. I drop down to the dining room on the main deck and grab a hot drink with Chris, slowly warming up.

"What a trip," says Chris over a steaming mug. "I can't believe we're back. It seems an age since we left."

Before I can respond, Greg joins us with the latest weather reports. We talk about the route we took and all we've seen, but it's clear he has other things on his mind.

"What's up, Greg?" I ask, bleary-eyed.

Quietly, Greg tells us he's nervous about relaying multiple teams over such a long distance. If one of the Argos breaks down, we'll be stretched. The forecast shows there's a low-pressure system coming in within the next thirty-six hours and with it stronger winds.

"What are you suggesting, Greg?"

He pauses for a moment. "With another team delivered to Mawson's Hut, we'll have had an excellent couple of days. But we should move round to the east after that to allow us to dodge the worst of the weather. Tracey can be on the lookout for seals as we travel, and we can check out other penguin colonies for Kerry-Jayne. We can also get the rest of the team onto the continent more easily from there."

After the success of our trip, Greg is suggesting we leave al-

most immediately. Our euphoria is quickly turning to disappointment. Chris has real reservations about moving on to somewhere new; he's spent months working out the logistics of
shuttling people across the sea ice, with shelter set up along the
way for breaks. I have to confess I'm a little surprised too.

"Can't we just pull offshore and return in a couple of days
when this low has passed?" I ask. "We can then get other groups
out to the Huts to continue the work."

I want to get back and core the glacier above Cape Denison.
We only need a couple of days.

Greg has clearly thought about it. "We could, but we don't
know what the sea ice around here will look like if there's a
storm. It might not be possible to pick up any of the team left
behind. It will take a full day to get round to the east. We can
spend the time traveling while the low passes over and then get
to work shortly after."

I'm sorely tempted to tell him we're staying put, but what he
says kind of makes sense. There's loads more work we can do at
Mawson's Huts, but if Greg is saying it's safer to move off then
I'm loath to go against his advice. Chris shrugs his shoulders at
me, resigned to the decision.

"Okay, so be it," I say. "The next group out will bring in the
Mawson Hut guys and then we'll head east."

We pick up our cups of tea. Ziggy is back on board, finishing
breakfast with Graeme in the starboard dining room. They greet
us with congratulations.

"Awesome, dude," says Graeme, shaking my hand as we sit
down.

We go through the route to Cape Denison using the satellite
images as a map.

"Keep the ice sheet about half a mile to your right on your
way in and you can't miss it. Follow the GPS. Don't try to take
a shortcut. You'll just run into jumbled ice around the bergs or
risk getting lost."

They're both fired up for the journey. They might be following our waypoints, but it's still going to be a heck of an adventure. And if there are any problems, they can always call one of the expedition's satellite phones.

"Now, guys, we'll have scheduled calls at 1200 and 2000 hours so you can keep us posted on your progress," Greg says to them. "Any problems, remain with the Argos, and we'll come to you."

Outside the dining rooms, Alok is getting himself ready for the journey. They should be leaving shortly but he's still assembling his gear. Laurence is filming Alok's final preparations, the light from the camera casting an uncomfortable glare in the corridor. Alok looks understandably nervous.

With limited space in the Argos, Alok is going to have to do the work of two. Laurence has engineered an ingenious selfie-stick for the camera and given Alok a crash course in filming.

I feel a little guilty. Poor Alok has no real idea what's about to happen. He's going to be away from the ship on one of the most uncomfortable trips of his life. He's going to be bounced, pushed, and basically thrown about during a torturous twenty-four-hour journey. When they reach Cape Denison, there'll be no time to sit around. Every moment out there will be precious. Just because we had clear, warm weather doesn't mean the next group will. The katabatic winds could easily kick up at any moment.

Alok disturbs my train of thought. "Where are we going to sleep, Chris?"

I laugh. "You're not going to sleep, Alok. But you'll be fine."

I'm not sure he believes me.

The ship is now waking up as the team nears departure. Kerry-Jayne passes by, fully kitted out for the trip, her down jacket filling the corridor.

"All ready?" I ask her.

She turns, her eyes burning with intense excitement.

"Chris," she says earnestly in her broad New Zealand accent,

"I've been waiting for this for thirty years. Of course, I'm bloody ready."

I smile to myself and follow her on deck with Alok, Laurence diligently filming ahead.

Making up the last of the team is Estelle, the citizen scientist who won the draw. I'm really pleased she did. Estelle is quiet and confident and more than capable of handling the journey. Kerry-Jayne will need help with the penguin census, and I can't think of anyone better than Estelle in the fitness stakes for scrambling over all the rocky outcrops.

Graeme and Ziggy are already on the sea ice with the Argos doing the final checks. Within minutes, the rest of the team are in the Zodiac and casting off from the ship. I wave them good luck, feeling incredibly weary.

I need some sleep.

During the next twenty-four hours, we keep in close contact with the second team on the ice. Following our route, they make it to Mawson's Huts in under four hours. The weather is good—even better than the previous day—and they manage to do more than I dared hope. Graeme and Ziggy have drilled holes across the sea ice and taken hours of footage with GoPro cameras. A quick look at the film shows a scene of devastation. After three years of blanket ice, the seabed is now in perpetual gloom. What was once a thriving kelp forest is now in decay, replaced by marine worms and brittle worms that have moved up from deeper waters. There's been a complete ecological shift in just three years. Even if the sea ice disappears in the future with iceberg B09B, it's not clear whether the kelp will immediately recover; the scale of the change has been that large. As the guys drill down, they also find the ice is more than six feet thick, enough for the Antarctic Division to land small planes "offshore" and hopefully open up Cape Denison for future visits.

Alongside these efforts, Kerry-Jayne and Estelle walked almost the entire cape, counting Adélie penguins and noting any skua seabirds. Our worst fears have been realized. With the increase in sea ice across Commonwealth Bay, there are only 11,000 penguins left, a catastrophic collapse from the numbers of just a few years ago. What had been a short shuffle for the penguins is now an exceptional hike of more than thirty miles to open water. Hardly any of the adult birds seem to be returning, and those that have are struggling to feed new chicks. Cape Denison's entire ecosystem, on land and at sea, is dying. These are important new discoveries, and over the next few days we'll start posting our findings online.

Alok has also managed to capture impressive images with his one-man camera team and found time to visit Mawson's Huts, all to be reported in *The Guardian*. Ian and Jon are understandably disappointed to be heading back, but they've had double the time of anyone else, allowing them to make emergency repairs and set up monitors inside the Huts for collection during the next visit. It will have to do.

The next day is gray and overcast; the sun we've enjoyed is gone for now. The second Cape Denison team made it back at five in the morning. The Argos worked brilliantly well, but their effectiveness came at a cost. Everyone returned sore, beaten up by the journey.

"My bloody back," complained Kerry-Jayne, rubbing her spine tenderly. "That Argo shook me apart." Without waiting for a response, she headed off to bed. I never even saw Alok.

It's frustrating not to have had longer at Cape Denison but we can still get one more piece of science done in the area before we leave. While the recently returned team sleeps, Chris is keen to drill the seabed where we're moored. Before the expedition left New Zealand, research was published suggesting the massive expansion in sea ice in Commonwealth Bay may have caused a dramatic increase in the amount of carbon being laid down on the sea floor. The reason is due to small single-celled organisms known as diatoms that live in the ice, staining it a urine-yellow color. Diatoms are remarkably adept at using the small amount of light that can penetrate sea ice to photosynthesize carbon dioxide dissolved in the seawater. They only live for a few weeks, but in that short window of time can consume voracious amounts of carbon. When the sea ice melts, the diatoms fall to the seabed, making them very efficient at taking carbon out of the ocean. The paper argued that with the sea ice locked fast in Commonwealth Bay, the diatoms should be able to take full advantage of the long summer sun, potentially capturing lots of carbon. But how much wasn't clear. Over a couple of hours, Serge helps Chris and me drive a succession of four-inch-diameter cores into the muds below. It's a time-consuming business, but we soon have three sets of tubes filled with fine gray muds from the sea floor. These will have to wait until we get back to the university to be analyzed, but they'll provide precious data on how much carbon is being locked up under the ice.

By midday, we're ready to go. With one last check of the name tags, the *Shokalskiy* silently pulls away from the sea ice edge and heads around to the east.

Upon returning home to his love Paquita, Mawson received word from his old Antarctic mentor Sir Ernest Shackleton asking a favor. Shackleton was planning a new expedition to the Antarctic, and he needed the Australian's help. The plan was even more ambitious than Mawson's venture. It was to be a two-pronged attack on what many now suspected was a single continent. Shackleton's ship *Endurance*, named after his family motto "By endurance we conquer," was built with reinforced timber to take tourists to the Arctic to shoot polar bears. It was ideal for reaching the Antarctic continent. Shackleton wanted the *Endurance* to drop a team of men at the southern end of the Atlantic Weddell Sea. After overwintering in a purpose-built hut, Shackleton aimed to make full use of the summer sun and complete what many considered the last great journey left on the planet: to cross Antarctica via the geographic South Pole. Leading five men, dogs, and sledges, he planned to cover the 1,700 miles in a hundred days, mapping and collecting scientific samples as they went. Unfortunately, though, they wouldn't be able to carry enough supplies to complete the trek. Shackleton appealed to Mawson: Could he have the *Aurora*?

Mawson was conflicted. He faced crippling debts from the extra year in the Antarctic, and hiring out the *Aurora* would go a long way to writing off the money he owed. But Shackleton had helped raise a small fortune for the Australasian Antarctic Expedition; without him it would never have happened. After some hesitation, Mawson eventually handed over the ship at a knockdown price. The *Aurora* would deliver another team to the Ross Sea to put down supplies toward the Pole. Shackleton's team could then pick them up on the way over and complete the journey. It sounded almost easy.

When the news broke in 1912 that Roald Amundsen had beaten Scott to the Pole, Shackleton wrote a glowing tribute to the Norwegian explorer but remarked: "The discovery of the South Pole will not be an end to Antarctic exploration. The next work is a transcontinental journey from sea to sea, crossing the Pole." The Anglo-Irishman's failed attempt in 1909 and his near-death during the *Nimrod* expedition had made him an international household name. At only forty years of age, Shackleton had another big expedition in him, and with characteristic flair against the backdrop of an impending world war he raised the necessary £50,000, convincing a Scottish millionaire, Sir James Caird, to donate almost half the money with no strings attached.

Teamwork would form the backbone to Shackleton's plans. They were heading into the unknown and he needed both experienced expeditioners and fresh faces. His old teammate and right-hand man, Frank Wild, joined him, fresh off the ice with Mawson, while Irishman Tom Crean, recently returned from

Scott's expedition, was also central to the expedition. For filming their adventures, Wild had been so impressed by Mawson's photographer Frank Hurley that he assured Shackleton the Australian cameraman was the best man for the job. Shackleton immediately wired Hurley, who was in the outback on a job, and offered him a place on the expedition. The Australian jumped at the chance, the "glamour of Polar adventure" too much to resist.

Shackleton impressed the young Australian in turn. He was quite different to Mawson and had a style of leadership that would prove crucial for success over the next two years:

> *Shorter by half a head than Sir Douglas Mawson, in many other ways he bore little resemblance to my former leader. His square chin, strong face, with its masterly nose, and broad brows, was in sharp contrast to the finely-chiseled features of the Australian . . . They had some characteristics in common. Both possessed the fearless, indomitable will of the born leader. Both were strong men physically and mentally, able organisers and accustomed to having their own way . . . Shackleton planned on broad lines, and while exercising the greatest thought for the safety and comfort of his men, delegated the responsibility of carrying out details to others.*

Aside from Hurley, Shackleton knew or interviewed everyone else for the job. A famous advert was reputedly placed in the London *Times* newspaper: "Men wanted for hazardous journey. Low wages, bitter cold, long hours of complete darkness. Safe return doubtful. Honor and recognition in event of success." Whether this advert was actually ever used is uncertain, but it has Shackleton written all over it. His plan was audacious, exciting, and completely sensational. Over 5,000 people rushed to join, their applications placed in one of three piles: "Possible,"

"Hopeless" or "Mad." Those interviewed considered his methods eccentric, but in hindsight there was a touch of genius. Often pacing the room, he would inquire about an applicant's expertise, their teeth, their likes and preferences, and, most important of all, could they sing. Shackleton wanted specific skills but also needed people who were optimistic, would work well under pressure and could fit into a team—things you can rarely tell from an application form.

In no time, Shackleton had gathered a team around him. Serendipity played a large part in the selection. His captain, Frank Worsley, happened to pass the expedition office the morning after having a dream about ice blocks surging through London and applied on the spot. Medical student Leonard Hussey read about the expedition by chance in an old newspaper while in the Sudan. Captain in the Royal Marines, engineer, and skier Thomas Orde-Lees was only released from active duty after the personal intervention of the First Lord of the Admiralty, Winston Churchill. In the end, Shackleton had twenty-eight men, made up, as he liked to describe them, by ABs (for able-bodied seamen) and BAs (for the scientists and doctors). The level of preparation impressed Orde-Lees, who remarked, "in fact nothing was left to chance except the ice, a factor which no amount of provision could regulate." Happy with his final selection, Shackleton spoke of their chances with good humor: "We are a band of comrades, and, feeling that, we shall feel that we can do our seventeen hundred miles, if not on our heads, on our feet."

In a letter to his long-suffering wife, Emily, Shackleton swore this would be his last trip, after which he would settle down with the family:

> *I think nothing of the world and the public; they cheer*
> *you one minute and howl you down the next. It is what*
> *one is oneself and what one makes of one's life that*
> *matters.*

As the *Shokalskiy* heads north around B09B, the weather turns for the better. The barometer shows the low-pressure system was deeper than forecast but has since weakened, as expected, to reveal a bright, sunny sky. Up on the bridge, there's a hive of activity. Almost all of the team are there. Kerry-Jayne has snatched some sleep and resumed her post taking hourly bird observations. But most of the volunteers are there to help Tracey, Naysa, and Alicia spot seals. We've had to set up a schedule to take it in shifts.

Mid-afternoon, the *Shokalskiy* comes to a stop, and I go upstairs to find out what's happening. Annette and Cara are looking out on the port side with binoculars, sharing a joke. Cara spots me.

"Hi, Dad. Tracey's just seen a seal and they've gone over to check it out." She points to a nearby floe and passes me her binoculars.

I see Ben Maddison driving Tracey over in a Zodiac, her bright red Helly Hansen dry suit standing out against the black inflatable. A moment later, she's stepped onto the floe, stealthily approaching a dozing seal. In her hand, she's carrying a rifle. I peer more closely.

"Looks like a Ross seal." I pass the binoculars back to Cara and point. "You can just make out the dark streaks on its head."

In the distance, we see Tracey lying on the floe about twenty yards from the seal, taking careful aim. We hear a shot and a cry of anguish. The seal looks round angrily as if it's been bitten. Tracey has shot it with a dart gun that takes a small sample of skin and blubber that then pops out onto the nearby snow.

The makeup of blubber is strongly affected by what a seal eats, with krill and fish leaving distinctly different chemical signatures. By taking a sample from the seal, Tracey is hoping to find out what this individual has consumed during its life. Previous work has shown there was a massive shift in their diet away from krill across large parts of the Southern Ocean during the

1970s. Some scientists suspect over-fishing may be to blame, others climate change. Tracey needs more samples from the East Antarctic to find out why.

After just a few moments, the seal seems to have forgotten anything has happened and drops back off to sleep. Tracey gets up and cautiously collects the dart lying a couple of feet from the seal before returning to Ben in the waiting Zodiac. It's a huge improvement on the old method of killing the creature and taking the carcass home.

"Cool," says Cara. "That's the first one today."

I look up from the latest satellite imagery in my hand and smile. The route round to the east is all clear.

All being well, we should make the Hodgeman Islands and what's left of the Mertz Glacier tomorrow morning.

PART II
TRAPPED

CHAPTER SEVEN
An Armada of Ice

The Antarctic Factor: If anything can go wrong, it will. It's basically Murphy's Law on steroids and as frustrating as hell.

As a scientist, you're trained to keep uncertainty to a minimum, to have as much control over events as possible. But when it comes to working in the Antarctic, you have to be a lot more flexible. You have no control over the elements, so can't be too rigid in your thinking. As long as you accept the A-factor is part of the landscape and plan for it, you have a chance of getting home. But as soon as you get comfortable, as soon as you think you know the ice, you're in trouble. The important thing is to recognize your assumptions; to be alert to the fact that something may not be all it seems; to be open minded about other scenarios and willing (and able) to adapt to them. You should never take anything for granted in Antarctica. It's the one sacred rule.

The history books on Antarctic exploration are filled with expeditions that planned for the worst but still suffered for their actions. Overcoming adversity is a common theme in Antarctica, and no one, absolutely no one, embodies this better than Shackleton. His almost superhuman ability to escape the very worst of predicaments on the *Endurance* made him an inspirational leader in his own lifetime. Scientist and expeditioner Raymond Priestley famously described why you wanted the Anglo-Irishman on your team: "For scientific leadership, give me Scott; for swift and efficient travel, Amundsen; but when you are in a hopeless situation, when there seems to be no way out, get on your knees and pray for Shackleton."

If things headed south, Shackleton was the man.

I stir at the sound of the drums. I thrash out and turn off the alarm. It's five o'clock in the morning. Last night our estimated time of arrival at the Hodgeman Islands was six, and I want to be up to see our approach.

Although there was disappointment at leaving Commonwealth Bay, news of our planned visit to the Hodgemans was greeted with enthusiasm by the team. Kerry-Jayne was pleased, for one: "Fantastic, Chris. We can check how the Adélies are faring over there. It will be a really good comparison to Cape Denison." If she's right, B09B should be too far from the Hodgemans to have any real impact on the penguins. Tracey's also keen. She's had the least success of all the scientists and wants to try sampling elsewhere. This will be another chance for her team to find more seals. The plan is to spend a day at the Hodgemans, two if necessary, and then return to Macquarie Island before heading home. After a wonderfully refreshing sleep, I feel alert for the hour. We're nearing the end of the expedition.

Annette is soundly sleeping next to me. She's still taking seasickness pills, and they're proving highly soporific. Kneeling on the bed, I rub the condensation off our porthole and look out. We're passing a large berg, and in the distance I can make out some rocky outcrops. The *Shokalskiy* is already over on the eastern side. Igor's made good time.

I throw on my clothes, grab the laptop and satellite comms and leap up the stairs to the bridge.

Greg is already up, searching the horizon with a pair of binoculars. "Morning," he says cheerily and points off the port bow. "They're over there."

The sky is overcast and there's a light offshore breeze. Following Greg's direction, I can see the islands just a few miles away, a small archipelago sitting in front of the ice sheet. We may be only fifty miles to the east of Cape Denison, but Adélie penguins seem to be everywhere. A constant stream of birds is moving between the islands and the sea-ice edge. It's far busier than anything we saw around Cape Denison. The penguins are thriving here. It looks like Kerry-Jayne was right about B09B: The berg is giving the Cape Denison Adélies a killer commute.

Over the next two hours, Igor pushes and probes his way along the edge of the sea ice, looking for somewhere to lock the *Shokalskiy* in so we can get the team and gear off. He has no luck.

We have to come up with another plan. We want to get the team onto the islands, but how? We could push the *Shokalskiy* into the sea ice long enough to drop the quad bikes over the forward side, but not for anything else. We're going to have to transport the Argos and team from offshore.

The idea is simple. Using the ship's rear deck crane, we put the Argos over the side and drive the amphibious vehicles the hundred yards through the water onto the sea ice. The team can then be delivered from the ship to the sea-ice edge by Zodiac as normal.

The weather forecasts and sea-ice imagery show open water and a low-pressure system arriving tomorrow. We'll have to be away by then. That means a day to work around the islands.

After breakfast, I give the briefing in the lecture room. The place is packed, the scientists and volunteers talking excitedly to one another. Upstairs, Greg and Chris organize the unloading of the vehicles.

While I'm getting my presentation plugged into the projector, Andrew, the BBC man, comes up for a quiet word. He's already heard about our plans and asks if he can be on the first convoy out to the islands. He wants to get as much audio as possible.

"No worries at all, Andrew. We'll keep you out there as long as possible," I reply. He's been understanding about not going to Mawson's Huts, and I don't want the BBC to miss out on getting to the Antarctic continent altogether.

Over the next half-hour, I show the team where we are on the map and outline the program for the day: three convoys made up of Argos and quad bikes will operate between shore and the islands. I go through the weather forecast. The winds are expected to strengthen in the evening, but we'll be long gone by then.

An Argo can "comfortably" take five people plus emergency gear, food, and shelter if the *Shokalskiy* has to leave. Each convoy will therefore take a total of eighteen people, the first primarily made up of scientists, but also some media and volunteers. The estimated five-mile journey from the islands to the ice edge should take around twenty minutes. Chris will lead the first convoy, and Greg will stay with the *Shokalskiy* to coordinate the relays. The first team will be left on the island with the science leaders. The vehicles will then return to pick up a second group, which will rotate with most of the first team upon arrival at the island. And so on. If all goes to plan, we should have everyone back on the *Shokalskiy* some four hours after the first group heads out.

"Long enough to count all those penguins, Kerry-Jayne?" I ask.

She smiles back at me. "I suppose it'll have to do, Chris."

On the whiteboard, I draw up a list of who will go on which convoy; those who made it to Cape Denison will be on the final trip if time permits. A call will be made over the ship's tannoy system for each group to go to the lounge twenty minutes before departure.

Finished, we head up to the main deck to see how things are progressing. While I've been giving the briefing, the two quad bikes have been delivered onto the ice and parked up a couple of hundred yards from the edge. The first Argo has just been put into the water by the ship's crane and driven slowly to shore by Eleanor, its eight wheels effortlessly negotiating the sea-ice edge to ride up on the surface and park alongside the quads. The second Argo follows with similarly little bother.

The tracked Argo is a whole different affair, however. What was an advantage driving over broken sea ice is a limitation in the water: The tracks slow the progress of the Argo. Looking through my binoculars, I can see Greg alongside in a Zodiac, watching as Ben Maddison—conspicuous in his bright red dry suit—maneuvers his vehicle at a snail's pace. After several minutes of little progress, Greg connects the Argo to his Zodiac with a rope and tries to pull it to shore. The nose of the vehicle immediately dips and takes on water, lots of water. Poor Ben scrambles to the back of the vehicle as near-freezing seawater pours over the sides and into the engine.

"Oh, hell," I call out involuntarily.

The Argo is almost certainly buggered; there's no way it's going to be able to drive this afternoon. We need to get it back onto the *Shokalskiy* to dry out, and the number of convoy trips will have to be increased from three to four.

Furious instructions are relayed on the VHF radios as the stricken Argo is dragged unceremoniously through the water with Ben perched just above the surface. I can see Chris on shore, quickly shoving stakes in the ice, ready to help drag out the stricken Argo.

The team on the *Shokalskiy* are watching with bemusement. I can't share their good humor. I don't like delays in the Antarctic, and we've just lost our best machine on the ice.

The now-dead Argo is dragged up beside the others. I call Greg up on the VHF. He confirms what I feared. The Argo is out of action. The engine won't start, and he's not sure what the damage is. It could be the carburetor.

What a pisser. It was all going so well.

"What do you want to do, Greg? Are we still all right to proceed?" I ask.

"Yes, we're still good. We're just going to have to run another convoy. Rearrange the order of who's going in each party, and we'll get underway."

I look at my watch. It's eleven o'clock in the morning.

Okay, that'll work.

I call another briefing and re-organize the groups. Everyone seems happy enough. It's all part of the adventure.

The first convoy heads off at midday. The wind is gusting, but the sun soon breaks through the clouds. It might actually be a good afternoon.

Robert is excited. Annette has said she's happy to hold back for the fourth convoy, and let the volunteers go ahead. But Robert is champing at the bit to get on land, and there's space on the second convoy.

"All right, mate, but you stay with the group. I'll be driving out in the next convoy and I'll bring your mum and sister after."

Before I've finished the words, he's grabbed his down jacket and gone, off on his own adventure. I'd have loved it at his age.

Forty minutes later, my VHF announces the second convoy is heading back. The next group meet in the lounge and once ticked off the list, go out on deck. Graeme and Ziggy have their gear for drilling the sea ice around the islands to repeat the work they did at Cape Denison. They're chatting with some of the volunteers. Terry, Kerry-Lee, and Pat are talking excitedly about the prospect of reaching the continent.

"How is everyone?" I ask.

"Excellent, Chris, thank you," replies Terry happily.

"All name tags turned?" I ask. Nods of agreement confirm they're ready to go. The system is now second nature.

Greg comes out on deck, ready to shuttle our group out. "Everyone ready? Good."

I turn my name tag and adjust the GoPro camera set up on my chest. I should get some great footage driving across the sea ice. From her post at the top of the gangway, Nikki checks over my life vest before I join the rest of the team in the waiting inflatable.

It's about three o'clock in the afternoon. The sun has disappeared behind some clouds, but there's plenty of blue sky about, and the water is calm for the short journey. Everything is looking good.

It takes just a few minutes to reach the sea-ice edge, and I jump out first to help Graeme and Ziggy with their gear. A handful of Adélie penguins approach, peering inquisitively at the boxes piling up on the sea ice. Although we're not meant to get any closer than fifteen feet to the wildlife, the Adélies can't seem to help themselves. You start off with the best of intentions and keep your distance but in no time at all they invariably shuffle over to find out what's going on. After twenty minutes of avian inspection a single Argo arrives from the islands. Ben Maddison is driving and has three volunteers with him, one of whom is Mary.

"What's going on, Ben?" I ask. The two Argos should be traveling together.

"Mary's leg fell through a crack in the sea ice. She was getting cold, so I've rushed her back," said Ben.

"Are you okay, Mary?" I ask, concerned.

"Oh, fine, Chris. I just missed a step. It's nothing really." She cracks me an embarrassed smile.

"Well, you get on board and warm up." To be honest, this didn't need a solo return. If Mary was cold, they could have easily put up one of the tents and used some of the spare clothes from the emergency kits.

This is not ideal. The convoy system is out of balance, but it's done now. We're just going to have to modify our plans to meet the new situation.

I hear Greg talking to Ben about the return of the single Argo. He's in charge of this operation, so I need to check that he's happy.

"Greg, are you all right with me taking a team out or shall I just go on my own and return with a full load?" I ask.

"The visibility is dropping, but you should be fine, Chris," he replies. "Take your team out and expedite the return of those on the islands."

"Okay, out," I reply.

International events threatened to overtake Shackleton's expedition before it began. A few days before the *Endurance* was due to leave, war was declared on Germany. Shackleton immediately offered his vessel and men to the national effort, but within an hour Winston Churchill responded from the Admiralty with a single word: "Proceed." The *Endurance* sailed for Argentina and then on to the Norwegian whaling station of Grytviken on the south Atlantic island of South Georgia. On the way they discovered a castaway, nineteen-year-old Perce Blackborow. Furious but short of a man for the expedition, Shackleton challenged the young lad: "Do you know that on these expeditions we often get very hungry, and if there is a stowaway available he is the first to be eaten?" Blackborow was quick to retort: "They'd get a lot more meat off you, sir." Shackleton choked back a smile and offered Blackborow a place if he proved useful on the remaining part of the voyage to South Georgia, but just in case not, "Introduce him to the cook first." Blackborow soon lived up to Shackleton's high expectations and remained with the expedition.

Reaching South Georgia in November 1914, the whalers gave Shackleton the news he dreaded most: the Weddell Sea was unusually thick with ice. In fact, it was so bad they recommended waiting until the "end of February or the beginning of March" or even delaying a whole year. Hurley wrote: "Its waters were so congested with ice as to be almost unnavigable . . . According to the whalers, the ice fields extended as far north as the South Sandwich—an indication that the season was unusually severe."

Shackleton faced a quandary. He didn't have the time or money to wait, but the Weddell Sea had developed a fierce reputation in recent years. In 1903, Swedish explorer Otto Nordenskjöld had lost his ship, the *Antarctic*, to the crushing pressure of sea ice in the Weddell Sea and was forced to spend two winters there, extremely fortunate to lose only one life. In 1904, William Spears Bruce and his Scottish National Expedition had narrowly escaped being trapped in the Weddell Sea when a change in wind direction opened up the pack ice and allowed the *Scotia* to beat a hasty retreat north. And more recently in 1912, the German Antarctic Expedition led by Wilhelm Filchner suffered a *Lord of the Flies* experience when his vessel, the *Deutschland*, was trapped in the Weddell Sea for eight long winter months, the men close to mutiny with allegations of fighting, duels, and attempted murder. Filchner himself chose to sleep on the floor of his cabin with a loaded rifle so that the medic "can't shoot me through the walls."

No one entered the Weddell Sea without serious pause for thought. Shackleton knew this, but was also aware the Antarctic summer is notoriously short in the best of years, and they had a job to get done. He was already low on funds, and if they waited as the Norwegians suggested, there was a very real risk the *Endurance* would not be able to drop everyone off and get back out before the sea ice closed in for the winter, with the possibility of getting trapped like the *Antarctica* and the *Deutschland*. Shackleton decided he was going to try. Under ominously gray clouds, the *Endurance* left South Georgia on 5 December.

* * *

I take five volunteers in my Argo, leaving Graeme and Ziggy to get to the islands in the next vehicle on its return from the Hodgemans. It's nearly half-past three in the afternoon, and I'm keen to rotate the team on shore. Annette and Cara are waiting patiently for the fourth and final convoy. The sooner I can turn around the waiting group at the Hodgemans, the sooner I can get the rest of the team out from the ship.

I start up the engine and turn my back on the *Shokalskiy*. The high clouds make for poor contrast. One moment everything looks good, the next we're nose-down in a snowdrift. We bog twice. Both times everyone disembarks and good-naturedly push and dig the vehicle out with spades. It takes over twenty hot, sweaty minutes before we reach the islands, passing Ben Fisk as he drives the second vehicle back to the sea-ice edge. This time the vehicle is filled and on board are Andrew from the BBC and Laurence. I promised the two media guys they would get as much time as possible on the continent. They should have plenty of film and audio now.

I pull up along the nearest of the three islands where the rest of the expedition are working. Chris greets us as we arrive, his bright orange jacket visible for miles around. This is a world away from Cape Denison. Adélie penguins are everywhere. Some waddle across the ice in groups, others jump from rock to rock, many sit on the nests that litter the island, surrounded by mounds of creamy brown guano. As soon as I turn off the engine, the smell hits me. Even with today's cooler temperature, the place stinks. Penguins have a keen sense of smell; how they live with it is beyond me. On the lower slopes, I can make out Kerry-Jayne completing the bird count on the island with volunteers. They've clearly found a thriving colony.

My passengers climb out of the Argo gingerly, a little worse for wear from the journey.

"Kerry-Jayne is over there," Chris points out to the recent arrivals. "Go 'round to the left and you can climb up, but just be careful stepping over; there's a small lead of open water."

Robert sees my arrival and runs excitedly toward the Argo. "Hi, Dad!"

"Hi, Robs. Are you having a good time?"

Even with big ski glasses and a thick scarf over his face I can tell he's having the time of his life. "It's awesome here. I've been up on the island with Sean looking at the penguins." He runs off to re-join Sean. I can't help but smile to myself.

As soon as everyone's gone, Chris turns to me.

"Ben Maddison went off on his own!" he exclaims. "He passed me with only a few passengers."

I nod in sympathy. "I know, I know. He was worried about Mary."

Ben has done the best he can for Mary but it has thrown things out. "I'm just going to load up and head straight back."

The contrast is getting better. The clouds are breaking. There's some blue sky; even the odd ray of sunlight. It's almost pleasant, Antarctic pleasant. But we do need to get the next convoy of people back. Most of the team are on the island, but Chris tells me some are behind a nearby pressure ridge of ice with Medic Andrew and Tracey. In the Argo, I soon find Andrew helping Tracey collect blubber samples from two unsuspecting seals lying near a breathing hole. Tracey has taken the final shot of the day and is packing up the dart gun and samples when I arrive. With a cheery acknowledgment, they load up their quad bike and direct the others back round to the departure point.

Returning to the island, Chris makes an important suggestion: "Rather than you taking a group straight back, why don't you wait here until Fisky returns with the other Argo? We can then re-establish the convoy. If anyone gets bogged, they can be dug out quickly. It'll be quicker and safer."

I like it. Chris has years of ice experience and I don't feel comfortable maintaining a broken system. In the Antarctic, anything can go wrong. If my Argo breaks down on its own, it will only add more delays.

I dismount my vehicle and head toward the island, encouraging others to make their way down for the returning Argo.

I meet Kerry-Jayne halfway up the slope. She's just finishing the penguin survey. "They're loving it here, Chris. Completely different to Denison. They're even aggressive." She steps toward a nearby nest. The occupying penguin gives a warning squawk and snaps its beak. "See what I mean? They were almost comatose up the coast."

It's so unlike what we saw a couple of days ago. It's telling just how energy-sapping the commute must be for the birds at Cape Denison.

I hear an approaching engine and see Ben Fisk's Argo pull up. He speaks to Chris, who calls me on the VHF.

"Chris, Greg wants to get everyone back to the ship now. Conditions are changing out there."

There's urgency in his voice. I shepherd the remaining few down, helping some of the less-agile navigate the slippery slopes. I don't want anyone to fall. I hope Annette and Cara won't be too disappointed they haven't made it to the islands.

We now have both Argos and the two quads back together. The problem is we can't get everyone back to the ship in a single run. Trying to compress two convoys into one means there just isn't enough space for all. After our experience driving over, we don't want to get bogged in snow or, worse, have someone fall out and hurt themselves on the journey to the *Shokalskiy*.

I call out: "Chris, this isn't going to work. Rather than waste any time, I'll stay with three of the guys. Leave us one of the emergency bags and you get going. You'll only need to send an Argo and quad back for us."

And if the Shokalskiy *has to leave urgently, we can always*

Braving the storm. The first science expedition to Cape Denison, East Antarctica, 1912. *(Frank Hurley, Australasian Antarctic Expedition. National Library of Australia: nla.obj-141758511)*

Reflecting on the loss of two friends. Douglas Mawson (second from right) shortly before leaving Cape Denison, December 1913. *(Frank Hurley, Australasian Antarctic Expedition. Mitchell Library, State Library of New South Wales: aae_36558)*

The *Endurance* trapped in the long Antarctic winter night, 1915.
(Frank Hurley, Imperial Trans-Antarctic Expedition. Royal Geographical Society: S0000143)

Icebergs were an ver-present threat to the trapped *Endurance*, 1915. Note the two figures, circled at the base of the berg, for scale. *(Frank Hurley, Imperial Trans-Antarctic Expedition. Mitchell Library, State Library of New South Wales: a285010)*

Partying to keep up morale, Shackleton style.
Frank Hurley, Imperial Trans-Antarctic Expedition. Scott Polar Research Institute: P66/19/81)

Frank Hurley and Ernest
Shackleton at Ocean Camp[,]
November 1915. *(Reginal[d]
James, Imperial Trans-
Antarctic Expedition.
Mitchell Library, State
Library of New South Wale[s]
a423107)*

Launching the *James Ca[ird]*
for South Georgia, Ap[ril]
1916. *(Frank Hurl[ey,]
Imperial Trans-Antarc[tic]
Expedition. Mitch[ell]
Library, State Library [of]
New South Wales: a42309[...])*

seriously endangered species. A New Zealand sea lion on the subantarctic Auckland Islands.
(Australasian Antarctic Expedition 2013–14)

Refuge in the Southern Ocean: Perseverance Harbour, Campbell Island.
(Australasian Antarctic Expedition 2013–14)

Hanging out, communicating science with the locals, Snares Island.
(Anthony Ditton/Australasian Antarctic Expedition 2013–14)

Heading south on the MV *Akademik Shokalskiy*.
(Andrew Peacock/footloosefotography.com/Australasian Antarctic Expedition 2013–14)

The *Endurance* navigating sea ice.
*(Frank Hurley, Imperial
Trans-Antarctic Expedition.
Scott Polar Research Institute:
P66/19/39)*

Entering the "pack" hasn't changed
much in 100 years.
*(Australasian Antarctic Expedition
2013–14)*

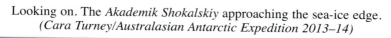

The *Akademik Shokalskiy* working through the ice.
(Annette Turney/Australasian Antarctic Expedition 2013–14)

Looking on. The *Akademik Shokalskiy* approaching the sea-ice edge.
(Cara Turney/Australasian Antarctic Expedition 2013–14)

Adélie penguins at the sea-ice edge, Commonwealth Bay.
(Annette Turney/Australasian Antarctic Expedition 2013–14)

My wonderful family at Commonwealth Bay.
(Australasian Antarctic Expedition 2013–14)

Erik and team members drilling sea ice in Commonwealth Bay.
(Australasian Antarctic Expedition 2013–14)

Kerry measuring seawater properties from the sea-ice edge
(Australasian Antarctic Expedition 2013–14)

Made it! Chris and I outside Mawson's Huts, Cape Denison. Now on with the science program.
(Eleanor Fogwill/Australasian Antarctic Expedition 2013–14)

The unstoppable all-terrain Argos parked up at Mawson's Huts.
(Australasian Antarctic Expedition 2013–14)

Two men and a dog. Ben, Stay, and I heading out from Cape Denison
on our 35-mile sea ice journey back to the *Akademik Shokalskiy*.
(Australasian Antarctic Expedition 2013–14)

Pyramids of ice, Commonwealth Bay.
(Australasian Antarctic Expedition 2013–14)

The view from the top deck on the morning we were trapped.
(Australasian Antarctic Expedition 2013–14)

The *Akademik Shokalskiy* trapped by a breakout of decade-old sea ice.
(Australasian Antarctic Expedition 2013–14)

Icebergs off the Antarctic coast.
(Australasian Antarctic Expedition 2013–14)

The team preparing the helipad for evacuation.
(Australasian Antarctic Expedition 2013–14)

The helicopter evacuation. *(Andrew Peacock/ footloosefotography.com/Australasian Antarctic Expedition 2013–14)*

Evacuation from the ice. *(Andrew Peacock/footloosefotography.com/Australasian Antarctic Expedition 2013–14)*

The view from above. Decade-old sea ice as far as the horizon.
(Australasian Antarctic Expedition 2013–14)

camp out. If the worst comes to the worst, we can always make it round the coast to Mawson's Huts.

"Yes, sounds good. The other vehicles can be stowed back on the *Shokalskiy* while we're fetching you," he says.

I call to Colin, Taylor, and Pat. "Can you guys stay with me? We probably won't have to stay here long, but there's no way everyone can get back in one run." I try to make it sound a positive thing, but if we do get stuck here for a few days or longer I want the youngest, fittest adults with me. They agree enthusiastically, happy to remain at the islands.

I make sure Robert is safely on board one of the Argos and wave everyone off. All the vehicles are packed to the gunnels with people and gear. Robert should be back with his mum and sister in twenty minutes.

Within a short time, the vehicles are just distant blobs on the horizon, and the penguins are our only company.

While we're waiting, we may as well keep busy and do some science.

"Right, guys, let's grab the bag and bring it over to the island."

Taking a handle each, we drag it over to solid ground and open up some of the chocolate for an energy shot.

Chris and Eleanor were trying to find rocks that had melted out and left behind when the ice sheet had been larger in the past, something they can date for comparison with Cape Denison. They had limited luck, but we might as well have another look while we're here.

Over the next half hour, we walk the island, weaving our way around the nesting birds. Whenever we get too close, the birds make their displeasure known.

We can't find anything that looks like it's been transported onto the islands by ice. Just shattered bedrock, nesting birds, and lots of shit. The smell is almost overwhelming.

Walking down off the high point of the island, Nikki calls me on the VHF.

"Hodgemans, Hodgemans, can you hear me, over?" Her normally cheery voice has been replaced with one of concern.

"*Shokalskiy, Shokalskiy*," I reply. "I can hear you, over."

"Hi Chris, can you guys make sure you're ready to be picked up when Ben and Ziggy get to you? Conditions are changing out here and the captain wants to get away."

Down below I can see an Argo and quad bike approaching fast.

"Sure, Nikki. We're just coming down now and will be ready as soon as they turn up."

As we step off the island, Ben and Ziggy pull up. Ziggy comes over and with no effort grabs the duffel bag and throws it on the back of his quad. I join Ben in the front of the Argo and the others pile in the back.

"Thanks, mate," I greet Ben as I climb in. I glance back: "Everyone okay back there? Keep an eye out for Ziggy. Any problems, shout straight away."

"Sure," comes back a chorus of replies.

Ben turns the Argo away from the island and accelerates, the engine protesting loudly.

In the distance, a thick dark bank of water sky hangs over the *Shokalskiy* and away out to the east.

Ben keeps his foot down all the way and, in spite of the contrast, successfully navigates the snow patches. The only time we slow down is to dodge a convoy of Adélie penguins that seems intent on walking under our wheels. We reach the ship in just eighteen minutes.

As we get closer, I can see the *Shokalskiy* has pushed her nose into the sea ice. Conditions are deteriorating, and fast. I'm shocked. A katabatic wind is in full flow, pouring off the ice sheet and whipping the open water into a frenzy. I look out and see ice moving beyond the vessel. It's completely different from what we had at the islands.

Where the hell did all this come from?

I've only been gone from the sea ice edge for two hours. It was all clear when I left. We've got everyone back quickly but now it's nearly a white-out.

Shit.

A small team led by Chris is busy around the bow of the ship. The first quad bike is being craned into the front hold. Meanwhile, Ben Maddison is getting ready to reverse the first of the Argos down the side of the *Shokalskiy*. The vehicle is connected to the remaining quad by rope and slowly being let out from the shore. Once Ben reaches the rear deck, he hooks up to the crane and is lifted up. The second soon follows.

Shouted instructions fill the air.

"Ben, check that link."

"Ziggy, watch yourself."

Within half an hour everything is on board.

I'm unnerved. This is no small local disturbance. Something dramatic has happened, but I can't work out what. Back on board, I flip my name tag. I double-check the rows of names. Everyone's back, including Robert.

They're all safe.

I look out the side window and see the *Shokalskiy* is already pulling away from the sea-ice edge. There's no messing about. The vessel immediately starts to turn and heads north.

I go out on the deck and look over the bow.

There's thick floes of ice everywhere.

This isn't good.

The *Endurance* headed east out from South Georgia to try to by-pass the worst of the ice before plunging south into the Weddell Sea. It didn't work. Three days after leaving Grytviken they met sea ice, far farther north than usual. The Norwegian whalers had been right: the summer of 1914–1915 was terrible. To the south, they faced a brilliant white "ice-blink" sky that warned of closely knit pack ice stretching seventy miles or so to the horizon; behind them lay the inky dark "water-sky" from where they had come. Shackleton chose the ice-blink. For some 1,800 miles, the *Endurance* was directed toward any patches of darkness in the sky that indicated lanes of open water reflecting off the underside of the clouds. It was a remarkably effective way of navigating through the ice-choked Weddell Sea. Hurley was optimistic, writing in his diary: "The ship cut her way through in noble style, leaving a long wake which could be traced, and remaining open, for a mile or so."

Buoyed with optimism, the expedition discovered new land on 12 January and named it the Caird Coast in honor of their major benefactor. Things looked hopeful. Large patches of open water allowed the *Endurance* to reach speeds of several knots. In spite of all the warnings, maybe they could set down Shackleton and his men after all. But as the latitude increased, so did the thickness of sea ice. At times it appeared impassable, and the ship would grind to a halt, apparently trapped. A few hours later, the winds would change, and they'd manage to break free, resuming their journey.

On 17 January, the wind swung round to the northeast and, gusting up to 46 miles per hour, Worsley noted it "drove all the ice in that part of the Weddell Sea down to us, and packed it solidly around the ship." Two days later, the *Endurance* was stuck, frozen "like an almond in toffee" as one diary entry remarked. At first the men thought it was just another temporary stop. After all, leads of open water still lay ahead. Shackleton organized attempts to reach them. The men threw themselves into the work with gusto. Long saws and crowbars were used to try to clear the way. Hurley filmed their efforts. It was no good.

New sea ice formed almost as quickly as they cut it out. With hindsight, it all seems rather futile, but at the time it gave the men purpose, something to do instead of sitting around dwelling on the situation. Eventually they were forced to concede defeat.

As the days turned to weeks, the reality of their situation started to sink in: they could be trapped for the winter. They had been so close to reaching their goal. Wild wrote with frustration: "We could see the land we were making for about forty miles away, but so far as effecting landing was concerned it might as well have been four thousand." Orde-Lees had even sorted out the stores and labeled up those for the "ship" and "shore." Shackleton remained optimistic, at least outwardly. "His unfailing cheeriness means a lot to a band of disappointed explorers like ourselves," remarked Orde-Lees. "He is one of greatest optimists I have ever known. . . . He merely says that this is but a little setback not altogether unforeseen and he immediately commences to modify his program to accord with it, even working his future plans out to given dates and to meet various possible contingencies." To everyone else, there didn't seem be a way out.

It's Christmas Eve, and we're not going anywhere. At least not for the moment.

We're stuck, and there's nothing we can do about it except wait.

We can't cut our way out as Shackleton and his team attempted—there's two to four miles of pack ice between the *Shokalskiy* and open water. Instead, I'm forced to try and will the wind to change direction so the sea ice might part, something like the old Bible story of Moses crossing the Red Sea. If I'm honest with myself, the odds are worse.

Christmas couldn't have come at a better time. It's keeping everyone's mind off what's happening outside. Decorations are going up, gingerbread is being made, presents are getting wrapped. We'd originally planned to be in open water, steaming north for Christmas. But here we are.

After lunch, Annette sits with me in our cabin. She pulls out a DVD. It's Kenneth Branagh's brilliant TV movie *Shackleton*, one from the pile of Antarctic films I brought on the trip.

"What do you think? How about putting this on in the lecture room later today?" she says with a mischievous smile.

I eye the case doubtfully. "Given what's outside, do you think anyone will want to watch it?"

"I think it will do them good. It'll remind everyone it could be much, much worse. These guys were stuck in the ice for months."

I pause for a moment. "You are wonderful, aren't you? Yes, why not? What's the worst that can happen?"

CHAPTER EIGHT
A Christmas to Remember

It's Christmas morning, and I'm struggling to get my head straight. Our situation has gone from bad to seriously horrible in just a few hours. How can it have changed so quickly? Everything looked so good when we brought the *Shokalskiy* round to the Hodgeman Islands. There was nothing but open water. I glance out of the porthole at the deceptively blue sky overhead. Now rafts of thick sea ice surround our ship.

"Dad, go on, open it," cries Robert, passing me a carefully wrapped present.

Annette looks at me questioningly.

"Sorry, mate, lost in thought." I'm sitting at our cabin table laden with brightly decorated presents, while outside . . . for the moment, I have to close my mind to what is going on outside. I try to give Annette a reassuring smile and turn the brightly colored package over in my hands. It's heavy. The card on the top has a short message: "To my darling husband. Happy dreams! Love Annette xx." I can't help but notice the wrapping paper is covered in snowflakes.

That's ironic.

"Dad, hurry up," pleads Robert, desperate to get to the next present.

I carefully undo the wrapping and find a massive, dark, medieval-looking tome: an omnibus of *The Sandman*, the fantasy tale about the lord of dreams, Morpheus. Neil Gaiman is one of my favorite authors, and I've wanted this edition for years. I open the book, admiring the lavishly decorated pages.

"Thanks, darling. This is brilliant." I lean over and give Annette a hug. "How on earth did you manage to get it on board without me noticing?"

She laughs. "Oh, a wife has means. But it did take up nearly all of our luggage allowance flying over."

I'm not surprised. It weighs several pounds.

"Great, my turn," says Robert, and dives on his next present, ripping the paper enthusiastically.

"You're such a freak," says Cara, smiling. Teenagers. You have to love them.

Over the next ten minutes, gifts are unwrapped, while the packaging assumes an impressive pile on the floor. For Annette, I've bought tickets to see her favorite musician, Sarah Blasko, on our return to Sydney. For Robert, a typewriter for his next story, though even Annette couldn't get this on the ship, so it's waiting for him at home. For Cara, books on fashion photography, one of her great passions. We must look like a picture postcard image of Christmas: a family surrounded by presents with snow outside the window, all apparently without a care in the world. It's amazing how looks deceive. Are we really trapped? I still can't believe it's true.

What are we going to do?

I look at my watch. It's eight-thirty in the morning.

I need to take stock of the situation. I have to get back to the bridge and find out if anything's changed. Maybe some leads of water have opened up and Igor is about to start up the engines. *Maybe*.

"Guys, I hate to do this, but I'm going to have to go back upstairs. Do you mind if we open the rest later?"

I'm expecting howls of protest, but instead I see resigned faces around the table. Cara and Robert don't look completely surprised. They know something isn't right.

"Sure, Dad."

"Okay, Dad."

I turn to Annette and mutter, "I just need to head up. I won't be long."

She nods, but I can see the concern in her eyes. After a kiss on the cheek, I go to the door.

I'm trying to keep things as normal as possible for the family, but this is going to be tough. I look back in the room. The kids have resumed their smiles and laughter. I love them all so very much.

Closing the door behind me, I step into silence. Even now, most of the team are still asleep. Well, it is Christmas.

As I climb the stairs, I see Igor pacing one of the side rooms off the bridge, Vlad and one of the other officers with him. Not a word is being spoken, but the expression on the guys' faces says it all.

This isn't good.

The bridge is deserted. I'm on my own while the Russian crewmen discuss their options. What to do next is completely their call. The *Shokalskiy* is their ship, their responsibility. I don't envy them one little bit.

Ironically, one of the reasons we came over here was to dodge the worst of the weather. Now a vast icescape has suddenly appeared, and the *Shokalskiy* is trapped right in the middle of it. Under the blazing sun, the whole scene is awash with light, but the beauty is only surface deep. Everywhere I look, one large floe lies jammed up against another, blocking our path—massive blocks and needles preventing us from getting home to family and friends, rising out of what the great polar scientist and expeditioner Wally Herbert once described as "the stew of ice debris." It was one of these bastards that pierced the hull of the *Shokalskiy* when we were trying to make our escape. The damage shows what the ice is capable of and just how vulnerable we are. We're now completely at the mercy of the elements.

I pick up a pair of binoculars and scan the seascape. There are no leads of water, there's barely even a puddle: just a jumble of ice filled with dead ends. Out beyond, the thick, dark-gray clouds of water sky lie over the horizon. They can't be any more than four miles from us. It's sickening to know open water is so close. On the flat I can walk four miles in just over an hour. It seems such a pathetically short distance, but for the *Shokalskiy* it's completely unreachable.

I walk to the starboard side and look out. In the twenty minutes I've been downstairs, the nearest icebergs have definitely moved. One berg is only a mile away. Over fifty feet high, it must have at least 200 feet of ice below the surface, an enormous underwater sail driven by the ocean currents. It must be doing two to three knots.

That's bloody fast.

I can almost feel the shocks as the bergs carve their way through the sea ice, chewing up the surface, breaking all before them, the water boiling in their wake. On the positive side, the bergs seem to be running parallel to the ship, which means these ones should miss us if they keep on the same trajectory. That's something, I suppose. There are more icebergs off the stern, but I can't be sure where they were before. Our ship is safe, for now—a tiny refuge set in a scene of devastation.

Igor steps back into the bridge. "Chris, can you get Greg and the other Chris? I need to speak to them."

His tone is somber. This isn't going to be for a festive drink.

"Sure, Igor. I'll go and find them."

The simplest thing would be to call them up on the ship's tannoy system, but that will wake everyone. The less we broadcast at the moment the better.

I head downstairs and meet Greg on the stairs.

"Morning, Greg. Igor wants to talk. I just need to get Chris. Can we meet in the bridge?"

"Sure," he says matter-of-factly. Greg knows it's not good news.

I head down two flights of stairs. It's so quiet. Sensible people are sleeping.

I find Chris's door and tap hesitantly, not wanting to disturb any of the neighboring cabins. I have an English reticence that I've never been able to shake off.

"Chris, Chris?" I whisper. "Are you up?"

I hear a grunt of acknowledgment.

"Sorry, mate, but Igor needs to speak to us. It's serious. Can you get up to the bridge?"

The voice on the other side of the door suddenly becomes alert. "Yes, of course. I'll just chuck on some clothes."

I return to the bridge, where Chris joins us five minutes later. Hardly a word has been said the whole time we've been waiting. It's almost like someone has died.

Igor is pensive, anxiety radiating from him. Big decisions are being made. The confident smiles of the crew members are gone.

Igor continues where he and I left off, almost pleading with us to understand. "No way out. *Shokalskiy* needs help."

Greg nods cautiously, "But can't we wait? Maybe in a day or two the wind—"

"No, not possible," Igor interrupts, sweeping an arm out toward the window. "*Shokalskiy* can't leave on own. This ice is too thick. I make call."

He's already pushed the distress button for help.

* * *

Shit.

It's official, then. We really are in trouble.

The general rule of thumb when trapped by sea ice is to wait it out. Eventually the ice should spit you out; it may take weeks, months or even years, but you should get home.

Not this time. The icebergs are too close, the pack too thick.

The silence of the room is broken by the printing clatter of a fax machine. Igor rips the message off the machine and lays it on the table in front of us.

We read it in silence.

From: Falmouth Coastguard
Subject: ATTENTION MASTER
IMMEDIATE
24 2025 UTC DEC 13
FM UKMRCC
TO AKADEMIK SHOKALSKIY C/S UBNF
<u>ATTENTION MASTER:</u>
YOUR INMARSAT C DISTRESS MODE HAS BEEN
ACTIVATED.
YOU MUST CONFIRM YOUR DISTRESS OR
INDICATE YOUR
VESSEL IS SAFE.
COMMUNICATE WITH UKMRCC AND PASS YOUR
POSITION

Igor turns to Greg: "You call, please. My English not so good."

Greg nods acknowledgment. He's been the point of liaison between the bridge and the expedition. He's worked hard with the crew to keep things running smoothly in the background. And that's just the way I want it. There's no way I'm going to start butting in and confusing the lines of communication. We need to keep everything working as efficiently as possible.

It seems bizarre that the Falmouth coastguard in the U.K. is handling our rescue. They couldn't be farther away. But Falmouth is one of the global hubs for rescue, switched on twenty-four hours a day. Anyplace, anytime, a distressed ship's call first goes to them and is then passed on to a local rescue center.

Greg rings the number and confirms the distress signal. He gives our coordinates: 66°52" south, 144°19" west.

We get a barrage of questions: *What's the state of the ship? Distance to the ice edge? How close are the icebergs? What's their trajectory?*

Greg delivers the answers, short and to the point. A few minutes later, he hangs up.

"Okay, they've got enough to be getting on with. They're going to call back in twenty minutes with further questions."

There's nothing to do but wait.

I look at the bridge clock above us. It's only nine-thirty. A lot's happened this morning.

My family are eagerly waiting downstairs to open more presents, but a toxic mix of pack ice, a hull breach, a drift to shore, and roaming icebergs are threatening to spin things out of control up here. Two different worlds: festivities in the cabin, an emergency on the bridge.

What a Christmas.

I absently glance outside. No change. Surely the wind will swing round, maybe not today but sometime soon. A few cracks in the ice would make a world of difference.

I want to be as far away from here as possible, but no amount of willing is helping so far. The ice is staying stubbornly locked around the ship.

The telephone rings.

Greg picks up and relays the question: "Do we need immediate evacuation?"

There's a helicopter at the French base Dumont d'Urville, seventy miles away. If we have to, we can get the passengers out onto the ice for pickup. It would be a challenge transporting a handful at a time over that sort of a distance, but it could be done.

Igor walks up to the windows and looks out at the bergs moving past us on the starboard side. He returns to the radar screen and takes another look.

After a moment, his mind made up, Igor shakes his head. "No, we're okay for now."

"You're sure?" Greg asks.

Worriedly, Igor shrugs his shoulders. "I think okay."

That's going to have to be good enough for now.

Greg relays the message, listens for a moment, and then hangs up.

"Okay, we're going to be passed over to the Australian Rescue Coordination Centre shortly. They've asked we send any photos we have of the ice and call back in forty minutes. In the meantime, they'll look to see what ships are nearby."

There's nothing around for at least 100 miles. Before we left Australia, I informed the Italians, French, and New Zealanders that we were going to be working in the region. But of these only the French have an icebreaker, the *Astrolabe*, and that left their base for Hobart several days ago. There is the possibility a Chinese icebreaker called the *Xue Long* might also be able to help; they're meant to be reconnoitering possible sites for a new base in the Ross Sea, but their current location isn't known.

Our best chance is the Australian icebreaker, the *Aurora Australis*.

"Right, I'll go up on the top deck and send over the photos," I say. "What's the email address?"

Greg writes it down on a scrap of paper.

"While I'm online I'll check on the *Aurora Australis*." The icebreaker could be anywhere. The Australian schedule has been screwed up due to getting trapped in sea ice earlier in the season. They've already crammed two voyages into one to make up for lost time, but since we left New Zealand I've lost track of their schedule. They could be back in Hobart or resupplying their base at Mawson.

That's the other side of Antarctica.

Greg nods. I grab my laptop and the comms case. Throwing on my down jacket, I stagger out onto the blustery deck. The frigid air catches me off guard; in the warmth of the bridge, I forgot about the forty-knot winds blowing outside.

Working against the wind, I sit up on the top deck facing the bow. The *Shokalskiy* is locked in the ice pointing almost due north, the ideal direction for connecting to Inmarsat's satellites over the tropics. On the port side, I can see the rocky stretch of coastline at Stillwell Island and behind that a wall of ice: the East Antarctic ice sheet. Somewhere beyond, there is Cape Denison. It looks close—too close for comfort. I take the requested photographs.

The high-pitched squeal shrieks at me for attention and I dash back. We're connected.

If we're lucky, the Australian icebreaker will be at Casey, only a week's sailing from here. We won't be popular after all the shit they've already endured this season, but in Antarctica an emergency trumps everything. Out here everyone looks out for everyone else. Government operator, tourist, it doesn't matter: there's never any question of refusing help. There's no one else out here. If you don't look out for one another, people can get hurt . . . or worse.

I open up my laptop and download the photos. I stare at the icy images—those bergs have definitely moved. I email them straight to the coastguard.

Waiting for the pictures to send, I access the webcam on the *Aurora Australis* and check the ship's schedule.

I breathe a sigh of relief. The Australians are doing a resupply at Casey. It's close, Antarctic-close.

I return to the bridge with the update.

"That's some good news, I guess," says Chris.

* * *

An hour later, I'm standing at the front of the lecture room on the lower deck. Every seat is filled, every spare patch of floor sat on. With the Heritage staff, we have fifty-four people packed into a tiny space. It's getting hot.

We couldn't keep the situation quiet for much longer. We've already closed the bridge—a first for the whole voyage—to manage the calls with the coastguard. It was only a matter of time before someone started asking questions, serious questions. If we don't lay out the facts and fast, rumors will start and things will only get worse. We need to brief everyone. It's what Shackleton would have done. It's the only way we're going to get through this.

Nikki made the announcement over the ship's tannoy in her normal bright, cheery voice. In fact, it was so bright and cheery you'd never know anything was up—perfect for keeping everyone calm. She's a real asset to the team.

Before heading down, I pop back to my cabin and explain what's been going on. The family heard Nikki and figured out what was happening.

"Are we going to be okay?" Annette asked after the kids left to drop the presents in their room.

"We should be fine, love," I said, trying to not show any worry in my face. "We're now in regular contact with the rescue center and they know where we are. Either the wind direction will change, or they'll send a ship to break us out."

I hope.

Now we have to bring everyone else up to speed. Igor is speaking to the Russian crew; the expedition and Heritage staff are my responsibility. The team are a mix of personalities, ages, and experience. Few are expeditioners in the traditional sense of the word. How they'll respond I don't know, but I'm not going to give them the worst-case scenario. The last thing we need is panic. Thankfully, most seem happy chatting about the morning's festivities.

I can see Annette, Cara, and Robert in the middle row. Annette's look of concern says it all; she knows it's worse than I'm making out. I smile weakly, and the kids smile back.

Chris and Greg are seated to my right, just as they have been every day for the briefings. We've worked well as a team on the subantarctics and Cape Denison. Now we're going to have to step up a gear.

I clap my hands for silence.

Remember Shackleton: keep it positive.

"Morning, everyone. Happy Christmas."

Boisterous cries of "Morning, Chris" and "Happy Christmas, Chris" come back in reply.

That's a good sign.

"As I'm sure most of you have seen, the sea ice from yesterday hasn't broken up. There's a persistent easterly wind that's keeping the ice locked around us and unfortunately the forecast suggests this is not going to change appreciably for several days yet. That means we're unlikely to be able to get out under our own steam. Because of this, the captain has shut the engines down."

There's no need to talk about a possible blocked rudder, the breached hull, the icebergs, or the drift toward the coast.

"The good news is that the weather is looking better than forecast, but we can't rely on this. As a result, Igor has made a call for help to get us out of here."

There's a murmur across the room.

Earlier, Greg warned Chris and me that Igor thinks we may be here for ten or more days and might need to start thinking about rationing. At the moment, the *Shokalskiy* is all right for food, but if we get stuck much beyond ten days we're going to need a resupply.

Probably best not to mention this just now.

"At this stage, there's not a lot we can do. It's important we're patient and focus on looking out for one another while we wait. To bring you up to speed, I've asked Greg to give you a rundown from the perspective of the bridge."

I want the team to hear it from our point guy. Greg's wealth of experience will help reassure them.

Calmly, Greg outlines the morning developments and what's likely to happen. "As you've just heard, the captain has requested assistance to help break the *Shokalskiy* out. The Australian Rescue Coordination Centre—you may know them as the RCC—are now looking after us. We're in regular contact, and they've directed three vessels to our position: the Chinese *Xue Long*, the French *Astrolabe,* and the Australian *Aurora Australis*. These are all icebreakers, and should be with us in three to four days' time. The *Xue Long* will probably get here first. It was on its way from Fremantle to the Ross Sea to scout out some locations for a new research base, so we're rather fortunate. It's a majestic vessel and should be able to cut a way through to us. I'll make sure we get a picture on the noticeboard upstairs with some details about the ship."

There are looks of approval around the room.

"There's nothing else we can do for the moment, as Chris said. We'll hopefully be out soon, so just enjoy Christmas. But it's important we don't spread panic. I've been in situations like this before, and phone calls home can cause confusion. So when you speak to loved ones today, please don't let on about our current situation—including those of you in the media." Greg nods toward Alok, Andrew, and Laurence.

I'd already spoken to the media guys to give them the heads-up about what's happening. They've agreed not to report our immediate situation because of these concerns, and signal an acknowledgment to Greg as he sits down.

I'm standing back up to finish off the briefing when a sudden succession of sharp, hollow bangs resonate through the ship.

The good humor in the room immediately vanishes; worried looks are exchanged.

I put up my hands and try to sound reassuring. "As you can hear, the crew are making repairs to some damage the ship received on the way out from the Hodgemans. It sounds far worse than it is. There is a break in the hull, but it's above the water line. It's all under control."

The metallic ring of the repairs cuts right through me.

We were lucky—very, very lucky. If the ice had been any deeper we would be in serious trouble. The rest of the team don't need to know that, though.

"Any questions?"

Janet puts up her hand. "So with the ships coming, am I right in thinking they can reach us without much trouble?"

"Yes," I reply. "The *Xue Long* can cope with sea ice over three-feet thick, so it should be able to cut a path through. Once she gets to us we'll most likely follow closely behind her to open water."

I look to Greg for confirmation, and he nods.

I continue: "The *Astrolabe* is unlikely to be able to reach us on her own, but the *Aurora* will be a few days behind if there are any problems."

"So why have they sent the French ship?" asks Rob.

"That I can't say, Rob. Igor was most insistent the sea ice is too thick and they won't be able to help, but they're coming anyway." I pause. "Maybe they don't want to miss out?"

There are hoots of laughter. It's a welcome sound, breaking the tension.

"Now it's Christmas Day, so everyone relax. Nikki has put up a schedule of events for the day, and Nicola and Brad have been working hard preparing a fabulous dinner for later tonight. Isn't that right?"

I turn toward our two cooking maestros who are standing by the door.

"Absolutely, Chris," Nicola says, smiling. "It's going to be fantastic."

During their first few months trapped on the *Endurance*, Shackleton's men faced an uncertain future. Hope still lingered that they could get out under their own steam. Sure, the currents and winds were taking them away to the west, but if the pressure on the ice would ease up just a little, they might yet escape and even drop Shackleton and his team off. Leads of water did sometimes appear near the ship, but would then close shortly after, taunting the men on board. Shackleton remained positive, telling the men it was "better to be in an open pool than a closing crack, for that means pressure, the greatest peril a polar ship has to face." All perfectly sensible, but still deeply frustrating. The icescape was too chaotic, too broken "to get the hut and all our provisions ashore, some 50 tons of gear at a minimum, taking fuel and dog-food into consideration," wrote Orde-Lees.

By mid-March, their northward drift was all too apparent. With the approach of winter, the days were now noticeably shorter and temperatures were dropping. Repeated attempts to set up the radio system had failed; no one in the outside world knew where they were or what was happening. Shackleton re-signed himself to the inevitable. They were stuck and needed to prepare for the winter darkness. The expedition doctor Alexander Macklin commented:

We could see our base, maddeningly, tantalisingly. Shackleton at this time showed one of his sparks of real greatness. He did not rage at all, or show outwardly the slightest sign of disappointment; he told us simply and calmly that we must winter in the pack, explained its

dangers and possibilities; never lost his optimism, and
prepared for winter.

The boilers were shut down, and the stores and equipment moved so the men could sleep in a part of the vessel better insulated to cope with outside temperatures of -30°F. To free up space on the deck, flamboyantly designed "dogloos" were built on the ice to create "Dog Town." Shackleton kept his cabin, now in a cold part of the ship, to give himself the space for thinking and planning; if men needed a confidential word with him, they could do so without fear of being overheard.

With winter, the winds became stronger. The grinding and crashing of the *Endurance* against the sea ice was replaced with the eerie creak of timbers. They were surrounded by "an immense chaos of hummocks and ridges, ice needles and broken blocks piled up in the wildest confusion" and completely at the mercy of the elements. Time and time again, storms struck the ship, some inflicting serious damage. On August 1, 1915, a "terrific blizzard sprang up," and blocks of ice crushed the *Endurance*, smashing the rudder and starting a major leak. Another time Dog Town was destroyed by two twenty-foot-high floes, the dogs fortunately saved by an alert Shackleton who had stayed up during the night.

There was no way out. They were trapped with no chance of rescue.

The expedition had failed to reach its goal. Now all they could do was stick together as a team and hope the ship stayed out of serious trouble.

Six hours later, I step outside, alone.

It's been the weirdest Christmas ever.

The warmth of the ship instantly dissipates as the heavy door closes behind me and the polar wind sweeps into the doorwell, snow blowing in my face. Zipping up my jacket, I adjust my scarf and hat, trying to keep as much of the cold air out as possible.

Somewhere out on the port side is Stillwell Island, but it's disappeared from view, hidden by one of the thickest fogs I've seen in years. The visibility has crashed to just a hundred feet. I can't see anything out there. The *Shokalskiy*'s isolation is now complete. We're in our own cocoon, cut off from the rest of the world. On the broken ice below, the only thing I can make out are two Adélie penguins jumping between floes, single-minded in their undertaking.

I walk along the side of the ship, the beams of light from the windows piercing the gloom. It feels unearthly. The hiss of the snowflakes blowing across the deck remind me just how alone we really are.

There have been some good developments during the day. The wind has let up, and the icebergs have come to a standstill. And now we've stopped drifting to the shore; there's enough ice packed between us and the coast to stop the ship smashing on the rocks. That's a massive relief. Otherwise we'd be dealing with a completely different scenario.

I can just make out the muffled singing and laughter on board. I look in through one of the windows. After the sumptuous Christmas meal cooked by Nicola and Brad, everyone has moved to the lounge. Chris, Eleanor, and Erik are singing a carol next to the tree, Stay the Dog sitting attentively next to them, red and green antlers perched on the mascot's head. Annette and Cara are seated in the far corner chatting to Kerry; Robert is showing off the card tricks he's been taught by Graeme. The team are relaxing, enjoying the end of the day. We're surrounded by snow and ice. It doesn't get any more festive than that.

Brad walks across the lounge, still wearing his Santa outfit. Completely lost in character, crying, "Ho, ho, ho," he gave out the gifts from the tree this afternoon. During the lead-up to the expedition I asked everyone to bring a small gift for a Christmas lucky dip. The presents were a mixed bag. I did rather well— someone had generously bought a bottle of wine worth far more than the suggested $10 value. Poor Greg, though, opened his elaborately wrapped item and found one of the expedition fridge magnets inside.

The immediate threats have gone for now but this fog is a worry. Earlier today the barometer was showing rising atmospheric pressure, suggesting the forecasted low was tracking to the north, away from our location. Everything changed in the afternoon. The pressure held steady, but the wind swung round to the north and with it this fog has rolled in. In the Southern Hemisphere, the air in low-pressure systems flows in a clockwise direction, the opposite to their northern counterparts. As a result, you can sense their approach when the wind switches to the north; after it's passed, the wind is funneled up from the south, slamming any vessel in its path with blasts of frigid polar air. It looks like the low is now heading our way, and we're forecast a blizzard with wind speeds over forty-five knots. I don't even want to think about what it's going to do to all that sea ice out there.

I look up at the weathervane. If it would just swing to the west, we might still be able to get out of here on our own.

Shift, you bastard, shift.

I have no idea how Shackleton survived months of this. One day is enough for me.

CHAPTER NINE
The Home of the Blizzard

The blizzard is far worse than I feared. Through the driving sleet and snow, I can just make out Chris on the other side of the Zodiac.

Chris is looking toward me. He's gulping for air as he shouts something, his words carried away by the storm-force winds screaming between us.

"What?" I bellow back.

He tries again. "This is ridiculous."

I know what he's saying. It's Boxing Day morning. Most normal people would be lying in bed after a day of over-indulgence. We, on the other hand, are stuck on a ship, 1,400 miles from anywhere, surrounded by sea ice and bergs. It's only eight o'clock, and I'm having the air choked out of me by a raging snowstorm.

We're checking the lashings of the Zodiacs on the rear deck. They seem firm enough, and I'm sorely tempted to let them be and hope for the best, but in these winds you can never be sure. With the slightest slack, they'll rapidly unravel. The last thing we need is twenty-foot-long inflatables breaking loose and fly-ing off the deck.

The wind shrieks through the rigging.

Today's weather chart makes sobering viewing. Just like topo-graphic maps, the closer the barometric pressure lines, the steeper the change. This morning's chart shows a tightly jammed low out to the west heading our way, meaning what's happening now is just the start. The atmospheric pressure has dropped fifteen mil-libars over the last few hours and with it the winds have cranked up. The *Shokalskiy* is now being buffeted by sixty-plus-mile-per-hour winds and it looks set to stay this way for most of the day.

It's a good job we're not in open water. We'd have towering waves to contend with, as well.

What the hell am I doing here?

There's a momentary drop in the wind and I shout to Chris: "All good on this side, I'll try the next Zodiac."

He nods in acknowledgment, and I move on to the last re-maining inflatable.

This blizzard is more violent than anything I've ever been caught in before. The deck is treacherously icy and I hold on tight, grabbing anything to keep my balance. The wind on the other side of the ship's funnel is even more fierce, blowing vi-cious darts of ice in my face. I gasp in shock and get down on all fours, keeping low. There's a very real chance one or both of us might get blown off our feet, and the last thing we need is a bro-ken limb—or worse. Fragments of ice hurtle off the rigging. I make sure my snow goggles are firmly in place and drop my head. Only one word can sum this up: violent.

A distant roar of wind warns me another blast is about to hit. It builds in strength, howling and screeching around the ship. I can feel the *Shokalskiy* shaking as if it's about to be torn out of the ice.

Come on, you bastard! I scream at the ropes, and finally feel the knot tighten. With the inflatable secure, everything is locked down. *Thank Christ for that.* Chris makes to come over but I wave him away: *don't bother; it's all good.* There's no point shouting; he'll never hear me. Chris gets my meaning and moves to the shelter of a nearby doorway. I'm out of breath by the time I reach him.

"This is bloody crazy weather," he says.

It is bloody crazy, but we're done. When the winds worsen, at least we know everything is lashed as securely as possible.

"I need a coffee," I shout, and heave open the door into the back of the lounge.

We step from the raging apocalypse into another world. Inside, all is calm and warm, lights ablaze. It's almost too warm. Ben Fisk is cleaning up, and greets us as we fall into the room: "Morning, guys. Bit wild out there?"

I smile to myself. Ben is one of life's positive people. Always upbeat, he's the first to volunteer for any task, going out of his way to find out what needs to be done. It's typical Ben would be one of the first up and helping out on Boxing Day.

"Morning, Ben." I shake myself clear of snow. "Is the coffee machine on?"

"Turned it on a few minutes ago. Should be warmed up by now."

I'm gasping for a coffee. Early on in our planning I insisted we have decent coffee on the expedition. No crappy instant. I'm a caffeine junkie, and I knew many of the others are too—if we were going to fuel this expedition properly we had to have a near-inexhaustible supply of good beans. Behind the bar, I've set up a Breville espresso machine and grinder.

Without asking, I make a long black for Chris. He takes the steaming cup gratefully, the aroma filling the room.

We collapse on the sofas and savor what has to be the best damn coffee in the world.

* * *

Unfortunately, the media had learned about our predicament.

The first we knew about it was during Christmas dinner when Vlad called for me over the tannoy.

"Chris, Chris, please come to bridge."

Faces turned toward me. I smiled back weakly, knowing it must be important if I was being asked for now. I rose from the table, leaning over Annette's shoulder to give her a kiss. "Don't worry love, it'll be fine."

I climbed the three flights of stairs to the bridge nervously.

Vlad met me at the door. "Call for you, Chris." He signaled to the phone next to the chart table.

It was a journalist wanting to know whether we were okay.

It completely caught me off guard. I did the only thing I could think of: I stalled for time.

"Oh fine, fine," I replied. "We've run into some thicker-than-expected ice, so we're just waiting for a change in wind and then we'll be on our way."

"So nothing to be concerned about?"

It was bizarre speaking to someone while we're . . . trapped. The journalist was talking to me as if I was just down the road.

"Oh no, we're all good. Just having dinner. Everyone's in fine spirits." I wished the journalist a happy Christmas and put the phone down.

I hoped it was just a case of an enthusiastic journalist on a slow news day, maybe checking the ship's location online and seeing we hadn't moved.

No chance.

Then we learned the authorities had put out a press release. It's causing unintended mayhem. The ship is being inundated with calls. There are Russian reports that we've been hit by an iceberg, that we're sinking, that several people have died. This morning a confused newspaper article came out in Australia. At first, I didn't recognize what it was describing: a tourist ship on some sort of botched historic recreation. I'm struggling to rec-

oncile our expedition with how it's being reported; the journalist hadn't bothered to do the most cursory of research. There's a
danger the story is about to become very twisted, very quickly.

What is a difficult situation has now become a whole heap
worse. We have enough to be getting on with without journalists
firing out lazy reports. The *Endurance* expedition never had to
deal with this. When Shackleton and his men were caught, they
were off the map and no one knew what they were grappling
with. The newspapers could speculate and criticize, sure, but the
men on the expedition didn't have to deal with any of it at the
time. They just concentrated on the one and only important thing:
getting through it together.

The conditions are too bad to go outside again, so I send a
message to the head of the Australian Antarctic Division via the
ship's email; we need to coordinate our efforts to minimize any
more garbled stories being published. The last thing we need is
the crap being scared out of everyone at home. I hope we get a
response soon.

I'm nervous about how the team is going to take this. Breakfast hasn't finished yet, but already family members and friends
are starting to call the *Shokalskiy* in panic, jamming the only
phone in the bridge and preventing the authorities getting through
to us. If this continues, it threatens to wreak havoc with morale.
Christmas helped keep everyone's minds off the situation. Now
it's passed, we need to keep everyone busy. We don't need
panic. We could be here for a while yet.

"Chris, can I speak to you?"

I turn to see Mary chasing me down the corridor.

I breathe deeply. *Here we go.* "Morning, Mary. Everything
all right?"

Just behind her, volunteer Rob steps through a door, slamming it shut on the raging storm outside. A flurry of snow follows him in, the notices on the walls momentarily flapping in

the wind. Brushing off his camera and ice-covered hat, Rob mutters about the weather.

"Have you seen this article?" Mary holds up a printout from a newspaper website, shaking it crossly. "It's complete rubbish. What is wrong with them? We're not a tourist ship. We're a science expedition. Any journalist worth their salt could have found that out."

I sigh with relief. I could give her a big hug.

"I know. I've just seen it. I've no idea what they're on about. How are the others taking it?"

"The same. They're incensed. What are we going to do about it?"

I'm energized by the morning briefing. Rather than being despondent, the team are fired up. There's an old notion in expedition circles that you need a bogeyman on the team, someone to bond against. We don't have anyone like that, but no matter—the newspaper article has done the same trick. It's had an electrifying effect on morale, taking the focus off the blizzard outside. *We need to respond. We need to tell everyone what we're doing.* I would never have dared believe it.

Janet is particularly cross. "If we don't do anything, they'll continue to make a hash of it."

I see lots of nodding heads.

Greg sums it up nicely: "We can push back on this. Don't let them take control of our story. We need to tell everyone we're all right and the expedition is scientific."

We all agree. Alok, Laurence, and Andrew have already started sending in their own reports to *The Guardian* and the BBC. I don't know what they're saying, but anything will be better than the garbage we've seen this morning.

Our social-media network seems an obvious way to reach out: Twitter, Google+, Facebook, Vine, YouTube, and the blogs. We've been posting daily science updates to all of these. Now we can use them to tell everyone we're all right. Alongside these efforts, Tracey has the great idea of writing an article for the on-line newspaper *The Conversation,* to counter the screwy views at home.

We will tell our story.

Reassurance is the name of the game. "If you have a satellite phone, please do feel free to call friends and families and tell them everything is okay; it will hopefully put their minds at rest. We also have the office phone and can open this up for a few hours for calls. Nikki, can we put up a schedule in the lounge?"

The pressure of the ice hit the *Endurance* in waves with a noise likened to a "train passing or a heavy sea on a rocky shore." Each time, the ship would shake and the timbers groan. There was nowhere to hide. It must have been a terrifying reminder of the danger the men found themselves in. At any moment, the ship could be crushed and everyone with it. Nightwatchmen were posted to alert the others of impending danger and keep the stoves alight; Shackleton's burner required attention every half-hour, and the men would anticipate an interrogation about the conditions outside. The Anglo-Irishman was soon preparing for the worst. As early as 31 July he asked Orde-Lees to make a list of supplies to sustain the men on the ice for seventy-two days and store them on deck in case they needed to abandon ship.

It was an unsettling time, and the men were desperate to find ways to anticipate what might happen next: rumbles in the distance meant ice floes were colliding and might threaten the vessel; falling snow and light drift might signify an approaching blizzard. To help keep their minds off the horrors outside, Hurley wrote, "At first the gramophone proved a godsend, [but] no sooner did the music begin than the ice-pressure commenced, and the vessel began to quiver and creak . . . The belief became so strong that eventually the gramophone was placed under a ban." No more records were played for fear it would be the end of the *Endurance*.

Unfortunately, the pressure around the hull was just one of many risks for the *Endurance*. The floes around the ship were large, but the icebergs in their vicinity were enormous. One moment they were frozen around the ship, the next they were heading off at great speed, threatening to collide with the *Endurance*. Eight miles from the ship they spotted a "monster," a berg 180 feet high, ploughing through the sea ice. Other smaller bergs came dangerously close. Ship's carpenter Harry McNeish described one near-collision: "We had a rather narrow squeak with a berg this morning. It passed us about half a mile away going NE. It caused a lot of pressure but is well away now." McNeish was not a man with a sunny disposition, but this comment is remarkably positive. "Half a mile" is as close as you want your vessel to get to a moving berg. It's one thing waiting trapped in the ice, entirely another for your ship to get smashed to bits with you on it.

Over the next few hours, the wind continues to increase in intensity. I can feel the ship responding. It's not just being buffeted—something else is going on. It's almost like we're being plucked from the ice. I realize the *Shokalskiy* is starting to tilt. It's only slight at first, the sensation subtle, but it's definitely there.

Up on the bridge, I walk over to the window and look down.

The wind is blowing from the north. Finding their path blocked, the ice floes are rafting up, piling alongside the starboard side of the vessel.

The visibility is bad. If anything, it's worse than last night. We can't see any of the icebergs or what they're doing, but they're somewhere out there. I squint into the gloom, but it's futile. The radar has become our only eyes. Involuntarily I find myself checking the screen every few minutes. I'm not the only one. Bald-headed chief mate Nikolai is on the bridge. A good-natured man, Nikolai is normally supremely confident in the ability of the ship to weather any conditions, but even he is making a regular passage between the radar and the windows.

"It's okay," he says reassuringly, almost to himself. The bergs glow ominously green, but so far they seem to be staying put. That's a relief. If one or more of these Goliaths make a bee-line for the ship, we won't have long to react. I hope to God they don't. The last thing we want to do is evacuate the *Shokalskiy* in these conditions.

The wind is screaming again. The tilt meter on the wall is showing the ship at 1.5 degrees. I can feel it. I pace the room nervously, something I always do when I need to think.

I go down to find the kids. Both are in their cabin: Robert watching a film on his iPad, Cara reading. Annette and I are fiercely protective of them. We need to keep them as safe as possible in this situation.

"Guys, no going up on deck today. It's really wild outside and I have to know you're both safe. Is that okay?"

"Fine, Dad," says Cara, barely looking up.

"Sure, Dad," says Robert cheerily, completely unfazed by my instructions. *Dad sounds like he's making a fuss about nothing. Kids.*

It's a relief to know they're not completely freaked out by what's happening outside their window.

This weather is mad. It's like something out of a bad movie. There's a howling wind outside, we have massive icebergs within a couple of miles off the starboard side, and there's almost no visibility. And to make it worse, the constant pressure from the ice is pushing the ship over.

If we ever wanted a helicopter evacuation, we can forget it. The wild winds and zero visibility make that impossible. We're on our own and no one else can help us. The A-factor is working overtime.

I head along the corridor to find Greg. I need to talk through our options. We drop into his cabin to speak.

"What choices do we have if we get into further trouble, Greg?" I'm almost whispering. The walls are wafer thin, and I don't want anyone to hear what we have to say.

"It depends on how bad things get, Chris. We'd only leave the ship if it's at risk of sinking. The icebergs look like they've stopped for the moment. But if that changes, we do have the Argos."

I grimace. The wheeled Argos would be hopeless trying to cross the rafting ice outside. Thankfully, Serge has repaired the tracked vehicle after its swim in the ocean. He very proudly showed it off to me working in the forward hold. If necessary we could crane it onto the sea ice next to the *Shokalskiy*. I wouldn't want to push it too hard, but we might not have much choice.

We talk through possible scenarios. If things get dire and the ship is threatened, we'll have to get everyone onto the ice and try to make for the continent. If an iceberg does head toward the *Shokalskiy*, we'll probably get everyone into the lifeboats for shelter while we do relays. Stillwell Island would be our best bet, but it would be a huge ask of the team—some might say impossible—to cut a path through unfamiliar terrain in dense fog with winds reaching over 60 miles an hour. And all accompanied by a group with virtually no experience of extreme conditions. It's not a situation that fills me with confidence.

I look out of the porthole over Greg's shoulder and shudder. There are ten miles of moving ice between us and the continent.

Shit, I hope it doesn't come to that.

I'm struggling to see us keeping everyone alive in the conditions outside.

There's no way I want to introduce this scenario to the team unless it's definitely happening. Morale is good, but not that good. Panic will just set in, and that won't help anyone. There's nothing anyone can do at the moment anyway. The radar should give us a couple of hours' warning if any of the icebergs start moving in our direction—enough time to get everyone fully dressed and ready to go. Preparing for this eventuality now would only unsettle everyone.

With the strengthening wind, the ship is now listing to port big time. It's no longer just a feeling. And it's getting worse fast.

We both head up to the bridge. Terry calls after us. "All okay, guys? It doesn't feel good."

"All fine," Greg answers over his shoulder as we hurry on.

Terry isn't the only one concerned. I'm seeing a lot of worried faces about the ship.

Up on the bridge, Nikolai is still pacing between the radar screen and the starboard window. The tilt meter is now reading 5 degrees. That might not sound like much, but for a vessel the size of the *Shokalskiy*, 5 degrees is a big deal. The cabins and corridors are noticeably askew.

"It's not a problem, Chris," Greg says quietly. "It's disconcerting, but we can manage this. If necessary, Igor can flood the ballast to correct the ship."

"Can you make an announcement on the tannoy and tell everyone this? I know the team would appreciate hearing all is okay."

I walk over to the window and let Greg make the call from the ship's control panel. I glance down. The weather station readout on the nearby computer screen has flatlined. The conditions outside are so extreme it can't cope. The last reliable wind measurement was 54 knots and rising.

I gaze into the gray whiteness. The storm just seems to keep getting worse.

And we're completely on our own.

*   *   *

The weather is too wild to go out on deck to give interviews. Even if we found somewhere sheltered outside, the high-pitched screaming of the winds would kill any chance of us being heard. So most of the afternoon is being spent in my cabin taking satellite phone calls. After three days of being stuck, almost everything that was carefully stowed in the room has been used. The floor and seating are now strewn with science kit, clothing, boots, bundles of wires and other electronic gear. Along the walls, batteries and consoles hum contentedly as they're being charged.

For the phone calls, I've fed a magnetic antenna out through one of the portholes and slapped it onto the outside of the ship. With the open window, the small orange curtains flap wildly with each gust of wind, the temperature in the room approaching that of the outside. We don't always manage a clear link to the satellites, and the signal keeps dropping out, but it's the best we can do. I don't want the bridge swamped with any more media calls; we need to keep that line open for the RCC and other emergencies. It may be Boxing Day, but New Zealand is up and eager to know what's happening. Luckily for them, we have one of their own on board. Kerry-Jayne is more than happy to oblige.

She's on the sixth interview, still enthusiastically answering the same questions fired at her by the journalists. "I'm actually rather pleased we're stuck," Kerry-Jayne says with remarkable cheerfulness. "I wanted longer to study the bird life in the Antarctic, and thanks to all this ice I've got it."

The final interview complete, Kerry-Jayne turns to me. "You know, Chris, during four decades of expeditionary work, I've never mixed with so many different scientists. I'm learning so much." She gathers up her gear to resume the hourly bird counts from the bridge, stops at the cabin door and laughs. "I'm happy to do the interviews, but it must be a bloody slow news day back home."

I'm glad Kerry-Jayne's here. Even with all that's happening, Kerry-Jayne remains completely unflustered

Back in Sydney, our media man Alvin has seen the news and stepped into the breach. Most of the university seems to be on holiday, but not Alvin. This is a major news story, and his team are at the frontline. Before we left, he kindly agreed to be point man for inquiries, but little did he suspect he was going to have to give up his holiday time.

The afternoon calls from New Zealand are now turning into international requests, including from the United Kingdom and United States. Alvin is already proving his worth, fielding inquiries and keeping it at a manageable level. I just don't have the time alongside my other responsibilities on the vessel to answer everything. I hope this works to convince everyone at home we're okay. An email from my Dean, Merlin, is particularly reassuring, and just what I needed to hear: "Keep up the good work . . . Take care and ensure you have some tales to tell your future grandchildren."

Annette is looking after the children, answering their questions, reassuring them. But we also have our own families at home to think of. Annette and I agreed it was important to phone our parents—it is the holiday season, and, with our predicament in the news, we needed to reach out and tell them we're okay. Annette's mum and dad were reassured. Almost matter-of-fact, they wished us all a happy Christmas and ended with, "Oh, do you know what happened to your sister's present? It hasn't turned up." My parents, on the other hand, were both struggling with their emotions, worried sick about what was happening. It was a heartbreaking call. I can't believe how lucky I am to have Annette by my side, but I would give anything in the world to have the family safely at home, away from all this. *Anything.*

*   *   *

At the same time as Shackleton and his men were trapped on the *Endurance*, a dramatic series of events was playing out on the other side of the Antarctic. Poorly financed, the *Aurora* left Hobart for McMurdo Sound in the Ross Sea on Christmas Eve 1914. The plan had been to lock Mawson's former ship in the sea ice over the winter and use it as a base, from which the men could deliver the supplies toward the Pole that Shackleton expected to pick up on his way over. The *Aurora* departed six weeks late, and time was pressing. The leader of the party, Aeneas Mackintosh—one-eyed due to the result of an injury sustained on Shackleton's previous venture south—was concerned the Boss might have been dropped off early in the Weddell Sea and was already making his way across the Antarctic. Unfortunately, the telegram reporting the *Endurance*'s delayed departure was never sent from Grytviken. Unaware, Mackintosh immediately set about laying caches of food down to 80 degrees south before the summer ended. This would at least give Shackleton a fighting chance of getting to McMurdo if he was already on his way.

Returning in March, Mackintosh and his men were exhausted and dispirited. They had laid the depots as planned, but the man was not a good leader. Even though he was with Shackleton on the *Nimrod*, Mackintosh lacked any real knowledge of expeditionary work. He had driven the dogs too hard and too quickly after their long voyage, and many of the unfortunate creatures had died. Poor sledging technique only exacerbated the terrible conditions by making the journey far harder and longer than it needed to be. Furious arguments had ensued. The *Aurora* collected the disgruntled men on their return and decided Cape Evans, just offshore Scott's old base, was a safe anchorage for the winter. It was not for long. On 7 May 1915, the *Aurora* was struck by a storm. Breaking free of her anchors, she was swept out to sea, leaving ten men stranded on the shore, including

Mackintosh, with "only the clothes on their backs." The expedition faced disaster.

Realizing their ship was gone and unlikely to return, the men of what became known as the Ross Sea party moved into Scott's Hut. Morale was terrible, rescue uncertain. And they faced a huge challenge: They now had to lay the full schedule of supplies Shackleton was expecting. To accomplish their task they needed food, stoves, sledges, tents and clothing, virtually none of which had been brought off the ship. The men had to improvise. They set about organising themselves, salvaging what supplies they could find. A large tent was found and from this trousers and jackets were fashioned for everyone; food left over from Scott's expedition was prepared for the summer journey; old tents, sledges and stoves were repaired as best they could be; seals were killed for meat and fuel. The following summer, during a staggering 199 days of sledging in largely defective gear, the men somehow laid down the supplies Shackleton had asked of them, all the way through to 83 degrees south. Hardly any of the dogs had survived the previous year's effort, which meant the men had to drag the sledges and supplies themselves. It was an incredible achievement, particularly given the bitter disagreements that plagued the group. One of the men, however, died from scurvy and, impatient with the conditions, Mackintosh led another man across desperately thin sea ice, never to be seen again.

Remarkably, after the *Aurora* was swept out to sea, it too became trapped in sea ice, just like the *Endurance*. It was a dreadful year for sea ice in both the Ross and Weddell seas. In a little-known part of the story, Shackleton's second vessel drifted helplessly for 700 miles over nine very long months. When leads of open water appeared close to the vessel, the men tried to cut their way out but to no avail. They faced crushing sea ice and terrific storms, and watched bergs narrowly miss the ship. Released from the sea ice in February 1916, the ship was barely recognisable when it limped into New Zealand two months later. It would not be until January 1917 that the *Aurora* made it back to McMurdo to rescue the seven surviving men.

It's the end of Boxing Day. The team have just finished dinner, and a movie is on in the lecture room. The day is ending more positively than it began. The storm seems to be calming down outside, the rip in the hull has been patched up, and Igor has shifted the water in the tanks to tilt the vessel back upright. The ship doesn't feel like it's in so much peril now. But even more promising, the *Xue Long* and *Astrolabe* have made better progress than expected and called with the news they could be at the edge of the sea ice by mid-afternoon tomorrow. Things are looking up.

I head to the medical center, where I find Andrew checking over his photos from the day. I shut the door quietly behind me and pull up a chair. "I just wanted to catch up. Are there any problems I should be aware of? Is everyone all right?"

I learned long ago that telling everyone you're available doesn't always translate into action. Sometimes people are shy; sometimes they're reticent about voicing issues for fear it might be taken as criticism. I've had lots of conversation with the team in the lounge and during mealtimes. I know Chris and Greg have done the same. But no one has sought us out privately to express concerns. Maybe there aren't any, but I need to be sure. An obvious person they might confide in is the expedition doctor. I need to hear if there's something I'm missing.

"No, they're all good," replies Andrew, smiling confidently. "Their biggest fear seems to be missing the arrival of the other vessels when they're in bed!"

I leave feeling much more relieved. If everyone is concentrating on the rescue, that's good. They're looking forward rather than dwelling on what might be. I go into the lounge to make tea for Annette and myself. Maybe we'll get out of here soon. The family will be safe and we might even still get to visit Macquarie. If we leave in the next couple of days, this will have all been just a bloody awful scare.

That's a wonderful thought.

I head upstairs, trying to avoid tipping scalding tea over my hands. I'm just about to knock on the door for Annette to let me in when I become aware of someone halting at the door next to mine. It's Andrew. He's just stepping into the captain's cabin . . . clutching his medical bag. We're not the only ones feeling the strain.

The morning comes as a devastating blow.

Everything outside has changed—again. The fierce winds of yesterday have packed even more ice in between us and open water. What had been a few miles of sea ice is now far, far worse. There is no dark-gray water sky anywhere. We're surrounded by the white glare of ice blink. There's no let-up all the way to the horizon. There must be twenty miles of ice. Twenty miles to open water. Four miles was bad enough.

And to make matters worse, what was a broken icescape is now a scene of complete devastation. Under cover of the fog, the sea ice has cracked, collided and rafted; two-storey-high blocks of ice create a vista strikingly reminiscent of a destroyed city. The pressure of the ice has formed long ridges around us, running out in all directions. Most disturbingly of all, the icebergs off the starboard bow have moved several hundred feet. If they'd set off in our direction, it would have been a disaster for the *Shokalskiy*.

Thank Christ we didn't have to evacuate the ship. The weather station is now running properly again after shutting down for eighteen hours during yesterday's storm; eighteen hours of the shittiest conditions imaginable. I try to banish the image of seventy-one people trudging across moving sea ice in a blizzard with next to no visibility. I shake my head—that would never have ended well.

It must have been one hell of a breakout of sea ice up the coast to cause all this. The question is, what are we going to do about it?

I need to find Chris and work through the different scenarios facing us. Fortunately, the ship is quiet, most of the team kept busy by the schedule devised by Ben Maddison and Nikki: with lab work and movies on offer, not many people are about. It's all helping keep a focus while we figure out what to do. We go to my cabin, a good place to talk with little fear of being over-heard. Chris collapses in a seat opposite me, haggard and worn, the aftermath of yesterday's storm clearly weighing heavily on his mind. We know what's at stake here. There's no point in wishing for the few miles of sea ice we had on Christmas Day. Twenty is what we now have to deal with. We set to work inter-rogating the latest sea-ice images and weather charts. A shift in the wind would help, but the forecasts insist we'll have strong easterlies for at least the next week. I know weather patterns can dramatically change in the Antarctic, but I can't shake the feel-ing it's a futile hope that we'll suddenly get a westerly breeze. Given that, we have to face the fact that the *Shokalskiy* isn't going anywhere without help.

The *Xue Long* is our next best hope. And if she does get through, we'll need to be ready.

There's a knock, and Greg puts his head round the door. "Morning, gentlemen. Can we speak?"

I clear some of the papers off a chair to make space.

Greg's not optimistic about the ability of the Chinese to break through. "It could be a three-vessel job to get us out," he warns.

My heart sinks further. I don't dismiss Greg's concerns lightly—he has decades of experience in sea ice. He's seen it all. He's even been trapped by it and had to be evacuated. If Greg is saying we might need three ships, we have to consider it seriously. The *Xue Long* is only capable of breaking ice just over three feet thick, and almost everything around us is thicker than that now; some of it is over ten feet.

Can they find a way through when they reach the sea-ice edge later this afternoon? If not, we could be here a lot longer.

Eight hours later, I'm on the top deck. It's late in the day, but there's hardly a cloud in the sky. I can feel a light breeze on my face. It feels good to be back outside.

Standing next to me is BBC Andrew, fully kitted out for a live interview back to the U.K., earmuffs on, microphone at the ready. Andrew's the broadcaster's man on the ground and is focused on the task at hand, in spite of all that's happening around him

From down below come shrieks of laughter. I peer over the side and see people milling about on the ice, enjoying the evening sun, grateful to be off the ship. After thirty-six hours stuck inside, we needed somewhere to break the cabin fever that was fast developing. By lunchtime, a safe area to walk was staked out with bamboo poles and flags on a large floe next to the ship. It might look like a prison yard, but it's a brilliant anti-dote to the claustrophobia some were feeling.

This afternoon the call came through to the bridge that the *Xue Long* and *Astrolabe* had reached the sea-ice edge. It seems extraordinary to think that just twenty miles away ships are freely moving about; just twenty miles from our frozen position. And yet, with almost no hesitation, the Chinese ploughed straight into the sea ice, leaving the French behind to repair a troublesome engine. The Chinese vessel seems hell-bent on getting us out of here, and they're reporting excellent progress. They're absolutely incredible. We're hoping to see them soon, very soon.

When the Chinese reach us, the idea is that the *Xue Long* will carve a path around the Russian vessel, cutting a doughnut shape that will relieve the pressure on our hull. Igor can then start up the engines and follow the *Xue Long* back to open water.

At least, that's the plan.

If by some extraordinary good fortune all this works, we'll be out of here by the early hours of tomorrow. We've been trapped for four days and survived miles of sea ice, drifting icebergs, a blizzard, a rip in the hull, the threat of being dashed against the coast and some crazy newspaper reports. That's enough for one lifetime. With the very real threat of choral singing on tomorrow's schedule, I'd like to leave now.

My earlier doubts about the *Xue Long* are fast disappearing. I'm feeling quietly hopeful.

Some of the team have joined us on the deck, looking expectantly off the starboard side. Andrew calls me to attention: "Right, Chris, we're just about there. London should be calling any moment now."

Suddenly I hear a roar of excitement and cheers. "It's here!"

I turn to see a small red object on the horizon: the *Xue Long*. I can make out the Chinese ship surging forward, fighting its way through the ice.

It looks like we're going to get out of here after all.

CHAPTER TEN
Frustration

We're still trapped.

I can't believe it.

It was all looking so positive yesterday. I almost completely forgot the A-Factor and chose to let myself hope. Bad mistake. The *Xue Long* appeared on the horizon and seemed to rapidly make progress against our icy prison. There was lots of cheering. I could almost feel the movement of the ocean swell again. Then the Chinese vessel ground to an agonizing halt.

You can never take anything for granted in the Antarctic. If we're going to get through this roller-coaster, we have to remember to hope for the best but anticipate the worst.

I look out over the windswept ice toward the *Xue Long*. I can make out so many details: the red hull, the bridge, the forward crane.

It's so close.

I hope the Chinese are all right. It is reassuring to see them there. But the *Xue Long* does seem ominously still.

There's a fresh north-easterly breeze of over thirty knots. I'm on the top deck uploading the latest blogs and science reports. With windchill, it's 10°F, and the weather forecast and charts seem to be taking longer than normal to download. I pull my hat firmly over my head and rub my arms strenuously to keep warm. Finally, the charts appear on the screen. Easterly and southerly winds for at least the next five days with the possibility of snow later. Nothing expected from the west. On the plus side, though, no big storms are forecast.

That's something, I suppose.

I pack up the comms and head down to the bridge.

It's wonderfully warm down below. And quiet. On the desk, there's an email from Captain Wang on the *Xue Long*. They've struck sea ice ten-feet thick. They've pushed as hard as they can but have only made two miles in the last eleven hours. That's tough going. No wonder the Chinese ship has stopped. It's a relief to read they're all right—I was starting to think they were actually stuck or worse, damaged in some way. The captain's email ends in a wonderful flourish: "So we propose a more powerful icebreaker could come to support this situation and help MV *Akademik Shokalskiy* to get out of stuck. We will stay here and standby in case of any unexpected situation." *What a lovely man.*

The Chinese have done their best. The *Astrolabe* remains standing by in open water but we're going to need something at least the size of the *Aurora Australis* to break out. And the Australian icebreaker isn't due to reach the sea ice edge for another three days. We're going to be here for some time longer.

The view from the bridge is brilliantly white. From the corner of my eye, I catch a large ice block collapsing off our port side. It may be beautiful, but the sea ice remains under tremendous pressure. It's all too easy to get lulled into a false sense of security. We're in a dangerous situation and I feel myself becoming resigned to almost anything.

Remember the A-factor.

I look off the rear of the ship and an alarm goes off in my head. I turn to Vlad, beside me on the bridge.

"Vlad, have those moved?" I point to the half-dozen table-topped bergs a couple of miles off the rear of the *Shokalskiy*. "They seem closer."

Vlad comes over and studies the radar screen. The Russians are responsible for keeping watch, but after the delay raising the bridge on our return from Cape Denison I need to be reassured someone is definitely looking out.

"I think okay, Chris. But we watch."

There's not a lot we can do about the bergs. It's just good to know where they are and that they're being monitored. After Shackleton's experiences, we know stalled bergs can suddenly start moving again in a completely different direction from before. Constant vigilance is needed.

I drop down the stairs to my cabin. There's no one around. The smell of cooking food tells me it's breakfast time. Our room is empty. I take off my jacket and fall into a chair.

God, I'm shattered. I'm used to a good eight hours of sleep. Over the last few nights, I've been averaging three to four. No wonder I feel so lousy.

There's a knock on the door.

That's my lot.

"Hello?" I call out.

It's Alok who pops his head around the door. "Chris, can we talk?"

In spite of my tiredness it's always good speaking with Alok. He's worked tirelessly the whole voyage, and his good humor is a welcome antidote to everything that's happening. His face is flushed from the cold after an early morning spent on the top deck.

"Sure, come in. What's up?"

"Laurence uploaded his report to *The Guardian* last night, and I've just gone online to check it."

Even in twenty-four-hour daylight we still talk about night and day; it's just easier that way. Since news of our predicament broke, Laurence and Alok have been posting articles at all hours, accompanied by stunning photos and movies. I'm amazed at their energy.

"Chris, you might not realize it, but we're in the middle of a media storm. The world's woken up to where we are. It's gone crazy about your social-media posts and the reports we're doing. The tweets, the Vines, the YouTube movies. The media are recycling them in their reports around the world. The story has really captured people's imaginations; trapped on a ship a thousand miles from home, posting photos and movies, blogging about what's happening. The Boxing Day blizzard has lit a fire under the whole story."

Alok rattles off a list of networks wanting interviews: CNN, CBS, ABC, BBC, Al Jazeera, SBS, Channel Seven, MTRK, the Weather Channel . . . the list goes on. I haven't heard of half of them.

"I've never seen anything like this. It's so big we're even on Buzzfeed, and that's just made it bigger."

"Really? It's actually been picked up by them?" Buzzfeed looks at what's trending on social media and then pulls it together into a news report. It's big news if it's on Buzzfeed.

I'm incredulous. As a scientist, I'm used to writing press releases on research and having hardly anyone pay attention. I haven't heard anything back from my email request to the Antarctic Division, but after our social-media blitz and Alvin's hard work coordinating interviews, the tone of the reports has changed. Now journalists seem to have realized we're scientists and have turned their focus to reporting what we're doing and how we're coping. We're on the edge of the known world, scientists and volunteers trapped on board a ship surrounded by icebergs. It isn't an everyday news story.

I hope our reports that the bergs have stopped moving are helping calm nerves at home, but I'm concerned about the media interest getting out of control.

"So what do you think, pull back what we're reporting?" I ask Alok.

"No, absolutely not. You're telling your story. Now you've engaged, you're going to have to keep going. I've seen this before. If you stop now, there'll be a news vacuum, and everyone else will fill it. The world is hungry for news, and if you don't take control, others will—and they'll make up the details if necessary."

My heart drops.

"Surely after we set the story straight on that Australian report we're okay now? The media can now just report what comes through the official channels."

"Seriously, Chris, they'll report anything. The world wants to know what's happening on the *Shokalskiy* and if you don't do it someone else will. On the plus side, everyone is waiting to hear what you have to say. You just have to keep up the conversation."

There's only so many hours in the day, and my priority has to be the team. We can't risk people getting scared and that fear spreading. Everyone needs to be seen around the ship; if Chris, Greg, or I disappear for too long it could be interpreted as a major problem happening behind the scenes. That's how rumors start. Everyone is working hard to try to maintain normality or be as close as we can get to it.

"That might sound easy, Alok, but I can't do much more. I have to keep on top of things here."

"Well, it's also a human-interest story now. How about a video diary? Film one team member a day, telling their story with a message for home. Can you give the job of filming and editing to someone on the expedition?"

Laurence would be obvious, but he has a job to do for *The Guardian*.

I know straight away: Taylor. He's young, enthusiastic, and studying media at university. When we did the last Hangout on

Air he was asking all sorts of questions. Yesterday I was concerned he seemed a little quiet, a bit more reserved than normal. Taking ownership of the video diaries will give him and everyone else on board a welcome distraction, as well as help to reassure families back home we're all right. Shackleton would have liked the idea.

We go down to the dining room and find Chris and Greg discussing the day's tasks over breakfast. Alok explains the situation and gives his opinion that we need to do more media, not less. They both agree.

"We need to keep everyone busy," says Chris. "The guys want to know what the world's saying. We can screen the daily videos in the lecture room before the evening movie. It'll help keep their minds off things."

Great. We have a plan. I find Taylor straight after breakfast and ask him whether he'd be willing to make the video diaries.

"Sure, Chris. It would be good to do something."

We have our director.

The morning briefing is a salutary lesson in handling disappointment, Antarctic style.

I was worried the failure of the *Xue Long*'s attempt might have dampened the spirit on board, but everyone could see what happened. A new situation has developed and psychologically they've moved on. Already the A-factor is being accepted as the way of things.

It crystallized something in my mind that the men on the *Endurance* were all too familiar with: Don't build up everyone's hopes unless you are 100 percent certain. And in Antarctica, that means promise absolutely nothing. Jack shit is certain when it comes to logistics down here. The sea ice can change, the weather can become violent. Instead, embrace the A-factor. Prepare for the inevitable delays, warn everyone what might happen and be ready to move if it does. The key thing is keeping everyone together, and for that you need to give people time to get their heads around a situation. Well, most situations. Highlighting the worst-case scenarios isn't going to help anyone. Then things will quickly go to shit.

I scan the room. The fifty-one team members look expectantly up at me for news. This isn't a bunch of testosterone-pumped adventure-seekers, or even experienced explorers. Instead, we have an eclectic mix of scientists, expeditioners, and amateurs, all with their own personalities, needs and demands. We're one of the most diverse groups ever trapped inside twenty miles of crushing ice. Now I'm speaking to the "lucky" ones—the ones Chris and I chose for the "adventure of a lifetime." At the moment, everyone seems to be hanging in there. But for how much longer?

"The *Xue Long* is standing by to offer help if we need it. In the meantime, we're going to have to wait for the *Aurora Australis* to reach us, which will take a few more days. We're keeping an eye on the weather and maybe, just maybe, the wind will shift round to the west."

Jon from the Mawson's Huts Foundation puts up his hand. "Is the Chinese ship stuck? I've been watching her this morning, and she doesn't seem to be moving."

I'm surprised Jon is asking a question like that. He's been visiting the Antarctic for more than thirty years. If the *Xue Long* is indeed stuck, that won't help morale on the *Shokalskiy*. Some in the room are genuinely scared, and I don't want to give them any more reason to worry.

"No, they're all good." I try to sound confident. "Captain Wang is in regular contact with the bridge and keen to help in any way he can. By holding their position, they will be able to help more quickly with their helicopter if we need it."

Jon looks unconvinced, but I move on quickly. Dwelling on potentially bad news isn't helpful. I switch focus on to the media interest and ask Alok to say a few words. It helps divert attention from any uncertainty that's arisen from Jon's question.

There's amazement that we're on the front pages of the world's newspapers.

"Well, it's good to hear we're no longer being described as a tourist ship," Mary says, and there's a chorus of laughter.

"It's true. Laurence and I have never seen anything like it. The thing is, we need to do more or others will start telling the story."

Alok describes the idea of video diaries, and there are nods around the room. Here's something to do, an opportunity for everyone to tell their story. I introduce Taylor as the director of this new series of films, and he bows at the back of the room to a spontaneous round of applause. There's a show of hands for volunteers, and we have the next week's worth of video diaries mapped out.

We're on.

"We are now six months out from England and during the whole of the time we have all pulled well together and with an almost complete lack of friction," Worsley wrote after the *Endurance* became stuck. "A more agreeable set of gentlemen and good fellows one could not wish for shipmates." Incredibly, Worsley wasn't the only one to express this sentiment.

The secret on the *Endurance* was teamwork and optimism. Shackleton encouraged the team to work and play together. He actively discouraged negative comments, recognizing it could poison the atmosphere and morale on board, with Orde-Lees remarking: "Pessimistic prognostications are not popular." Shackleton united what was a disparate group of individuals by rotating tasks so everyone was capable of working in almost any role. Quarrying ice for fresh water, scrubbing the floors, exercising the dogs, making scientific measurements—it made no difference if you were a BA or an AB, everyone had to take part. He encouraged team spirit at all times and took part in jobs, however menial.

Shackleton spent time talking to the men individually. As Macklin later wrote, "He would get into conversation and talk to you in an intimate way . . . This communicativeness in Shackleton was one of the things his men valued in him; it was also, of course, a most effective way of establishing good relations with a very mixed company." Sometimes he would fool with the men. When Orde-Lees asked about his interview, Shackleton lamented the officer had come at all; he told Hussey he was only accepted because "I thought you looked funny." But if needed, men were also indulged. When Orde-Lees was struck down by a particularly bad case of sciatica—a complaint Shackleton also suffered from—the expedition leader personally nursed the officer in his own cabin for two weeks, giving up his bed to do so.

It wasn't all chores on the *Endurance,* though. Spare time was spent playing football and hockey on the ice, in the evening cards and slideshows. Alcohol was frequently allowed, just enough for everyone to enjoy but not to get drunk. Saturday was enjoyed with a toast to loved ones: "To our sweethearts and wives, may they never meet!" Another time they experienced what Hurley described as a "form of mid-winter madness" when all the men shaved their heads, with Shackleton the first to be cropped. Singing, that much-sought-after ability in interviews, was a regular part of each evening's entertainment, accompanied by Hussey playing the banjo. During their time trapped, Hurley would take the most spectacular photographs of his career, capturing the frozen *Endurance* on glass plate negatives, the men helping him set up the shots that would go on to define the expedition.

Celebration was also a significant part of life on the *Endurance*. Birthdays and anniversaries were big events, something for the men to look forward to, a focus away from the ship's entrapment. The midwinter feast on 22 June was a major deal; surrounded by sea ice and roaming icebergs, the men partied in the heart of the winter darkness. A meal of delicacies with roast pork, apples, peas, and plum pudding must have tasted like heaven after months of eating penguins and seals. In the evening, a concert of skits, songs, dressing up, and banjo-playing completed the day's celebration.

Even those who did not enjoy all the activities recognised their value. A self-confessed bad singer, Orde-Lees complained in his diary about being forced to join in with the others: "I suppose it's all right for those who smoke and appreciate the liquor but for those who don't it is a nauseating penance." But he grudgingly admitted, "There is no doubt though that teetotalism and conviviality are somewhat incompatible and it is probably this that has mitigated more than any other factor against the abstainee's propaganda."

The result was a remarkably content team who seemingly reveled in their situation. An amazing example of this was a conversation Macklin had with Third Officer Alfred Cheetham during a sledding trip around the ship. Reflecting on their situation, Cheetham asked the doctor whether he agreed they were better off than the king. Macklin was surprised at the question, so Cheetham explained, "Well, I'm happy, Doctor, and you're happy, and here we are . . . looking at the wonders of the world; it goes into your soul, like, don't it, Doctor? The king with all his might and with all his power couldn't come here and enjoy what I'm enjoying."

Greg caught me in the corridor shortly after lunch: "Chris, can we meet with Igor? He's keen to go over our options."

"Yes, absolutely." I haven't seen much of Igor in the last twenty-four hours, basically since Andrew's visit to his cabin. But now the hoped-for arrival of the *Xue Long* hasn't come to pass, it's important we all sit down and discuss where to go from here.

Half an hour later, I'm crossing a threadbare carpet to sit at the table in the captain's cabin. It's the first time I've been past the door. I'm struck by the sparse, almost austere decoration. A few books lie neatly stacked on the floor, a map on the wall, some pictures on the side, and not a lot else. This is Igor's private space, effectively his home, and there's very little of the man anywhere to be seen.

I turn my attention to the haggard, sun-tanned faces of the three other men in the room. Chris, Greg, and Igor look back at me. The last five days have been wearing, and who knows when we're going to get out of here. Hopefully after this meeting we'll have a better idea. We have a lot to talk about and we need to do so freely.

Greg starts. "It's been a busy few hours. The RCC wants information on how best to proceed."

He sums up the questions the team at the rescue center have. Their immediate concern is whether we remain in imminent danger. It's not whether icebergs are in our vicinity; they want to know if they're moving around.

Thankfully, they aren't at the moment. The nearest bergs lie just a couple of miles off the *Shokalskiy* but they don't appear to have moved recently.

"If that's the case," continues Greg, "they will release the *Astrolabe* so it can resume its voyage to Hobart. But if critical, they say they have room to evacuate twenty-one passengers by helicopter."

What does that mean? If we need to evacuate, surely we need to get everyone off, not just twenty-one. Are we meant to start drawing lots? Everyone is going to get home, not just some. My family, the team, everyone. We all have to be safe.

The Chinese are remaining on station. There is, of course, the one elephant in the room.

"Is the *Xue Long* stuck?" I ask.

"Perhaps," says Igor seriously and shrugs.

I grimace. The one ship that we can see could be in the same predicament as us. The situation might now be twice as bad.

For the RCC, the focus of the rescue now falls to the Australian icebreaker. Igor is keen for the *Aurora Australis* to push on. *It will be able to break through. It will reach us.* He's almost imploring us. The Australian captain, however, is arguing they're no more capable than the *Xue Long*. If the Chinese vessel is struggling, his won't get through.

Igor disagrees, shaking his head: "They can do more. The Australians know these waters better than anyone. Their captain will be better able to find a way through the thinner, weaker floes. They should continue."

Greg makes notes.

"Otherwise we wait for westerly wind," Igor states matter-of-factly.

My hopes rise. If the wind does swing round, the pressure of the sea ice around *Shokalskiy* would immediately ease. A strong westerly wind could open up a lead of water as quickly as everything closed in.

I pull out the latest weather forecasts we've downloaded, and we compare them to the synoptic charts from the bridge. They all show the same thing: a low-pressure trough is sitting to the north of us, and with it easterly winds for several more days. There's no prospect of escape.

This is going to take a monumental effort to manage. Boredom and frustration could easily become major problems if we spend days cooped up, even with exercising off the ship. We need volunteers to offer classes and fill the hours. Ben Maddison has done an amazing job with Nikki so far, but now we need to plan activities that stretch over days. We've already had offers. Eleanor is keen to start cutting up the ocean sediment cores we took in Commonwealth Bay. Naysa and Alicia have suggested Spanish lessons, Andrew photography classes. These will all fill precious hours. The video diaries should help too. Anything to keep people occupied and safe.

And in the meantime?

"We watch."

That means time on the bridge. Those bergs haven't moved recently, but I'm skeptical they're lodged on the seabed. The water around here should be several hundred feet deep. It's highly unlikely they have that much submerged ice. If the icebergs start moving again . . .

What happened to the *Endurance* is all too clear in my mind.

After ten months trapped in sea ice, the *Endurance* had zigzagged 1,000 miles around the Weddell Sea. Seven degrees of latitude separated the men from their point of first imprisonment; ten months amid the restless, grinding ice. But with the arrival of the spring sun, Shackleton and his men met a new and terrifying prospect. Rather than finding themselves released by melting ice, the breaking floes jostled one another with renewed enthusiasm, creating new pressure ridges that squeezed the *Endurance* once again. Hurley described the strain on the vessel:

The decks gaped, doors refused to open or shut. The floor coverings buckled and the iron floor plates in the engine room bulged and sprung from their settings . . . we began to rise from the ice, much after the manner of a gigantic pip squeezed between the fingers.

No one was more aware of the danger they faced than McNeish, who at times "thought it was not possible the ship would stand it." During one bout of pressure, he feared "it won't do so much longer as we have sprung a leak. I am working all night trying to stop the pressure getting worse."

For the Boss, the men had to keep positive and busy. They weren't allowed to dwell on their situation; they had to do something about it. All hands were put to the pumps, but it wasn't enough to hold back the water. Trenches were cut around the ship to try to relieve the pressure on the hull. None of it made any difference. The vicelike grip of the ice was too much for the *Endurance*. The three lifeboats on board were taken off the ship and hauled to a safe distance.

By 27 October 1915, it was clear the *Endurance* couldn't take any more. To Shackleton "the ship presented a painful spectacle of chaos and wreck" and he lamented in his diary:

It is hard to write what I feel. To a sailor his ship is more than a floating home, and in the Endurance I had centred ambitions, hopes and desires. Now, straining and groaning, her timbers cracking and her wounds gaping, she is slowly giving up her sentient life . . . she was doomed. No ship built by human hands could have withstood the strain. I ordered all hands out on the floe.

For most of the time "he stood on the upper deck holding onto the rigging smoking a cigarette with a serious but somewhat unconquered air." The men salvaged what they could, dumping supplies on the ice. It was a depressing sight watching the ship, their home, slowly have the remaining life crushed out of her, the hold filling with water as Hurley captured the last moments on film. But she did not sink. Held in the grip of the ice, the *Endurance* was "well down but by no means entirely submerged" when the emergency lighting suddenly switched on, seeming to "transmit a final signal of farewell." Watching from the ice, Orde-Lees confided in his diary that "even Wild, as courageous a man as there is amongst us, admitted it gave him a pain in the stomach."

Just when the men on the *Endurance* didn't think it could get any worse, it did. The A-factor stepped up a notch. The men were about to find out just how bad things could get in the Antarctic.

Five days into our enforced stay, I'm starting to question my sanity. The A-factor is running me ragged. I know we have to build it into our planning but the range of possibilities for what might happen is numbing. For now, we're all right. But the worst-case scenarios, most of them with the prospect of little to no warning, terrify me.

It's eight in the evening, and I'm in the lecture room. I'm standing in front of the team, about to start my evening briefing. The room is packed, and it feels claustrophobic, but my family's expectant faces immediately catch my attention.

This really wasn't such a great idea. Why on earth did I bring them here of all places?

Late yesterday, we were cheering as the icebreaker *Xue Long* smashed its way through the sea ice toward the *Shokalskiy.* Our release seemed only a matter of time. *We're going home.*

Now the Chinese vessel has been stopped on the horizon and quite possibly trapped. The ice is too thick. Nobody can reach us.

I have to try to explain what happens next, but I have no real idea of how we're going to get out. With the forecast showing easterly winds, the pressure around the *Shokalskiy* isn't going to let up. The *Xue Long* was our one realistic hope of breaking out of here in the next few days.

The enormity of our situation appears to have sunk in during the day. This isn't just a slight delay; no one is getting out of here anytime soon. And with this realization, there's a palpable change in the mood. With Christmas gone, the team focus is threatening to disappear. With an indeterminate timeline, the drudgery and tension of life on a stranded ship is taking its toll.

We're completely at the mercy of the elements and everyone can sense it. The storms, the bergs, the rip in the hull—all we've experienced is throwing our situation into sharp relief. We're as vulnerable as you can be. *How much can the Shokalskiy reasonably take? For that matter, how much can we take?*

There are no longer any faces smiling at me. Even Kerry seems deflated by the failure of the *Xue Long*.

"The good news is, the icebergs have stopped moving around us and probably grounded on the seabed."

Faint smiles are shared. I don't draw attention to the convoy of icebergs off the ship's stern. I can't.

"Although the *Xue Long* can't get through, the captain has decided to stay on station to make sure we're safe."

That's what he's saying. He's quite likely stuck as well. The ship hasn't moved one little bit in twenty-four hours.

"We can still be broken out. We'll just have to wait for the Australian icebreaker, the *Aurora Australis,* to arrive."

There's a murmur across the room.

"So how long will it be?" someone asks.

I don't want to tell them this, but delay is the least of our problems. Igor is now talking about a fifty-fifty chance the *Shokalskiy* might not get out at all without a break in the winds. The ship could remain trapped for years, meaning we will need to evacuate. How and when I don't know. The Australians don't have a helicopter, which means we need the Chinese, the same Chinese who appear trapped on the horizon. That's just made any evacuation a whole heap more challenging.

Greg stands up at the back of the room. Quietly spoken, he says, "At least five days," and sits down promptly.

There's an audible gasp across the room. In spite of all that's befallen the *Shokalskiy*, the first talk of a longer delay seems to have made our predicament more real. The younger guys—normally smiling and laughing—sit stony-faced. Joan appears almost in tears. Annette, sitting next to her, offers a comforting hand.

Think of Shackleton. Keep it positive. Keep it hopeful.

"Remember," I say, "the weather can change at any moment. We're keeping a close eye on the forecasts and if the winds reverse, we're out of here. If all else fails, the American icebreaker *Polar Star* is in Sydney and can reach us in two weeks." That's one bit of good news that came through a few hours ago, but the timeline is horrendous. There's a palpable air of shock in the room, but I keep going. "The *Polar Star* is capable of getting through twenty-one feet of ice so won't have any problems with what's outside."

After a few final words on housekeeping, the briefing is over, and everyone shuffles out.

That could have gone better, I think, *but at least we were honest with them. For the most part.*

I daren't share my greatest fears. No one knows what those other icebergs are going to do, and the weather forecast looks crap.

Am I holding it together? Am I losing the group?

If anyone knew how worried I was, things would only get worse on board. I hope most of it's in my head. *We'll be all right.* I have to stay positive.

But I'm starting to doubt myself. I can't help but think over all that's happened, going through it all in my mind, time and time again. *How can it have got so bad? It looked good when we were sailing in to the Hodgemans. We had the best comms available. All the satellite imagery showed clear, open water.*

Why did that bloody ice have to sweep in so fast?

Annette looks toward me, worried. I smile at her from across the room.

It'll be fine.

The only happy face appears to be Kerry-Lee's, the Chinese banker.

"Kerry-Lee, was that okay?" I ask, concerned she may not have understood everything.

She beams back at me. "Oh, yes. I okay. Tomorrow more hopeful, yes?"

"Yes." I smile to myself. *At least someone's all right.*

As I climb upstairs, my thoughts are interrupted. Two of the volunteers, Peter and John, stop me in the corridor. They're worried about the delay and whether they're being told everything. I try to reassure them, but Greg joins us. Frustration suddenly erupts. Greg loses his temper.

"Of course, we're not going to get home when scheduled. It's bloody obvious, isn't it? We've been held up five days, so we're going to be at least five days late. It could be a lot, lot worse. Take responsibility and work it out for yourself."

The corridor is packed with onlookers by now, and there's a shocked silence as Greg storms off. I'd never guessed he was feeling the pressure. He seemed to be doing so well. A little distant at times, perhaps, but nothing out of the ordinary.

If Greg's this stressed, we're in even worse trouble than I thought.

Everyone else seems to be thinking the same. Terrified looks are exchanged along the corridor. People are starting to realize that this is more than just a temporary hold-up; we're not in a safe situation.

I need to take the heat out of what's just happened.

I offer a faltering apology and after promising fresh news tomorrow, I wearily climb the stairs to the bridge in search of Greg. I close the door on everyone else. Words are said. It's a bruising half-hour.

Afterward, I search out the kids in their cabin. Cara and Robert are sitting on a bunk with the iPad.

"Hi, Dad. How's it going?" asks Cara. "Want to join us for a movie?"

I breathe a sigh of relief. Normality . . . or as close as I'm going to get.

"Make way," I demand, determined to sound as calm as possible. They smile and silently shuffle apart. I drop into the middle, hugging them both, and settle down for the rest of the evening.

I'm never letting you go.

CHAPTER ELEVEN
Teamwork

The *Shokalskiy* isn't getting out of here anytime soon.

Everyone is sensing it, even Greg.

The morning after his outburst, Greg knocks on my cabin door and apologizes. I'm glad Annette has already left for breakfast. It's big of Greg to do this, but he's a private man.

"That's okay, Greg. Forget it happened. Let's just move on."

The stress isn't just telling on him; we're all feeling it.

Chris joins us shortly after. We sit down to plan the morning briefing. I lay out the latest satellite sea-ice imagery downloaded from the top deck an hour ago. It makes grim viewing. Where there was thick, decade-old ice out to the north of the Mertz Glacier, there's a large, gaping hole of open water. It's the same region where some of the biggest increases in sea ice have been reported in recent years. No wonder we can't get out. All this ice has been dumped along the eastern side of Commonwealth Bay by the Boxing Day winds. And we're slap bang in the middle of it. The weather charts show that the day before we were trapped, a tightly jammed finger of barometric pressure stretched over this vast region, driving the broken ice right into our path. It means the sea ice was following hard on our heels as we sailed into the Hodgemans. We were already trapped when we arrived; we just didn't know it. Whether the breakout of sea ice is from climate change seems a moot point at the moment.

"It looks like this might become fast ice," muses Chris as he pores over the images. "Shit, we've been caught by a major re-alignment of the Antarctic coastline. This could be here for a long time yet."

"If so," says Greg, "we might have to accept the *Shokalskiy* will remain stuck without some serious ice-breaking capability. I can't believe the *Aurora* or the *Xue Long* are going to reach us on their own."

Not good.

If the *Shokalskiy* isn't released, the only other real possibility is a helicopter evacuation—and that means working with Captain Wang on the trapped *Xue Long*.

I reach for my coffee. I slept fitfully during the night and feel groggy with tiredness. This is my second cup, and it's not even touching the sides.

"The alternative is the *Polar Star*," Greg continues. "She could get through." Igor has told us the Russian owners of the *Shokalskiy* have been in contact with the U.S. Coast Guard, who run the biggest icebreaker of them all. En route to the Ross Sea from Seattle and about to arrive in Sydney, the *Polar Star* is a god in these waters. Its distinctive red and white hull is known to all in the Antarctic. If anyone can get us out it's the *Polar Star*. But it could be another fortnight.

That's a heck of a long time to keep the team together.

We're showing signs of fracturing already and it's only been five days. And to make it worse, the bridge monitors show us surrounded by bergs that bear an uncanny resemblance to prowling sharks. At the moment, they're keeping at bay. With another two weeks, who knows?

After sitting with the kids last night, I went up on the top deck to clear my head and ran into Terry and Janet. They had some ideas that have got me thinking,

"Chris, it's not that we don't think you're telling us everything, but the uncertainties are playing with people's heads," offered Terry.

"Yes, it's not just what we do know," said Janet, "what would really help is what we don't know."

I hadn't thought of this.

It's not just what we plan on happening but what other factors might yet come into play. A sort-of list of unknown knowns. It's a brilliant idea, though I'm not sure Donald Rumsfeld would approve.

Chris loved the idea and offered to put the key points together for this morning's briefing. From now on, we'll have a series of slides specifically addressing what we know and don't know.

The briefing in the next hour is make or break. Last night unsettled a lot of the team and we need to present a clear plan of action that gives hope. But there's no way in hell I'm going to draw attention to the chance a rogue berg may suddenly appear along the starboard side.

We need to run our ideas past some of the team to get a sense of how they'll be received by the wider group.

We call in Nikki, Erik, and Ben Maddison. Nikki and Erik look exhausted; I'm not sure they're getting much sleep either. Ben seems remarkably chipper, though, apparently unfazed by all around him. Nothing seems to unsettle Ben.

We go through each of the scenarios. To start with, I lay out the weather forecasts and charts across the table. "The last few days have consistently shown the same thing: easterly winds. The barometer on the weather station is nudging a little higher than the pressure charts, suggesting the low may be tracking a bit farther north than forecast, though it's nothing to write home about. It looks like the easterlies are here to stay."

With little chance of a westerly opening up this pack, we're stuck and likely to remain so. We look at alternatives: the *Xue Long* breaking free and releasing the *Shokalskiy*, the *Aurora Australis* or *Polar Star* getting here. If the icebreakers can't reach us, we're left with the prospect of an aerial evacuation, especially if Igor feels there's a real risk to those on board; it's our only other chance of rescue. This could happen any time after the *Aurora Australis* arrives along the sea ice edge about thirty-six hours from now.

Visibility is forecast to be poor tomorrow; after that there could be a window of good weather.

We can still get everyone home.

It's not ideal. Helicopters don't have the safest record in the south. Earlier in the season, the Australians lost a helicopter at their Antarctic base Davis. Thankfully no one died, but the accident received a lot of media attention at home, which means some of the team will probably know.

Not a great thing to take into the briefing.

If an aerial evacuation is called, we're going to need to be ready. Bags have to be packed and a landing area prepared. We'll have to start thinking about a helipad on the ice.

Ben chips in: "The large ice floe the guys are exercising on next to the *Shokalskiy* would work. It must be a hundred feet across."

Great. We'll check it out later this morning.

If we get taken out by the Australians, they might return to Casey and finish off their resupply before heading back to Hobart. If so, we could be looking at a late January return: that's three to four weeks from now. It seems a minor inconvenience compared with other possibilities, but better to warn everyone now in case it does happen.

I turn to Nikki. "Will the team cope with this news?"

She hesitates for a moment before responding. "Yes, I think so. The general feeling is surprisingly good."

That's a relief.

Greg stresses the Russians won't leave regardless. Igor has made it clear his team will remain on the *Shokalskiy*. This is their home, where they will stay, wait, and hope. If the sea ice hasn't released the Russians by the end of the summer in late February, the French could evacuate them through Dumont d'Urville. The Russians may even remain on the *Shokalskiy* over the winter. If so, they'll need a resupply from the two years' worth of food kept on the *Aurora Australis* for this kind of eventuality.

Jesus, with icebergs moving around? Really?

In the meantime, we'll open the phone lines again for calls. It's important the ship's communications aren't disrupted for long, but we need to give access to anyone who wants a few moments on the telephone. Nikki will print off a new schedule for people to sign up.

Finished, we head down to the briefing. I'm willing the *Shokalskiy* to make its escape. Damn this wind; just change direction and take us with you. After all we've been through, it feels wrong to even be talking about leaving the ship and crew behind.

The lecture room is packed.

I give a morning welcome. The mood is markedly somber. Everyone is tense. What a difference a few hours can make.

I briefly describe the latest situation and then pass over to Greg, who presents the slideshow.

It's important to show this is a team effort. After yesterday's blow-up, it's important everyone sees Greg is onboard. The last thing we need is rumors we're divided. And Greg's experience counts for a lot.

Greg talks about the latest sea-ice images and stresses we're in a highly unusual situation.

"The sea ice has plastered onto the fast ice surrounding B09B. The *Shokalskiy* could be stuck here for a very long time indeed."

Greg goes through the scenarios we discussed upstairs. There's a concerned murmur when the end of January is mentioned as a return date, but I'm sure they'll cope. Everyone needs to get their heads around being away from Australia for a whole heap longer.

After Greg's finished, I continue. "Of course, the best-case scenario is that the sea ice breaks out and we make our escape tomorrow. If so, only ten days' sailing and we could be home by 9 January, just a week after we'd planned." It's something to hold on to.

There are a few smiles.

Terry puts up his hand and asks: "And what about the French? I understand they may have left."

There's no beating about the bush. I'm not sure how they're going to respond, but best be out with it.

"Yes, Terry. They've gone."

There's a surprising roar of laughter. The mood in the room instantly lightens.

I breathe a sigh of relief. Igor's scepticism over the *Astrolabe*'s ability to reach us has given the team a confidence boost in our captain. It's not a shock the French vessel has left. It shows to any remaining doubters that Igor knows what he's doing. Another valuable lesson learned: give everyone the uncertainties early on. There's less fallout if things don't work out later.

The briefing ends in a completely different mood to the start. There's idle chatter, even some banter among the crowd. A full schedule of events is planned for the day. Lots to do, lots to keep everyone busy.

I see Peter walking up to the front of the room. He has a smile on his face. He offers his hand to Greg and apologizes for the previous night's disagreement. Greg returns with an embarrassed apology for his outburst. They shake hands.

That's helped clear the air.

We're back together as a team.
What a difference an hour can make.

The wreck of the *Endurance* lying nearby was a ghostly reminder of what might have been. The men were alone on the sea
ice, tired and frightened. Shackleton immediately took control
of the situation. He never wasted energy on things he couldn't
change: "A man must shape himself to a new mark directly the
old one goes to ground." The men needed hope, to be reassured
all was not lost. They were 350 miles southeast of Paulet Island
on the Antarctic Peninsula, where Nordenskjöld and his Swedish
expedition had been trapped by sea ice ten years earlier. After this
near-disaster, Shackleton himself had been hired by the Argentinian government to stock the hut there with supplies. The
sledges, provisions, and dogs were the last things taken ashore
from the *Endurance*. They were now going to be used to try to
reach Paulet.

Shackleton spoke to the men and told them of his plan to
march west. As scientist Reginald James remarked, Shackleton
was adamant:

> *that if we all worked together it could be done . . . At*
> *heart we were probably glad that the time of anxiety as*
> *to whether or not we should save the ship was over, and*
> *that the job was now up to us.*

Shackleton's talk had an instant effect on the team. "It brought
us out of our doldrums," wrote Hussey, "our spirits rose, and we
had supper." Shackleton may have been a picture of calm and
determination on the outside but inside he was seriously worried, confiding in his diary: "I pray God I can manage to get the
whole party to civilisation."

They spent three nights on the ice preparing for their journey.

The loss of the *Endurance* meant the men had little in the way of food to support them. Shackleton immediately introduced strict rationing. Because food was so short, the weaker dogs and ship's cat, Mrs. Chippy, were killed to save on supplies. Weight was going to be key. For the journey, Shackleton told everyone they were to carry a very specific and limited kit: six pairs of socks, one spare pair of boots, one pair of fur gloves, a packet of toilet paper along with a pound of tobacco or cocoa and another pound of personal gear such as soap and toothbrush. Shackleton led by example, publicly throwing away fifty gold sovereigns, his gold watch and the Bible given to him by Queen Alexandra—only tearing out the personal dedication on the front page and a section from the Book of Job. The men followed his move and dumped all their other gear.

Action of any kind was better than none. Two of the lifeboats went with them, dragged on the sledges over the rough and broken ice. A path was hacked though the blocks, ridges and dangerously angled pinnacles of ice. The dogs helped, but relays were necessary to transport the ton of supplies. Progress was painfully slow. With the summer sun, temperatures went over 25°F. The snow became soft and the men regularly sank up to their hips, cursing as everything became wet. Two days later, hot, sweaty and badly dehydrated, they realized it was hopeless. The best they had managed was three-quarters of a mile in one day, far off the four to five they needed to cover. Dragging the boats was taking far too long. The men were exhausted and using precious energy to achieve nothing of worth. Shackleton called it off.

They weren't going anywhere fast. They set up their tents on an old floe and christened it Ocean Camp.

I leave the lecture room an hour later, hearing hoots of laughter upstairs. There seems to be a party going on. It's only eleven in the morning. Shouting, hollering, and cheering are coming from the upper deck. The lounge?

Ben Fisk and Colin are giving a class in knots, aren't they?

I climb the stairs, curious. The corridor is packed with people. I see Annette nearby.

"What's going on, darling?" I ask.

She turns to me and smiles. "Ben and Colin have been teaching everyone how to make a rope stretcher. They're testing it out now."

Over the heads, I can make out Ben and Colin smiling as they carry a nervous patient buried under sheets toward the medic room.

"Whoa there," cries out a muffled voice as the would-be chair-bearers stagger along the narrow corridor, encouraged by shouts of approval.

Moments later they ceremoniously deliver their charge to the door. Standing upright, Ben puffs triumphantly: "And that's how you use a rope stretcher."

There's a chorus of laughter and a round of applause. With slaps on backs, the group returns to the lounge to resume the lesson. It's been like this every day. Lessons, gentle conversations, private words. Almost everyone has had a worried moment at some time or other, but there's always been someone around to talk things through with, if not in the lounge then on the deck or in the privacy of a cabin. No one's been left alone.

It's wonderful to see the spirit on board. Looking around the tables, I see Robert with Sean and Pat across the room. They're busy tying new knots, helping one another when they get stuck. I'm so proud to see my son. He came on the *Shokalskiy* a boy, but he's fast becoming a man. For Sean and Pat, adventure, good humor and fitness have been the order of the day. Robert has spent every waking hour with them, and they've taken him under their wings without batting an eyelid. He's looked up to them in admiration. For a young man of twelve, he couldn't have had better role models.

Cara is in another corner, sitting with Eleanor, Kerry, and Mary. With a hot drink, she's talking happily to the other women as they tie a respectable bowline, something Cara would never have known how to do before. Cara has really come out of her shell, mixing with people outside of her normal teenage circle. Annette and I have always encouraged the kids to talk to adults, but they've both found a new confidence on board. And I'm aware they've helped when some of the other team members have been struggling. You know you have to step up when children are in the room with you.

I look at Annette standing next to me. I don't know what I would have done without her. She's always been the one I've relied on, but this has been far, far more. We're sharing our biggest adventure, and she's kept me together. There have been times I've nearly imploded, when I've wanted to go and hide. But knowing Annette's close, that she's within reach, that there's someone I can always talk to and depend on, has given me the strength to get through this awful week. A smile here, a touch there, has made me feel anything is possible.

I reach out for Annette's hand and look on. We have a long way to go yet, but I know we're going to make it.

While the team is busy, journalists are contacting us at an increasingly frenetic pace, wanting to know how everyone is coping and whether there's any news on our rescue. Alvin is doing his best to manage the requests, but it's now in the hundreds since we were trapped.

"It's intense," warned Alvin. "They've gone crazy for news. I'm struggling to keep up, but we're managing."

Communication is important, but there are so many other things to do on board. To stop it taking over our lives I'm scheduling two-hour windows that best map onto key time zones around the world: mid-morning for Australia and New Zealand; late afternoon for the U.K. and Europe; early evening for the

United States and Canada. For the television networks, Skype is the preferred means of interview; for radio, satellite phone. Every interview I give, I drop in details on the science work we're doing. If we aren't available, family and friends are being called on by journalists desperate to fill their time slots. My brother William has found himself on several news shows in London, while Ziggy's father is now a local celebrity in Buenos Aires. It's as intense as Alvin promised, but we dare not stop, given the confusion when we first became trapped. Overall, the press has been positive, particularly the American networks, sending messages of support. It's really helped on board, reassuring the rest of the team that others are thinking of us.

But there's been a worrying development in some of the reports. Over the last twenty-four hours, I'm being increasingly asked to respond to comments made by climate sceptics, a group of people I have little time for in the best of situations. With more important things to worry about I didn't give it much thought at first; you may as well concern yourself with Flat Earthers or Moon landing conspiracists. Now they're becoming particularly vocal, drawing attention to our situation. At first, I'm at a loss to understand how our predicament informs on the science of climate change.

Fox News is apparently leading the charge, claiming: "They went to study climate change, and they froze solid! This proves there's no global warming." It seems a snap freeze is to blame for our plight; more sea ice around the *Shokalskiy* means the world must be getting colder. Another is claiming we have no weather forecasting capability; that we just came south hoping for the best. As a scientist, I'm all for healthy scepticism but they must be soft in the head. I know these guys are perverse, but they can't claim they don't have information on the expedition. We've been posting about the science every day, and we have described how we're using weather forecasts and satellite imagery to guide our program. The journalists are asking me what I think. I have to remind them we're trapped on a vessel, 1,400 miles from New Zealand, that there's yet another blizzard raging outside, and icebergs are surrounding the vessel. All we're focused on is making sure everyone is all right and gets home safe.

The social media is worse, especially Twitter, which seems to be posting all sorts of personal crap. Chris looked over my shoulder and saw a particularly vicious tweet about my family. "Don't read that, mate. It'll just screw with your head." I nod dumbly and shut it down. It seems incredible that with everything that's happening around us, some people are venting their spleen at us. The comms we've been using to reassure folks at home and report our science could suddenly destabilize things on the ship.

A big part of this expedition was the desire to share the excitement of scientific discovery. The message was, you don't need to be a scientist to think like one. You make an observation, you test your ideas as honestly as you can, and the simplest explanation is most likely the answer. It's not a new concept. In fact, the principle behind it is known as Occam's razor, and it's been around since the fourteenth century. There's no way a snap freeze can trap a ship behind twenty miles of sea ice. *The Day After Tomorrow* movie wasn't real. It takes a month of winter temperatures in the Antarctic to build up a foot of sea ice. We're surrounded by at least ten feet. It's clearly been driven from along the coast into our path—something we've posted online with the satellite images to show what happened. More generally, there's a wealth of material on the web about the changes happening in the Antarctic today, provided by learned institutions in easy-to-understand language. Ignoring all this, idiots are publicly celebrating their ignorance and somehow think they're scoring points by mocking us. It's hard to comprehend.

There's no way I'm showing any of their comments to the

family or the rest of the team. I close up the laptop. We have enough on our plate.

Although the attempt to reach Paulet Island had failed, the men of the *Endurance* were still confident they would get home. Yes, it would take longer than planned but all was not lost. After they had abandoned ship, Worsley, the very captain who had been in tears on the order to abandon ship, wrote, "I don't think we have a genuine pessimist amongst us all. Certainly a good deal of our cheerfulness is due to the order and routine which Sir E. establishes wherever he settles down."

Routine was something the men desperately needed. Structure to the day helped keep doubts at bay. Shackleton reasoned:

> *The task now was to secure the safety of the party, and to*
> *that I must bend my energies and mental power and*
> *apply every bit of knowledge that experience of the*
> *Antarctic had given me. The task was likely to be long*
> *and strenuous, and an ordered mind and a clear program*
> *were essential if we were to come through without loss*
> *of life.*

As a result, camp call was at eight o'clock in the morning, breakfast half an hour later. The schedule for the morning included hunting for seals, exercising the remaining dogs, taking weather observations, and tidying up the camp. Emergency drills were regularly held in case the ice suddenly broke up. Lunch was at one o'clock, and the afternoon was spent as personal time to allow reading, walking, and writing up diaries. A thick seal or penguin soup known as hoosh was served at five-thirty in the afternoon, followed soon after by sleep.

Now they were staying, gear and supplies were salvaged from the remains of the nearby wreck. A wooden observational tower was built on the edge of camp, and a clothesline put up. The food taken off the *Endurance* would only last so long. So, to supplement their meagre rations, hundreds of penguins were killed: "the skins reserved for fuel, the legs for hooch, the breasts for steaks, and the livers and hearts for delicacies," as Hurley macabrely described their diet after the ordeal. Hurley even managed to improvise a stove from salvaged oil drums that used seal blubber and penguin skins for fuel.

The men were divided between the five tents, each individual chosen by Shackleton to complement the others. Against every natural instinct, he shared a tent with those who might cause trouble or were struggling with their situation. With his big ego and combative style, Hurley joined the tent along with anxious scientist Reginald James and an argumentative navigator, Hubert Hudson. In the tent, Shackleton confided in Hurley and soon the Australian was waxing lyrical about the expedition leader in his diary; any immediate threat to the Anglo-Irishman's leadership had been averted. Meanwhile, the men were encouraged to talk, to keep their minds off their predicament. After a year together, there were still new topics to explore that would help pass the time. The progress of the war was a popular point of discussion, but conversations also went to weird and wonderful places. Hurley described the talks they had on

> the arts and crafts of Ancient Egypt, comparisons of the social life of London, New York and Paris, etc. Then we had debates on such varied subjects as the birth rate, the liquor question, the mysteries of lighthouse optics, ship construction . . . disputations were referred to the arbitration of the Encyclopaedia Britannica.

In a later interview, James remarked upon Shackleton's lack of formality in the tent:

We had great discussion about all manner of things. One
of his great arguments was in favour of "practical" sci-
entific research as against pure. He had, or said he had,
little use for pure science and thought our efforts should
be directed to practical lines. I used to take the other
view and we would argue at length but never get
anywhere.

To avoid any accusations of favoritism and ill-feeling, Shackleton very publicly shared everything. He couldn't risk any dissent or bad feeling; if anyone was given special treatment, the rest would soon learn of it. There were few secrets among the men. All decisions were made in full public view to stop whispering and future dissent. Lots were drawn for the extra-warm sleeping-bags. Everyone took a one-hour watch every other night. Shackleton used a tried-and-tested method for meals: "Whose-ing." A member of the team would ask another to turn their back and give a name for each serving of seal or penguin steak. No one could claim they were badly treated. Any difference in size of portion was just down to luck.

The photographs taken by Hurley remained on the wreck, left on board when they evacuated. With the march to Paulet Island temporarily halted, he returned to retrieve what he could. Most of the vessel was now submerged, barely on the surface. Stripping to his waist, Hurley hacked through the walls and recovered his photographic glass plate negatives soldered in boxes under "four feet of mushy ice." They were far too heavy to take on any future march, so a few days later he sat down with Shackleton and chose the best 120 images, destroying the remaining 400 to stop the temptation of going back. He kept a small Kodak camera and two rolls of film for the rest of the journey.

Entertainment remained an important focus for the men.

Hussey later recalled Shackleton retrieved his banjo from the wardroom in the near-destroyed *Endurance*, leaving the gramophone and its perceived bad luck behind. Hussey was concerned about its weight and asked Shackleton whether they should take it. "Yes, certainly," Shackleton replied. "It's vital mental medicine, and we shall need it." After this, Hussey went from tent to tent most nights, where the men sang, smoked, and laughed. When it was warm enough, the gloves could be taken off and cards played; bridge and poker became hugely popular for a time, and generous winnings were promised on return to civilization.

It seemed to work. Shackleton reassured himself, regularly noting the words "everyone cheerful" in his diary entries, but the men do appear to have been genuinely happy. The expedition doctor Macklin expressed a common view: "I feel just as happy here as I did when I was in hospital with all the comforts . . . If we come through alive and safe it will be a great experience to look on." And yet observations by Worsley showed their camp was drifting north, but only very slowly. They were in a precarious situation. "It is beyond conception, even to us," wrote Hurley, "that we are dwelling on a colossal ice raft, with but five feet of ice separating us from 2000 fathoms of ocean and drifting along under the caprices of wind and tides, to heaven knows where."

The sun has come out this afternoon, and there's not a breath of wind. The temperature is above freezing. It's actually warm.

It's too good an opportunity to pass and we reopen the large ice floe alongside the ship. Most of the team have taken the opportunity to stretch their legs on something that's not a metal floor, turning their name tags and going out on the ice with life vests. Half a dozen of the team are acting as lookouts for any problems. It's a perfect day for a walk.

With the improvement in the conditions, some dark-gray clouds have appeared to the southeast. It's the first water sky we've seen since Christmas Day. Igor immediately calls up Captain Wang on the *Xue Long* and asks whether the Chinese helicopter would explore the area to see how distant the sea-ice edge is. It's possible it might be breaking up.

"No problem," comes the reply.

Might we still get out of here? I don't dare to hope.

Leaving the bridge, I go out onto the floe, where around thirty of the team are milling about. Down on the ice, I'm immediately struck by just how large the surrounding pressure ridges actually are. They seem big from the ship, but down here they really are enormous, with many of the blocks towering above. I feel a pang of pity for Shackleton and his men trying to drag sledges and boats through this stuff. How on earth did they cut a path through miles and miles of sea ice? I'm just grateful we haven't had to make an attempt to reach the continent. It looks completely impassable. I shiver at what we were forced to consider just a few days ago.

And we're only seeing the 10 to 20 percent on the surface.

No wonder the poor *Xue Long* hasn't made any further progress.

At the bottom of the gangway stairs, I step around a large block of ice toward the floe when I suddenly hear Robert. "Hi, Dad."

I turn to see the little man dressed in full outdoor gear. He's hard at work with Sean and Kerry, digging out and carving the ice to make a slide. He's hot and sweaty but having a great time. Climbing a few steps he's cut, he says: "Check this out!"

He promptly slides down to my feet, laughing.

"That's awesome, mate. You've done that quickly."

"Oh, we've been put to work," Kerry says meaningfully.

They have grand plans to make a theme park, and I leave them discussing the next stage of the works. Nearby I can see Annette and Cara taking photos of a curious Adélie penguin that's come over to find out what all the fuss is about. No matter where we are, Adélies always seem to pop up.

I suddenly hear an unusual noise in the distance and make out a large red helicopter approaching. There are cries of excitement as people point out the aircraft. The helicopter circles the floe and ship, the sound of the blades cutting the air with a deep throbbing. It's a double rotor Kamov Ka-32. Normally a threatening-looking machine, today it's one of the most beautiful things I've ever seen. It's our first tangible contact with other human beings since Macquarie Island. It hovers only a couple of hundred feet above us. Everyone stops and waves excitedly. It seems so close.

Surely, we're going to get out of here soon?

Our would-be saviors don't stay long, however. A bank of fog rolls in from the southeast, and the captain calls the helicopter back to the *Xue Long*. The search to the southeast will have to wait.

Maybe tomorrow.

Silence returns. We're on our own again.

I inspect the surface. The warmer conditions are turning the snow to slush. It's getting so soft around the *Shokalskiy* that the ship has tilted 4 degrees back the other way; Igor is going to have to readjust the ballast to level the ship up. I'm sinking up to my knees in places. I find Chris and we decide to send everyone back on board. It would be safer. The call is made on the VHF and slowly people head back to the ship.

We linger behind to speak. I enjoy the brief moment of freedom to talk about anything but our predicament as we grab the last of the gear left on the floe. After a few minutes, we have everything and stumble through the slush back toward the *Shokalskiy*.

I suddenly hear a howl of laughter from the ship. I can't make out whose it is, but stepping forward I see Ziggy on the rear deck, his head thrown back in laughter, pointing toward Robert's ice slide. The only clue to what's going on is Ben Fisk looking aghast on the other side.

There's a high-pitched shriek of mock indignation.

"What's going on?" I ask Chris, who appears equally perplexed.

Suddenly I make out a white bikini-clad figure struggling to
cover herself in front of a camera tripod.

It's Kerry-Lee taking a selfie on the ice.

Why not?

It's been a roller-coaster of a day. We've gone from narrowly
averting a major breakdown in team morale to a bikini shoot.
Bloody Antarctica. Nothing is ever straightforward.

I'm up on the top deck finishing off the last of the interviews
Alvin has arranged for today. I need some sleep but hear steps
behind me. Turning, I see Igor walking over, wearing a remarkably dark pair of glasses.

"Chris, I want to speak to Russia TV."

The Russian press has been some of the most fiercely interested in the expedition. After all, we are on a Russian ship with
Russian crew. So far, however, the team on board have been reticent about doing interviews. Vlad has asked me to send a message to his wife, but no one has wanted to do anything public. It
struck me as odd, given some of the media over there started reporting our predicament with a loss of life. The panicked calls
from Russian families was a major factor in our decision to report what's happening. Igor now wants to speak to Russians to
reassure anyone left in doubt.

Two Russian television networks have been particularly keen
to speak to Igor. I call them up on Skype and they jump at the
chance. It's getting late, and the sun is dipping in the sky. Igor
seems completely oblivious to the falling temperature and speaks
calmly in Russian, almost matter-of-factly, taking each interview
in turn, evidently describing all that's happened. It's a remarkably calm performance.

I can't help but be impressed. Here's a man at whom Nature

has lobbed a massive grenade. He's under immense personal pressure, but carries on with courage and fortitude, completely composed.

Finished, Igor passes me the microphone. "Done, Chris. Good."

Satisfied, he nods at me, turns and heads back to his bridge, his ship.

CHAPTER TWELVE
Keeping It Together

Through a fog of sleep, I can hear the heavy strike of snow on the cabin porthole. A snowstorm must be blowing outside. I know it's time to get up and find out what's happening, but after only a few hours' rest, I'm struggling to open my eyes.

It's 30 December. We've been trapped for a week.

Annette stirs as I'm dressing.

"I don't want you to stay on the *Shokalskiy*," she says abruptly.

Last night, Annette was deep in conversation with Tracey. I hadn't thought much of it at the time.

Tracey has spent many seasons in the Antarctic. She's been on the *Aurora Australis* trapped in sea ice. She's seen it all before, and she's worried. I don't blame her one bit. I've tried to allay Tracey's fears during and after briefings, but you can't brush off years of experience; you have to respect people's concerns. It's a fine line, especially when you don't want fear spreading through the wider group.

"I know you want to stay, but Tracey says those icebergs could start moving any time. If something happens, no one will be able to help you."

Annette's almost in tears. I go to hug her, but she backs away.

I've lost sight of how distressed my wife is. I don't quite know what to say.

Over the last couple of days, I've started thinking about remaining with the ship and continuing the science if the others are helicoptered out. Chris and a few other team members are keen. We might be stuck for weeks or even months, but if the *Shokalskiy* dodges the bergs and is released from the ice, we could finish the work we set out to do. Annette is terrified at the prospect and reminds me of my obligation to the volunteers.

"They came here because of you. You can't send them off alone. You have to make sure everyone gets home safe. And that includes you. If an iceberg comes through after we leave . . ."

She leaves the sentence unfinished, hanging in the air.

My mind is in turmoil. On one hand, I'm desperate to continue the science program and return home in the ship I've brought south. On the other, I'll be putting the team in someone else's care, on a ship I don't know, and taking a terrible risk staying.

Annette is absolutely right. I'm letting my desire to carry out science muddy my first priority. Everyone needs to get home safely, together. *Just as Shackleton would have done*. Nothing else matters.

"You're right, love. I'll leave with everyone." I feel a complete tit for even considering it.

"Thank you, darling," she says quietly.

We hug. I'm so glad Annette's here, always supportive but challenging me when it's necessary. Remaining behind would have been a terrible call.

I go up to the bridge in a somber mood. Nikolai is alone.

"Morning, Nikolai. How are things?"

He shrugs and shakes a downward-facing palm. "Not so bad, not so good."

Looking outside I can see what he means.

The weather has lurched to another extreme. The wind has picked up, and the fog has returned. A steady thirty knots is blowing snow around the ship in visibility no more than a couple of hundred yards.

Flicking through the logbook, I see the entry at two o'clock in the morning: the *Aurora Australis* was just forty miles away.

They're making steady progress at six knots and heading east. Only twenty-four miles to go.

Getting closer.

Up on top, the wind, snow, and now rain are making the top deck treacherous. It's absolutely miserable. *We're in the Antarctic, and it's actually bloody raining.* Mawson was at Cape Denison for two years and never saw a drop of rain. It wasn't something we expected. I am really starting to loathe the A-factor.

I check the weathervane. The wind has edged round to the northeast, bringing with it warmer air and this thick fog.

The higher temperatures and change in winds don't seem to be having any tangible effect on the sea ice. It may be over 30°F but we're still locked solid.

Chris joins me up on the top deck.

"Morning, mate," I call as he comes over.

"Morning," he replies. "Lovely day."

I'm trying to shield the computer from the elements while I download the latest forecast and sea-ice images. I need a clear line of sight for the satellites, but the electronic gear is at risk from all the water blowing around. Chris quietly stands over my shoulder, sheltering me from the worst of it as I finish off.

The top deck is one of the few places we can speak freely. The *Shokalskiy*'s engine stack offers some shelter from the wind. I look at my friend more closely. Heavy eyes stare back. It's not just me. We're both exhausted. Chris has been extraordinary, working behind the scenes with Greg, keeping everything together. It's come at a price. This expedition is ageing us both terribly.

We speak about Annette's concerns, and Chris nods his head sympathetically. "I think she's right. I'm not so sure about staying either."

I'm relieved. It's good to know Chris is thinking the same. The different scenarios for getting out of here are paralyzing. I'm still clutching to the vain hope the *Shokalskiy* will be able to break out on its own, but even if today's temperatures persist, I can't see us getting out of here anytime soon. We'll almost certainly have to be evacuated, and if so, we all need to go. We can't risk anything happening to someone on the team. The science has to come second.

Chris seems to read my mind. "I can't see them flying us out in this visibility though."

It's true. The weather really has crapped out, and the forecast suggests it's set to remain so. The *Xue Long* is somewhere out there, but it's completely disappeared. We're back on our own.

The one thing I can just make out are the bergs lurking at the edge of the fog, threatening. They're an ominous reminder that everything could change in a moment.

I'm acutely aware our entrapment is playing out in people's homes. It's the ultimate modern contradiction. In Shackleton's day, the public only saw the amazing photographs and film of their plight once they returned home. Now we're telling our story live. Although we're in the wildest, most inhospitable place on Earth, we're sending images and giving interviews around the world. We can be seen and heard . . . but we can't be reached. It could all end in a matter of hours and no one outside can do a damn thing about it. A-factor or not, I have to blot this one out of my mind, at least for now.

Yesterday Chris spent the day trying to sort the scientific gear with the volunteers. It was a rushed job just in case the call to evacuate was sprung on us. Now Chris wants some of the team to help him pack the gear properly.

"Good idea. And let's keep everyone else busy with sampling. How about we cut up one of the cores we took in Commonwealth Bay? It'll keep the science program moving forward and help take people's minds off the conditions."

Chris nods. It's time for the briefing.

Shackleton once commented to teammate Leonard Hussey that his venture was "to keep the spirit of adventure alive." We might be on a very public adventure, but I'm not feeling particularly brave about it. I need some rest to get my head straight, but that's not going to happen any time soon.

How did the men on the Endurance do this for months on end?

Repeat the mantra. *Remember Shackleton: keep it positive, keep everyone busy.*

Just under a month after the men abandoned ship, the ice finally took the *Endurance*. Late afternoon on 21 November, Shackleton spotted the ship make a sudden movement and called out: "She's going, boys." The men rushed across the camp to get a view and saw the *Endurance* going down "bows first, her stern raised in the air." It was their last tangible link to home. They were entirely on their own. No more salvaging wood from the ship, no more extra gear. The men shared nervous looks of apprehension. Privately Shackleton was distraught, noting in his diary: "She went today . . . I cannot write about it . . . Sunday always seems the day on which things happen to us." And to make matters even worse, the nearby icebergs had changed direction and moved closer, threatening the expedition's fragile refuge. But to the men, he spoke clearly and confidently: "Ship and stores have gone—so now we'll go home." An increase in rations that evening "soon neutralised any tendency to down-heartedness."

Shackleton continued working his men hard. They had to believe they would make it home. To some, the loss of the *Endurance* was a relief. Hurley claimed: "We are not sorry to see the last of the wreck . . . being an object of depression to all who turned their eyes in that direction, it was becoming more dangerous daily to those visiting it." Others were feeling their first real doubt and Shackleton had to be on the lookout for any negative comments. Orde-Lees was told off when Shackleton overhead him saying it was "bunk to say we shall be in England by Christmas this year." Confiding to his dairy, Worsley commented that "Sir E. optimistically discusses an expedition to the Lands N. of Canada. We . . . wax enthusiastic about our next trip before we can definitely settle how the devil we are going to get out of this one." There was a whiff of dissatisfaction in the air.

Three weeks later, the ice floe they called home continued to drift in a northwest direction. But it was erratic. At times, the ice would suddenly veer east before dramatically returning to its original trajectory. There was a very real risk they could start moving away from the Antarctic Peninsula, their only real hope of getting home. Meanwhile, boredom and despondency were threatening. Shackleton had to keep the crew positive and focused on the future. He made up his mind and spoke confidentially to a few of the men that he wanted to march west to reduce the distance to Paulet Island. In no time at all, word swept through the camp. Even though their last attempt to drag the lifeboats and supplies had failed, morale soared. Here was a chance to do something, anything, instead of sitting around hopelessly. Christmas Day was brought forward to 22 December so they could leave soon after. Sledges were packed and repacked to take as many supplies as possible. Not everything could come with them, so the men had the last good meal they would enjoy for eight months: "Anchovies in oil, baked beans, and jugged hare made a glorious mixture such as we have not dreamed of since our school-days," Shackleton described happily.

Harnessed up to the sledges and boats at night to take advantage of the colder temperatures and harder surfaces, the men set out at three o'clock on the morning of 23 December. Even though the sun was lower in the sky, they soon started breaking through the surface: "at each step we went in over our knees in the soft wet snow. Sometimes a man would step into a hole in the ice which was hidden by the covering of snow, and be pulled up with a jerk in his harness." It was backbreaking work to break a path through the icescape. On the positive side, progress was better than before. Sometimes they made more than two miles a day. But for each mile reached, they had to cover three miles in relays.

During each march, Shackleton would go ahead with Wild to find the best way through the ice and direct the men forward. On the fifth day, Shackleton returned from scouting to find the men were standing around. McNeish had suddenly stopped working, refusing "to obey Worsley's order, using at the same time abusive language." There was a standoff. Shackleton was furious. This was a direct threat to everything they had worked so hard to achieve. If the men gave up now, all would be lost. They needed to keep together as a team. Shackleton immediately took McNeish aside and angrily told him to get back to work, even hinting he would shoot the man if he did not fall back into line. McNeish morosely returned to his place, and the men resumed their trudging. At the end of the day, Shackleton called everyone together and read them the ship's articles: The *Endurance* may have gone, but they were still under orders and as such they would be paid until they made it home.

Shackleton knew it was pointless to continue, but more important, the men now knew it too. They had pushed as far as they could. They were only ten miles from Ocean Camp and could go no farther. There was no point anyone complaining about the lack of action. The next day was New Year's Eve 1915, and with the foggy weather Shackleton stayed put. He was shattered: "Everywhere surface of ice breaking up . . . all cheerful . . . I am rather tired. I suppose it is this brain." The tents were put up at what became known as Patience Camp and there they remained. With supplies running low and seals in short supply, the remaining dogs were shot. There was precious little else to do now but hope the ice continued to drift north so they had a chance of sailing to land.

Shackleton was impatient to be off. "Waiting, waiting, waiting," he wrote in his diary. They had to get out of there, but there was nothing more they could do.

Negative people are a curse. Having people around you who only see problems is debilitating. At home, I avoid them like the plague.

My grandfather once told me as a young man: "Keep away from the miserable buggers." It's a philosophy I've taken to heart. You can't let the negative voices get inside your head. The emotional cost is exhausting. In a group, just one pessimist can destroy a team. If the team start to listen to them, if they dwell on what might go wrong, morale can collapse; if a team loses purpose and stops communicating with one another, what is a bad situation becomes a whole heap worse. On the *Shokalskiy*, there's enough to do without thinking the worst or worrying about what others might be saying. Negativity is positively dangerous.

It's the morning briefing, thirty-four days since the expedition began. Day seven stuck. I give the situation report, including the latest weather forecasts and the position of the other vessels. I just want to curl up and sleep.

Must concentrate.

Smiling faces look back at me. Kerry is sitting in the front row beaming. Even Tracey seems happier. Word has spread that the *Aurora Australis* is close. We could be out of here soon.

I go through the uncertainties. The location of the *Polar Star* is top of the list. We've also just heard Russia might send its own massive icebreaker, the *Fedorov*, which is at the Mirny base on the other side of the Shackleton Ice Shelf; the downside is if it does come, it won't get to us before the end of January. The Americans and Russians could even arrive at the same time. *That's a scenario that wasn't considered even remotely possible until today*. I finish off with the schedule for the day and remind those doing their video diaries to make sure they meet up with Taylor. The response to the video diaries has been overwhelmingly positive, and we've had messages from family members saying how comforting they are. It's something we're going to continue.

I look around the room. We've done well choosing the team.

All the scientists were hand-picked. Everyone has stepped up and done what they've had to do. If we'd been on a government-funded trip, I wouldn't have had nearly as much freedom.

One part of the team I had little choice over was the Mawson's Huts Foundation. Chris and I were keen to have it represented on the expedition. No one had been to the historic buildings for two years, making the conservation work an important part of our program. Ian has been supportive, but over the last few days I've become increasingly concerned about Jon. He hasn't sought me out. Instead, his views have become more vocal in the briefings, his line of questioning more confrontational. What was an irritation at first is now unsettling some of the other team members. The last thing the more vulnerable on the team need to hear right now is what can go wrong, especially from someone with his experience of ice.

"This could be the worst-ever environmental disaster in the Antarctic," he boldly declares at the end of the briefing.

The threat of a massive oil spill if the Shokalskiy *sinks is a scenario I just can't think about at the moment*. And judging by the shocked faces on the rest of the team, neither can they. All our hard work yesterday keeping everyone together is threatening to unravel.

I wanted to do something different on this expedition. To take our own ship south and discover what's happening in the East

Antarctic. And now this. We're trapped in a highly dangerous situation. Evacuation is a very real possibility, and the Russians are openly discussing whether they might also have to leave. If so, the *Shokalskiy* will be left to face the elements alone. Jon might well be correct. It would only be a matter of time before a berg struck, causing untold environmental damage. The worst spill that's ever happened in the Antarctic was the Argentinian supply ship, the *Bahia Paraíso,* which was caught by sea ice near the American research base Palmer Station in 1989 and sank. One hundred and thirty thousand gallons of diesel smothered the west Antarctic Peninsula coastline, devastating the local wildlife. The demise of the *Shokalskiy* could cause much worse. Could I end up being responsible for the worst environmental disaster in the Antarctic? It just couldn't happen. *Could it?*

Hushed tones fill the room as people discuss the implications of Jon's statement.

The immediate priority is the team. We can't start thinking about yet another worst-case scenario. We have to hope it will all come right or the group will implode. I have to address this head on or these kinds of statements will become the norm, unsettling the team and making things far, far worse.

"Jon, there's absolutely no reason to believe this is the case. The *Shokalskiy* is away from the coast and all the bergs have stopped moving," I reply.

Greg steps up. "The *Bahia Paraíso* was lost on the Peninsula back in '89, but that's a completely different situation. There's no immediate risk of sinking. The *Shokalskiy* is okay."

Greg sits down quickly to end the conversation. Jon mutters something under his breath but decides against pursuing it.

I don't want to dwell on it any longer. I move to close down the briefing, and invite Ben Maddison to outline the day's events. Ben stands up and enthusiastically encourages any budding writers on board to attend the writing class he's starting this morning, seemingly oblivious to the very public disagreement that just happened.

"Alok, I presume you're attending?" he asks, turning to the *Guardian* journalist.

There's a ripple of laughter.

The team shuffle out, some of the damage repaired.

I'm furious. What on earth does Jon think he's doing? With all his experience, he should know better. A week of pent-up frustration is about to erupt, and I'm ready to put Jon right.

I watch Annette pass by the door, making reassuring noises to those around her. I desperately need someone to tell me everything's going to be all right, but I can't be so selfish.

Greg stays behind with Chris.

"What is wrong with that guy?" Greg asks.

"Let him go. Hopefully that'll be it now," Chris says.

Chris is right. Nothing is going to be gained by losing it and risking an escalation. We need to take the heat out of the situation, not make it worse. After all, everyone is feeling the pressure, even Jon.

I stagger up to my room and pass out on the bed.

I wake to a knock on the door and look at my watch.

Fifteen minutes. *No wonder I feel so bloody awful.*

"Chris, Chris?" Nikki calls. "The *Aurora* is at the sea ice edge."

I have to get up and find out what's happening.

Up on the bridge the news is mixed.

Since the operation began we've been in regular direct contact with all the ships involved in the rescue. Now the Australians have arrived, Captain Murray Doyle on the *Aurora Australis* has assumed charge of the operation. Unfortunately, the *Aurora*'s first attempt to reach us seems doomed to failure. Heavy ice and bad visibility are making conditions dangerous.

With decades of experience sailing these waters and already having been trapped once this season, the Australian ship is beating a hasty retreat. There's a very real chance they could get caught again.

That would be bloody awful. The *Xue Long* is still on station but remains suspiciously still on the ship's display. It would be a real mess if the Australians ended up stuck as well. The sea ice report from the Antarctic Division isn't particularly promising either. The imagery was taken just before the visibility deteriorated. The sea-ice edge remains twenty miles out.

Greg says Igor now feels there's a 70 percent chance they will want to evacuate us.

The odds have just shifted from evens to it being more likely than not we'll be flown out. The sea-ice images show we're surrounded by multi-year ice that may well be on the way to becoming fast ice and a more permanent feature of the Antarctic coastline. It doesn't look like the *Shokalskiy* is getting out of here anytime soon. The Australians are anticipating they won't be able to reach us and have asked for the ship's manifest, including our preferred cabin allocations. If they fly us out, each individual will be allowed sixty-six pounds of personal gear, with a further 1,700 pounds for the expedition's samples and gear. In the meantime, the *Aurora Australis* is going to keep trying to find a way through the sea ice.

I'm amazed at the prospect of us having cabins. I was expecting to sleep on the floor, maybe even in the corridors, anywhere there might be space. Surely the ship is filled with scientists and logistics staff?

"Apparently not," says Greg. "Odd, isn't it?"

I'm not going to complain. If they have space, brilliant. I just want everyone home safe. In the meantime, keeping everyone busy is the order of the day. With word spreading of a possible evacuation, there's a new energy on board. Just as Shackleton found, with a little bit of hope you can move mountains. The main deck lab is now a hotbed of activity. If we are going to be evacuated, we need to take the samples we worked so hard to get. Eleanor leads the charge, slicing and bagging one of the ocean cores from Commonwealth Bay. Other groups are working on filtering the last of the plankton net trawls, chipping rocks and sorting other samples. Annette is helping gather it all together and compiling the list for departure. Everything is being packed down, ready to go, all under the careful eye of Chris.

There might still be another way. Chris has raised an enticing idea. The thick ice to the north and east is holding up the *Aurora Australis*. But what about to the southeast? After all, that's where we last saw water sky. If the sea-ice edge is closer over there, the *Aurora* might be able to get in amid the fast ice and free the *Shokalskiy* from behind. Ironically, it means sailing past the Hodgemans where it all began. Greg heads off to the bridge to call the *Aurora* and see what they think.

I leave the lab the most hopeful I've felt over the last forty-eight hours. We have a plan that might just work. But Igor is pessimistic. We look at the charts and synoptic charts. The wind is stubbornly forecast to remain from the east. Igor doesn't think there's much prospect of the sea ice weakening enough in any direction for the *Shokalskiy* to be freed soon.

Okay. If not, we still have the *Polar Star*. The American ice-breaker is starting to look like a serious option. The Australians don't have a helicopter with them, only the deck helipad. They need the Chinese, and that means taking what is already a complex logistical operation and making it several times more difficult. Two ships, two languages. It's something that's rarely attempted even in warmer climes, let alone the Antarctic. The alternative is the U.S. Coast Guard vessel, a beautiful ship four times the size of the *Aurora Australis* that can effortlessly steam through six feet of sea ice at a steady three knots. It's even been known to bash its way through more than twenty-one-feet-thick ice when it's had to. The *Polar Star* should be able to reach us without any problems.

And if *that* doesn't happen, there's also the *Fedorov*.

We do have options.

As long as those bloody icebergs stay put.

Greg comes up to the bridge and hands me a sheet of paper. "Chris, check this out."

It's an email from the Chinese.

"They are stuck after all. It's exactly what we feared."

There it is. The Chinese look like they're trapped. They kindly offered to remain on station but are now in trouble themselves. Two ships now need help. Two ships surrounded by icebergs. The situation has gone from bad and jumped straight to bloody terrible. If only the wind would change direction.

The men from the *Endurance* spent six months at Patience Camp, six very long months waiting. As they drifted north, the conditions became warmer. Rain, fog, and wet snow became the norm. It was a miserable period. Most of the men suffered from cabin fever, cooped up in their tents for large stretches of time. During most of March, Worsley became depressed and withdrew from everyone, including Shackleton. Arguments would break out, often about something Orde-Lees had said or done. Many had bad dreams, with Hurley describing how he tried to "drown multicoloured hounds . . . My endeavours were not fraught with great success, for the Dachshunds, after assuming the form of seals, eyed me complacently with gummy eyes." They needed a change in the wind to break up the ice and allow them to sail for land on the salvaged lifeboats. If not, there was a danger the ice could swing south and they would be trapped for another winter. The wind became a major point of conversation. James wrote at this time:

*We also suffer from "Anemomania." This disease may be
exhibited in two forms, either one is morbidly anxious
about the wind direction and gibbers continually about
it, or else a sort of lunacy is produced by listening to
other Anemomaniacs.*

With their northward drift, cracks started to form around the
camp, revealing small leads of water that promised future escape. In case the call came to break camp urgently, the men
would often sleep in their day clothes, only taking off their
socks to dry. In early March, they saw the ice rise and fall. It was
the first time the men had felt the sea in over a year. They must
be close to open water.

Shackleton used this time to plan for every contingency, to
prepare for the worst. The expedition was split in two watches,
so half the men were always on lookout. They needed to be alert
for anything. One day, Worsley described how two icebergs
suddenly set a path toward the camp, ploughing through the
pack. Shackleton ordered the men to be ready to move, but destruction seemed inevitable:

*For miles behind them there was a wake of chaos, floe
piled on floe and crashing in all directions . . . Suddenly,
some freak or eddy of the current—or was it some
greater Power?—swept the bergs off on to a new line.*

The danger passed . . . at least for the moment. This was just
one of the myriad risks the expedition faced every day.

At eleven o'clock in the morning, 9 April 1916, a crack dramatically appeared through the middle of the camp. The men
suddenly found the sea ice below their tents was breaking up to
reveal a large lead of water. Here was their chance, an opportunity to get away before winter choked the area with ice once

again. Shackleton wrote: "Our home was being shattered under our feet and we had a sense of loss and incompleteness hard to describe." But it was time to go. It was just sixty miles to the nearest land, Elephant Island, at the very tip of the Antarctic Peninsula. Mixing experience and temperament, Shackleton assigned the men to one of three boats that would take them to safety.

At sea, the men fought new hazards. They had to contend with storms and ice floes that threatened to crush them at a moment's notice alongside the very real risk of being eaten: killer whales followed the boats, blowing "blood-curdling blasts." The men were fearful that a slight nudge would toss them into the sea. Sleeping on and off nearby floes, the men of the *Endurance* slowly worked their way into open water. After six terrible days, they reached Elephant Island. The twenty-eight men were frostbitten, hungry and completely and utterly spent. They had been in the ice for an extraordinary 497 days. Some staggered around the shingle beach, struggling to find their balance. Others lay on the beach and joyfully dropped stones on themselves.

It may have been one of the most desolate spots on the planet, but they had reached solid ground.

I sit bolt upright, wide awake.

Annette is sleeping next to me. I take a deep breath, but nothing seems to have changed. The ship is silent. We're not tilting. We're okay.

I don't normally sleep well in the Antarctic. It's something to do with the twenty-four-hour light, but this time around it's been so much worse. Different scenarios are constantly flickering through my mind, most of them not good. I'm hardly getting any sleep, and it's running me ragged.

It's five in the morning, New Year's Eve. Eight days trapped.

No point in lying around.

I rub my face wearily and gingerly get out of bed, careful not to disturb Annette.

I drag on my clothes and climb the steps to the bridge as I've done every day on this expedition. In the bridge, I check the logbook. Not a lot to report. The *Aurora Australis* hasn't made any progress toward us and the monitor shows the *Xue Long* remains obstinately immobile. I zip up my jacket, throw on my hat, and step outside.

It's colder this morning, and the deck has turned treacherously icy. I walk with exaggerated care. The last thing I need now is to break my bloody leg.

The satellite connection works straight away. I load the video diaries from Erik and Janet up onto YouTube and check the viewing figures on the others; Terry's entry from yesterday already has a couple of thousand views. It looks like Alok's idea has really worked, and it's noticeably helping morale on board.

I download the weather forecast. Conditions may be improving sooner rather than later. Sunny, clear skies are predicted for 2 January. If so, a helicopter flight might be possible. It looks like the winds could change as well.

Could the winds really change? That would be fantastic. With just a couple of hours of westerly winds the *Shokalskiy*, *Xue Long,* and *Aurora Australis* might get out of here. It would all be just a bad dream.

I keep hold of this beautiful idea for a precious moment.

After breakfast, we talk logistics in my cabin. Chris is looking better, rested after a good night's sleep. Ben Maddison, well, Ben looks like he always does: completely relaxed and comfortable with everything that's happening. Even Greg and Nikki are smiling.

Unfortunately, in carrying out Chris's suggestion to approach from the southeast, the *Aurora Australis* met with thick ice and has had to retreat. The weather may be crap at the moment, but the forecast has suddenly brought the helicopter evacuation forward. If so, we need to organize. We'll need a landing area, preferably near the ship—the closer the better. We might be getting more familiar with our surroundings, but it remains dangerous outside and after all the recent warm weather we've had, who knows how solid it is underfoot.

"We checked out the exercise floe just off the starboard side and it's a perfect place to land," said Ben. "We can put the helipad there."

"What can we use for marking out the area?" I ask. Putting a chopper down on a white surface is notoriously dangerous. With no real contrast, it would be all too easy to come in too close and plough straight into the snow and ice. Trying to estimate distance in these conditions is not something you want to do without help.

"Milo," Nikki replied with a broad smile. "We have tins of the stuff and hardly anyone's touched it."

A genius idea. When I saw all the malt chocolate powdered drink being loaded in Bluff, I was mystified about what we were going to do with it. Now it's found a purpose.

Milo it is.

"We'll need to prepare the helipad," Ben said. "How about after lunch?"

There are nods of agreement. We'll use the whole team. It will be good to get everyone off the ship and take some exercise. We're going to have to flatten a very large area. There'll be lots of linking arms and stomping back and forth. Knowing Ben, there'll be singing. It should be a lot of fun. Shackleton would have approved, I'm sure.

"Great," says Nikki. "I'll go and let everyone know."

A moment later, her cheerful voice comes out over the ship's tannoy, announcing our plan for the helipad. Everyone is to be at the gangway at two o'clock, fully kitted up.

"But before lunch," she continues, "today's movie showing in the lecture room is the ABBA sensation *Mamma Mia!*"

I hear a roar of approval downstairs.

We really do need to get out of here.

CHAPTER THIRTEEN
Escape from the Ice

"Ten, nine, eight . . ."

We're on countdown.

"Five, four, three, two, one . . ."

It's 2014. A new year. The *Shokalskiy*'s horn blasts three times in celebration, its sound carried away by the Antarctic wind. No one has reached us; no one can hear us.

Cheek by jowl in the lounge, everyone is here. We've had moments of doubt, of uncertainty, but tonight is about celebrating hope and a new start. Whatever lies outside, whatever is still to come, we've made it this far together. Our isolation and fears momentarily put aside, it's time for heartfelt hugs and cheers. There's nowhere else I'd rather be.

This afternoon was typical of what this remarkable team are capable of. Under heavy cloud, fifty men and women, young and old, linked arms and, under Ben Maddison's watchful eye, happily paraded outside. Singing "Auld Lang Syne," they stomped snow as if their lives depended on it, Annette in the middle, with Kerry and Cara, Robert with Sean. When someone fell over, they were helped to their feet, accompanied by laughter and cheering. And when the bedraggled line reached the edge of the area, Ben would get it back in some sort of order, turn them around and off they would go again. In an hour, the helipad was done, as flat and compact as you could hope for. Returning to the ship, all that remained to be done was watch from the decks, clutching steaming mugs of tea and coffee as Graeme and Ziggy marked out the landing area with our vast supply of Milo, and in a final flourish, an enormous "H." If the helicopter does come, we'll be ready.

I've no idea what the next days will bring, but nothing is going to get the better of us. The men on the *Endurance* knew all about the value of celebrations. New Year's Eve couldn't have come at a better time. After eight days being trapped, it's become a target, something to hold on to, keeping everyone's mind off the uncertainty.

As the music cranks up, I look at my wonderful family. We've been through one of the most grueling experiences imaginable. It would have broken many people, but my kids have taken it in their stride without missing a beat. I don't know where they get it from; it's certainly not from me. Annette has been a tower of strength to us all while Cara has a new-found confidence and Robert has become a man, all in just over three weeks. I'm very proud and very grateful.

Tomorrow is another day, but I know we'll always have one another.

Elephant Island wasn't the safe haven it first appeared to the men of the *Endurance*. Ship wreckage lay strewn along the back of the rocky beach, testament to a high-water tide, something that could happen at any moment with a strong north-easterly wind. They had to move, but Shackleton let the men get some much-needed sleep before wearily rowing along the sheer-cliffed coast to find a more protected area. Seven miles away they discovered a spit of land that sat far above the high-water mark. As Shackleton remarked, their new home "was by no

means an ideal camping-ground; it was rough, bleak and inhospitable—just an acre or two of rock and shingle, with the sea
foaming around it except where the snow-slope, running up to a
glacier, formed the landward boundary." Covered in guano, the
place stank, but at least it meant there was a plentiful supply of
local wildlife to supplement the expedition's meagre rations.
Two of the boats were immediately upturned to make a shelter.
They were safe . . . for now.

The twenty-eight men had made it to land, but they faced a
distressing fact: There was almost no chance of rescue if they all
stayed. It was mid-April. They were over a hundred miles from
the nearest whaling area, and the end of the hunting season was
fast approaching. Even with the local wildlife, they didn't have
enough food to survive indefinitely, and with the approach of
winter, sea ice was threatening to surround the island. They had
to get help, and fast. It was then that Shackleton made one of the
most courageous decisions of his life. A small group would have
to sail to South Georgia, the very island where the expedition
had set out from. The journey would be an epic in its own right.
Eight hundred miles across the stormiest seas on the planet. The
men were exhausted, the boats completely unsuitable, and if
their navigation was off by only the slightest degree, they would
miss the island and disappear into the South Atlantic, never to
be seen again.

For the trip, Shackleton chose the *James Caird*. Twenty-three
feet long and six feet across, she was the largest of the three
boats and capable of taking six men with thirty days of supplies.
The men would need to be able to sail, navigate, cook and make
repairs on the go, all in a space no larger than a small hatchback.
Shackleton needed experienced hands, but he was also acutely
aware that some couldn't be trusted to behave in his absence;
left to their own devices they could easily poison the minds of
those left behind, threatening the team's morale and ultimately
survival. To this end, Worsley, Crean, sailor Timothy McCarthy,

and malcontents McNeish and John Vincent were chosen to go
with him. Wild was given leadership on Elephant Island, with
strict instructions that if they were not back by spring, he should
take one of the other boats and attempt to reach Deception Island some 180 miles into the prevailing winds, where supplies
and help might be available.

Although McNeish had pessimistic tendencies, he was a fine
carpenter, and Shackleton immediately set him to work improving the *James Caird* as best he could. Cannibalising wood from
the other boats, McNeish went about raising the gunwales of the
small boat and covering the top with tent cloth to keep out the
worst of the elements. For caulking the planks, the Scottish carpenter used anything he could lay his hands on: flour, seal's
blood, paint, scarf wool. Anything. The result was a boat as
watertight as it could be, with space inside for three men to
sleep. They were ready to go. The men were rowed out to the
waiting boat, but in the heavy surf on the beach, McNeish and
Vincent were tossed out. Coming ashore, swearing and sodden,
Vincent refused point-blank to change his clothes. The men later
discovered he was hoarding some of the gold sovereigns so publicly discarded by Shackleton months before. It was a good job
he was leaving.

In a moderate westerly wind, the *James Caird* left on 24
April with the six men aboard, cheered on from Elephant Island.
She was "soon lost to sight on the great heaving ocean," wrote
Orde-Lees, "as she dipped into the trough of each wave, she
soon disappeared, sail and all." Shackleton immediately set
about establishing a schedule: three men on, three men off, rotating every four hours. Of the men on duty, one had to look
after the sails, another the tiller and a third bailed "for all he was
worth." The men fought waves and storms, in full knowledge
that if they failed they would also, in all likelihood, be condemn-
ing the men on Elephant Island to death. The ice that formed on
the boat became so thick during the voyage that it threatened to

capsize the craft, forcing the men "in turns to crawl out with an axe and chop off the ice . . . after four or five minutes—'fed up' or frostbitten—[they] slid back." The weather was so bad, Worsley only managed to get a sighting of the sun four times.

In the early hours of 6 May, Shackleton called the men's attention to a clearing in the sky. His excitement quickly changed to horror when he realized the "brightening" sky was in fact the crest of an enormous wave. "During twenty-six years' experience of the ocean in all its moods I had not encountered a wave so gigantic," wrote Shackleton later. "It was a mighty upheaval of the ocean, a thing quite apart from the big white-capped seas that had been our tireless enemies for many days. I shouted, 'For God's sake, hold on! It's got us!' . . . We felt our boat lifted and flung forward like a cork in breaking surf." The crew bailed for their lives, and the small craft somehow stayed afloat.

Dog-tired, the men sailed on, hoping against hope that Worsley's dead reckoning was right. Were they on the correct course? Or had they already sailed past South Georgia? Fifteen days after they'd left Elephant Island, seaweed and seabirds appeared. Hope was renewed. They were close, and they knew it. On the afternoon of 8 May, McCarthy suddenly cried, "Land oh!" The men looked, and "there, right ahead, through a rift in the flying scud, our glad but salt-blurred eyes saw a towering black crag, with a lacework of snow around its flanks. One glimpse and it was hidden again." With teamwork that no doubt surprised McNeish and Vincent, they had made the greatest ever journey in a small boat, just as Shackleton said they would.

Up on deck it's warm, 34°F and rising.

It's a perfect day.

Almost too perfect.

I undo my jacket and look off the starboard side. Never still, the icescape around the *Shokalskiy* is changing again. Under a beautifully intense blue sky, everywhere seems to be melting.

What had been rough, sharp-edged blocks of chaotically thrown ice are now being softened, moulded into weird and wonderful shapes. Floes are splitting, and water is starting to pond on the surface. And with the break-up of the pack comes the sobering risk that the nearby icebergs may resume their travels. I nervously look toward the flotilla off the rear of the ship. If they have shifted, it's nothing substantial.

Igor is on the bridge. He's not confident we'll be able to get out on our own just yet. His immediate focus is on the helipad. If it melts much more, the helicopter won't be able to land and we'll remain trapped.

The change in conditions seems to be having different effects across the area. Looking at the monitor, the *Xue Long* is drifting with the ice away to the northwest. It's not by much—only 0.2 knots—but over the last few hours the ship's movement is enough to show up as a track on the screen. By contrast, the *Shokalskiy* remains firmly locked in place; the ice is so closely packed in against the coastline, we're not going anywhere. Meanwhile, the *Aurora Australis* is resolutely probing to find a way through. The Australian ship is about twelve miles away but reporting thick, old floes of ice. There's still no way through.

Captain Wang calls the bridge, wishing us a happy New Year and enquiring after the helipad. We tell him about our preparations but relate our concern over the temperature outside.

"Thank you. No problem. Too windy for flying today. Maybe tomorrow."

Greg replies in thanks.

"We try to move out to open water today."

Poor man, he's been saying that for a while.

"Is difficult. We trapped in ice."

"*Xue Long*. This is the *Aurora Australis* speaking." Captain Murray joins the conversation. "We will attempt to reach you today."

Over the radio, the Australian outlines his plan: with no flights possible, the *Aurora Australis* will try a different tack and break out the *Xue Long* before resuming their efforts on us.

We'll just have to see what happens.

Down in the lounge, Nikki is printing off messages that have been sent to team members through the ship's email. It's helping a lot. We may be far from home, but supportive messages from loved ones are proving priceless for those on board. We know we're not alone.

I'm idly chatting to Nikki when Alok puts his head around the door, a note of urgency in his voice. "Chris, they're nearly ready for us in Times Square."

I'd completely forgotten about doing our interview for New Year. Poor Alvin has been swamped with requests. He's had over a thousand requests and, apart from a few loonies, most have been hugely supportive and sympathetic. It's helped reassure everyone on board that the rest of the world really does care. The team at CNN have been one of the best and are keen to do a live feed to New York.

I grab my jacket for the top deck. "How's it going up there?" I ask as we leap up the stairs.

"All good. They're ten minutes out. Seventy million viewers, apparently."

What? Seventy million tuning in? It's a number that's hard to grasp.

With all the rain and wind we'd been having, Chris has tied up a large red tunnel Hilleberg tent to the railings. It's our new media hub, offering shelter from the fickle elements. Inside, cameras, microphones, laptops, and piles of paper cover the floor. Laurence is already inside checking the settings, while medic and photographer Andrew is standing by in case of technology failure during the broadcast. A laptop and a tripod-mounted camera are set up at the front of the tent. I manage to find a space at the back, Alok and Laurence beside me, the tent furiously flapping in the wind.

On the screen, the neon lights of Times Square are being beamed into our tent. In the foreground, *360°* anchorman Anderson Cooper and actress and comedian Kathy Griffin are dressed heavily for the New York winter. They look colder than we are.

A distant voice calls out over the computer: "We can see you. You will be live in five, four, three, two . . ."

After a moment's pause, the speakers crackle to life.

"Hello there, hi, Times Square," I call out.

Anderson replies: "Hi, that's great. We can hear you loud and clear." There's just a slight delay, but his friendly New York accent is unmistakable.

I can't believe I'm doing this.

"How did you guys ring in the New Year? We saw that video of you all singing."

"We had a special song written by the team," I reply. I feel hopeful after all we've gone through together. "We came up on the top deck and broadcast it live. It's now four o'clock in the afternoon and looking good."

Alok continued: "It's like all the great poets of the time telling stories of what's happened to us. This is our *Odyssey,* and we're telling it as we go along."

I can hear singing in Times Square. We're a world away, and we can actually hear singing in New York. This is bloody amazing technology.

"Now you guys are waiting for a helicopter, but I've never met people who are jollier and happier," Anderson says meaningfully.

Kathy quips mischievously, "You're like *Sex in the City* having mimosa!"

It wasn't really the inspiration we were going for, but good to know.

"We're working hard to keep everyone going," I answer, not quite sure how best to respond. "Everyone has been fantastic.

There's a great team spirit, and we're just looking forward to getting home."

It's bizarre to be talking to two celebrities I've watched at home, but I'm enjoying the experience. It makes a welcome change from everything else we've been juggling.

"We're doing the same here," says Kathy. "We're just waiting on the helicopter to rescue us. Me in particular."

Everyone laughs.

There's just one thing I want to do. "Anderson, we see you're cold. We've got you this coat." I pull out one of our blue expedition jackets.

Laurence takes it forward toward the camera and says: "We're going to send it to you via penguin."

Anderson looks genuinely surprised. "Thanks. We can use it here."

Kathy gives a look of mock concern. "You're losing your minds. You need psychological help." She twirls her forefinger at her temple.

You might be right there.

Touchingly, Anderson wraps up the interview on a personal note. "I think you guys are really inspiring in the face of all that, and we wish you the best. We hope you get to your families soon. Chris, thank you so much. All the best."

The world really is watching.

The *James Caird* rolled up onto the pebbly beach. The men on board had spent the last two days sailing along the west coast, desperately trying to avoid being thrown against the rocky shore. Finally, Worsley spotted a small cove through a break in the cliffs that looked like it might be the refuge they so desperately needed. Some of the men would not survive another day on the small boat; they had to go for it. Bringing in the oars, they rode the swell over the shallow reef and jumped ashore. Their tongues swollen with thirst, the men were seriously dehydrated. They leaped on a nearby stream and drank their fill. It "put new life into us," wrote Shackleton. "It was a splendid moment."

They had made it to land, but salvation lay on the east coast where the Norwegian whaling stations were based; Stromness was only thirty miles away. It sounded so close, but how to get there was another question. They had survived the Southern Ocean, but it would be foolish in their weakened state to head back out to sea; the currents and weather could easily sweep them far from land and away into the South Atlantic. The only other option was to climb over the mountains, across the "precipitous slopes, forbidding peaks and large glaciers" that formed the backbone of the island, a path no one had ever taken before. True to form, Shackleton made the call. The men on Elephant Island were depending on them.

Only three of the men were fit enough to make the journey: Shackleton, Worsley, and Crean. Staying behind, McNeish, as the most senior man, was left in charge with Vincent and McCarthy. The night before their attempt, Shackleton barely slept. "My mind was busy with the task of the following day . . . No man had ever penetrated a mile from the coast of South Georgia at any point, and the whalers I knew regarded the country as inaccessible." Traveling light with no tent or sleeping bags, the three men planned to cross the mountains as quickly as possible. Trudging their way up through the mountains, climbing steep, icy slopes, they looked for a pass that would take them over to the east coast. Three times they met a dead end, three times they were forced back to try again. On the fourth attempt, they discovered a pass at the very end of the day. They were dangerously late. The sun was setting. With no shelter, there was a strong possibility they would freeze to death on the mountain peak.

The three men had to keep moving. Their only option was a steep slope of snow and ice that disappeared into the darkness. Shackleton declared: "It's a devil of a risk, but we've got to take it. We'll slide." Coiling their rope to form a sledge, they sat one behind the other and pushed off. Worsley wrote afterward how they launched into the unknown with trepidation but: "Then quite suddenly I felt a glow, and knew that I was grinning! I was actually enjoying it . . . I yelled with excitement, and found that Shackleton and Crean were yelling too." The men dropped 900 feet in just a couple of minutes, jubilant to have survived.

The trio pushed on. They were now on the very edge of existence. The physical exertion was almost too much. Freezing winds had blasted them for most of their journey. They were hungry and thirsty. At times, they were close to delusional, imagining another traveling by their side. They urgently needed rest. At one point, Shackleton let the two men sleep while he kept watch. Fearing they might not wake up, he stirred his companions after five minutes and told them they'd been asleep for a refreshing half-hour. They stumbled on, slipping through the darkness. They were close to collapse and couldn't continue for much longer. Not a moment too soon, Stromness Bay suddenly broke through the gloom. With the sun rising, the early-morning steam-whistle calling the whalers to work cut through the air. "Never had any of us heard sweeter music," wrote Shackleton. "It was the first sound created by outside human agency that had come to our ears since we left [Grytviken] in December 1914." They were close, really, really close.

Thirty-six hours after leaving the west coast and having had virtually no rest, they staggered into Stromness whaling station. They were a terrible sight, a "trio of scarecrows," with rags for clothes, salt-matted hair and beards, and faces blackened by months of blubber smoke. The first people they saw were two children playing in the street who ran on sight, terrified by the vision before them. A man pushing a wheelbarrow stared blankly at Shackleton when he asked for help and passed by with just a grunt. Finally someone agreed to take them to the station manager's office. They were kept waiting outside until the manager appeared at the door. He looked skeptically at the three bedraggled men standing at his entrance. Shackleton described the encounter:

> *"Well?"*
> *"Don't you know me?" I said.*
> *"I know your voice," he replied doubtfully. "You're the mate of the* Daisy.*"*
> *"My name is Shackleton," I said.*
> *Immediately he put out his hand and said, "Come in, come in."*
> *"Tell me, when was the war over?" I asked.*
> *"The war is not over," he answered. "Millions are being killed. Europe is mad. The world is mad."*

Even with all the fighting dominating the world headlines, the disappearance of the *Endurance* was well known. No one had heard a word from them for over eighteen months. Some believed Shackleton and his men had crossed the Antarctic, others that they were trapped in the sea ice; a widely held view was they had died. Calls for rescue attempts had been made, but nothing had happened. Shackleton's sudden appearance at the manager's doorstep was astonishing—a miracle in a bloody time. The news went round the station like wildfire: against staggering odds, Shackleton had returned to South Georgia.

It's five-thirty in the afternoon, and the *Aurora Australis* is struggling to reach the *Xue Long*. The Australians have been reporting young ice around them, but the Chinese are in the same thick multi-year ice as we are. They can't get out and are hoping the Australians can do a double rescue. The dangers are made all the more apparent by listening to the discussions between the captains in the bridge.

The Chinese are really concerned. "This ice very dangerous for us."

Is the Xue Long *saying they're at risk from icebergs as well?*

The Australians respond: "The ice is relaxing around us, but we're making slow progress."

My stomach is in knots. *Please don't let the* Aurora Australis *get trapped.*

"It's heavy going."

The Australians want out. They're not confident they can reach either of us. The sea ice is too thick for them to proceed. The safest way is to fly us out with Chinese support. But that doesn't help the *Xue Long,* and the Russians are steadfastly refusing to go anywhere.

"We stay," Igor insists.

That's his call. No one is going to question it. He's the captain, and the crew are his team. But we have to do what's right for us.

It now looks like a helicopter evacuation is going to happen. Maybe tomorrow. The weather is looking better for then; sunshine and light wind are forecast.

That evening, I introduce the briefing and then hand over to Greg, who has prepared a slide show on the helicopter evacuation. I almost collapse into a nearby chair as Greg starts talking. Weariness is threatening to overtake me. I'm exhausted by all we've been through and all that might have been. I desperately wanted to get us all home under our own steam. We should be sailing into Bluff, not beset in the Antarctic. I feel the terrible weight of responsibility.

The strain is showing on all the faces in the room. With New Years behind us, they need another focus. We can't stay much longer. It's been a terrifying ordeal, and many are on the edge of cracking.

Greg continues. "Don't forget your grab bags. These are meant to contain essential items. If the chopper comes down, the bags have to hold extra clothing, drink, food and any medicine for you to survive on the ice."

The shocked looks say it all: *too much information.*

* * *

It's Thursday, 2 January 2014. Ben Maddison is keen to host the inaugural Writers Festival at Cape Denison. Over the last ten days, his writing class has gained quite a following on board the *Shokalskiy*. What started out as a small group has now blossomed into a full-blown academy with essayists, poets, and novelists scribbling away at all hours. Many of the team members have waxed lyrical to me about rediscovering a love of writing they haven't known since they were children. This is something you often find in Antarctica, especially when you get trapped in ice: There's actually time to reflect and reassess what you love, what you want to do with your life when you get back home.

There's the possibility we may be evacuated by helicopter today . . . but maybe not. After ten days, I'm resigned to the uncertainty. Neither the Chinese nor Australians are saying one way or the other. There's only a hint of wind, ideal for flying, but bearing in mind the A-factor, I've given up assuming anything. If the Writers Festival will help keep everyone's minds off the uncertainty, I'm all for it.

"Great idea, Ben," I say eagerly. "We can put it in one of the large domed tents on the ice."

Within an hour, Chris has the ten-foot-high bright orange structure up on the helipad. Minutes later, a column of authors make their way off the ship for a morning of prose, chatting excitedly, notepads and paper clutched to their chests. It seems more like an academic procession than an Antarctic expedition. If we are evacuated by air, Chris assures me we can get the tent down in half the time. We'll be more than ready for a sortie if the call is made.

Back on the *Shokalskiy*, the corridors are strangely empty.

Medic Andrew catches me in the corridor on the upper deck. He's had an idea.

"Chris, I think we should leave the expedition photos up on the noticeboard with the blogs." He points to the images and text pinned to the wall outside the medical room. "If we leave and the ship is stuck for years, they'll tell our story to those who come after."

I'm suddenly thrown into the future. I imagine the *Shokalskiy* frozen among the bergs, silent as the grave, the corridors filled with hoarfrost. A small expedition chances upon the vessel, unmarked on any map, a refuge from the blizzard that's blowing. Stumbling up the gangway, they prise open the door and step inside, gasping for breath, shutting the storm outside. The strangers turn on their torches, beams of light falling on the corridor walls, their voices echoing in the empty space. Treading warily, they see the noticeboard. Images of the subantarctic islands, the Southern Ocean, albatrosses and seals, Erik and Chris's oceanographic work, Robert's minke whale, Mawson's Huts, Stay the Dog, the Hodgeman Islands, Christmas.

Precious moments made by an extraordinary team.

I snap out of the future. The here and now is all that matters.

"Great idea. If we're going to leave, let's keep it all up there." Andrew smiles and pins up the photos from the last couple of days.

I climb to the bridge to find out the latest developments. The Australians are asking about the dimensions of the Chinese helicopter. Can it land on the *Aurora Australis*? There's a breakdown in communication. Details are getting lost in translation.

This could be fatal.

"Greg, let's get Colin and Kerry-Lee up here. They're both Mandarin-speakers and can help out. That'll stop any confusion and make sure everyone knows what's going on."

Five minutes later, Colin and Kerry-Lee have agreed to leave the Writers Festival and join us on the bridge, answering questions and relaying key points between the Chinese and Australian captains.

Thank goodness we have Colin and Kerry-Lee. Antarctica is challenging enough without language issues.

The Chinese are insistent they can't land on the *Aurora Australis*: the Australian helideck is too small for the flying conditions. The Australians insist it isn't.

The Chinese almost cough with embarrassment and make an alternative suggestion. If they can't deliver us to the *Aurora*, we would be most welcome on the *Xue Long*.

What an incredibly generous offer. It is tempting. The Chinese vessel is closer to the sea ice edge and farther away from those bloody bergs. But we may be jumping out of the frying pan into the fire. We would be risking a helicopter flight—something that isn't ever taken lightly in Antarctica—and remain stuck in the sea ice.

After all that's happened, I'm seriously contemplating whether we should hold tight on the *Shokalskiy*. The bergs aren't moving, and if the *Xue Long* gets out there's a good chance we'd also be released.

But the Australians are really pushing for an aerial evacuation. They've concluded we're both stuck. If they persevere, they'll only get trapped as well. A helicopter evacuation is the only option.

The Chinese push back: *no, we really can't land on the Aurora Australis.* Given the helicopter rotors span nearly fifty feet, the Australian ship deck is just too small.

Maybe we are going to have to stay here after all.

Finally, the Australians relent.

An alternative plan quickly unfolds: we could be delivered to an ice floe next to the Australian vessel. We have our helipad. The Chinese are now searching for something suitable around the *Aurora Australis*. Their helicopter hasn't sighted anything yet.

Igor is getting increasingly restless at the delays.

"Chris, Greg, this snow is getting soft. Look,"—he points off the starboard side—"there's running water. And cracks." His arm sweeps across the waiting helipad. "The floe may not last.

We have to get passengers off now or cancel. It will be too soft later."

Things aren't looking good. The Chinese want a floe 100 feet across; so far they've found nothing even half that size near the *Aurora Australis*. The weather is good for flying at the moment, but the forecast shows it crapping out soon.

Greg goes to speak to Captain Murray on the phone. The *Aurora Australis* doesn't think it can help the *Xue Long*. The Australian feels we should evacuate now; with the impending bad weather we might not get another chance for several days. All bets would be off then. Even if we just get to the *Xue Long*, that's better than nothing, he argues. There are fewer icebergs around the Chinese vessel.

Murray's concerns alarm me. I look off the ship's starboard side at the threat. The fleet of bergs have stalked us for ten days, seemingly ready to pounce at any time. During most of this time, the team have treated them as part of the scenery. Could they still strike?

Oh, hell. What do we do?

As soon as Shackleton, Worsley, and Crean walked into the Stromness whaling station, the manager arranged for a ship to collect the three men waiting on the west coast. With their safe return, Shackleton was hell-bent on getting back to Elephant Island. Winter was approaching fast and he was worried about Wild's men. They had little shelter, limited food and few medical supplies. Three days after their arrival, Shackleton tried to get through with one of the whaling ships from South Georgia, but the sea ice proved too thick. Moving on to the Falkland Islands, Shackleton ran into a wall of British bureaucracy that offered little direct help. Frustrated, he appealed to different South American governments and relocated to the southern Chile city of Punta Arenas where he organized the rescue efforts. Attempt followed attempt with failure. They would try one more time.

On 25 August 1916, Shackleton set out with Worsley and Crean on a small Chilean steel-hulled steamer called the *Yelcho*. Five days later, his heart in his mouth, Shackleton saw Elephant Island—the way was clear of ice thanks to a southerly gale that had blown through.

Shackleton was just in time. Wild had done an impressive job leading the men, but they were now in dire straits. As the weeks had rolled into months, despair had begun to settle in. The men were responding in different ways. Wild wrote later in his memoirs: "At least half the party were insane, fortunately not violent, simply helpless and hopeless." Some anxiously watched the horizon for a ship, others hunted for penguins and seals, which had all but disappeared, still others just lay in their reindeer sleeping bags day after day. The men were down to their last few days' rations, and there was whispered talk of cannibalism, with a supposed plot to kill Orde-Lees that was only averted by their rescue. The team that Shackleton had left behind was on the verge of falling apart.

Hurley described 30 August as a "day of wonders." The Australian was the first to see the *Yelcho* and rushed back to the up-turned boats where the men were sheltering, crying out, "Wild, there's a ship. Shall we light a fire?" The men scrambled outside, tumbling over one another, tipping their seal hoosh on the floor as they rushed outside. A boat approached the shore and on board Shackleton called out: "Are you all well?" Wild, sobbing with joy, called back: "We are all well, Boss."

"This is the fourth attempt I've made to reach you blighters," laughed Shackleton in reply.

Shackleton kept his visit short; he didn't even go to visit the camp. He was impatient to be off. The last thing they needed was to be trapped by the sea ice again. The men grabbed their personal gear and within an hour everyone was on board the *Yelcho*. The Chilean ship cranked up its engines and headed north as fast as it could carry them. The men had escaped by the narrowest of margins. Although the Antarctic had thrown everything at them, they had pulled through a horrifying ordeal, together.

Shackleton was desperate to tell his wife Emily his news. As soon as they reached Punta Arenas, he dashed off a letter: "I have done it . . . Not a life lost and we have been through Hell. Soon I will be home and then I will rest."

Shackleton's men were going home.

"We found ice."

The ship's comms suddenly bursts into life. An excited Chinese voice clarifies the message: the Ka-32 helicopter has found a floe "to the right" of the *Aurora Australis* that looks big enough to land on.

They're hovering over it now. Can the Australians send someone to check how thick it is?

The evacuation looks like it might be back on.

"Greg, can we speak for a moment?"

I pull Greg aside.

"At the moment, everyone is safe on board. Flying them out is a risk. Do we have to go?"

I'm acutely aware of everything that's been risked to get us out, but I need to think about the team first. Is flying out really the safest option? After all we've been through, should we remain and hope for a change in the winds?

We talk it through. "We can stay, Chris, yes. But if one of these bergs starts moving again"—Greg pauses for a moment, searching for the words—"If people die, it'll be a bad call."

We don't have a choice. The weather is good, and we have a chance to get out. Shackleton would have taken this chance. We have to go. The Writers Festival is over, and the tent long since packed away, leaving the helipad ready for operations.

Ten minutes later, the Australians report over the radio that the floe is thick enough for the chopper to land.

The Chinese are happy.

It's six o'clock. The call is made to go.

Greg calmly announces over the tannoy system that we'll be evacuating the ship.

I feel terribly conflicted. Disappointed I'm leaving our ship, the vessel that's taken us so far, but relieved to know a decision has been made.

For good or bad, we're committed and the team springs into action. A human chain is quickly formed along the deck and gangway, bags and boxes thrown down the line to the waiting sledges on the ice below. There's a keen sense of urgency in the air. Everyone is here: scientists, expeditioners, volunteers, media, Russian crew. We're one team now.

Vlad is smiling. "It's good to be off ship," he says, dragging yet another sledge of kit out to the gathering pile at the helipad.

Stay the Dog is one of the first down. Perched on the top of Robert's ice slide, she watches unmoved over the proceedings. Stay's seen it all before.

The Chinese helicopter flies over, the heavy throb of its double rotor blades cutting the air. I stop talking and cover my ears.

The Ka-32 cautiously drops onto the ice, almost drunkenly wobbling into position over the Milo "H." Half a dozen Chinese crew jump out, throwing planks of wood onto the surface for a makeshift landing platform, along with buckets of frozen food for the *Shokalskiy*'s indefinite stay. The rotors slow down but keep spinning. If the ice is too thin and the chopper starts to break through, the pilot will need to floor the engine and pull away immediately; in a situation like that there is no time to fire up the engines from a cold start. Fortunately, the ice seems to be taking the weight.

That's a good sign. Hopefully it won't get much warmer and weaken the ice further.

With the Chinese crew off, the throb of the double rotors increases, the helicopter shifts its weight and, with a slight tilt of the nose, lifts off, heading away as quickly as it came, leaving the team on the ground to frantically make the final preparations to the landing area.

We have twenty minutes before they return and the first sortie flies out, twelve people per sortie. Twelve people safe. Little Nikki is heading out on the all-important first helicopter. As ship manager, Nikki has masterfully looked out for everyone on the *Shokalskiy*. Now we have to get the team settled on the *Aurora Australis* as soon as possible, and Nikki has agreed to continue in this vital role. Annette and the kids are on the second sortie.

Inside, the corridors are heaving with people. With single-minded pursuit, everyone is rushing in different directions, making final preparations before they fly out. Among the throng, Annette finds me and we duck into a quiet corner.

"I've just learnt Elizabeth is really scared about the flight. Can you get someone to be with her?"

Just like Annette to worry about others when she has something scary to do herself.

"Thanks, love. I didn't know that. Yes, I'll make sure."

Through the crowd I spot Ben Fisk, who is on the first flight with Nikki. I quickly explain the situation, and he kindly agrees to sit with Elizabeth. She's not the surest on her feet and after what Annette said, I know she'll need someone with her.

We head upstairs to get Cara and Robert kitted out in our cabin. Both have their full Antarctic gear on with life jacket and grab bags. I can't believe I'm letting them go. I want to remain with them, but Annette is insistent.

"No, love. You have to stay. We'll be all right. You have to make sure everybody is okay. We'll see you over there."

Cara silently gives me a hug. Robert is just excited.

"I'll be flying in my first helicopter. And it's in Antarctica!"

He's over the moon. I can't say I blame him, but now's not the time for excitement. This is dangerous. I kneel down in front of him and do up the zip on his jacket.

"Robs, I'm going to come out to the helipad, but you'll be on your own with your mum and sister on the helicopter. I need you to look after them. Can you do that for me?"

He nods seriously, understanding, and I give him a hug and rub his head.

In the distance, I hear a distinctive thud in the air. I glance up and through the cabin porthole see the helicopter approaching. *This is it. We really are getting out of here.* Hovering only briefly above, the bright red aircraft lightly touches down on the helipad, stark against the rafted blocks of ice that have held us firm. Below the furiously spinning rotor blades, the Chinese ground crew shepherd the first group on board along with Stay the Dog. Within moments the door is slammed shut and they're gone. The first group are away. The evacuation has begun.

Right, let's get going.

We go down to the lounge, where the second team is gathering for take-off. The space is filled with brightly colored clothing. But for all the people, the room is silent, the mood somber. Joanne is sitting pensively off to one side, visibly worried. Annette sits next to her and chats quietly.

Outside, the signal is made. The bridge has been called. The Chinese are on their way back.

We start to move out of the ship.

It's time for the family to leave. I don't want them to go, but the sooner they're away, the sooner they'll be safe.

We join the waiting group outside. Ben Maddison is there, talking about home, dinner tonight, the weather, anything to keep everyone's minds off the flight. Mary and Kerry turn and smile as we approach, barely recognisable in their full Antarctic clothing and snow goggles.

At that moment, the chopper flies over. I duck instinctively, feeling the powerful downdraught. Any closer and I'd be thrown to the ground. Near the landing, I can make out Chris and Eleanor lying across the pile of bags and gear, stopping them from being blown away.

Touchdown.

Chris makes the all-clear signal; the group are good to go.

I give Annette one last embrace and the kids a quick cuddle. They walk off to the helicopter bravely, Robert waving to me as he briefly looks back. I'm worried sick, but now is not the time to show it. Within seconds, the helicopter is back in the air and gone.

I return to the *Shokalskiy* along what's now a well-worn icy path. Back on board, the ship is starting to feel abandoned. Half the team have left; the few remaining are helping to shift the last of the gear out onto the ice. I go up to my room to make sure I have everything. With the family gone, our home for the last four weeks has suddenly become just another empty space. I feel an overwhelming sense of loneliness.

My thoughts are broken by the sound of the returning helicopter. Looking out the porthole, I see the Chinese land and the third group of twelve moving out.

I breathe a sigh of relief. That means my family made it okay. *Thank God for that.*

Now we just have to get everyone else out of here.

I leave my room and go downstairs. It's time.

I'm on the penultimate flight. Chris, Eleanor, and Greg are bringing out the science gear and samples at the very end.

I make one last visit to the bridge. Igor is at the port side window, watching the evacuation. Nikolai and Vlad are patiently standing by. We're leaving the Russians on their own to face whatever might happen, and it doesn't seem right, but Igor is certain about them staying.

There's not a lot left to say. We shake hands. "Good-bye," I say to Igor, "and good luck. I'll see you in Bluff soon." *I hope.* There are nervous smiles all round.

I join the others in the lounge, and we make our way outside.

Little is said; most are lost in thought, reflecting on the impending helicopter flight. Each trip is taking about twenty minutes. The Chinese are running the evacuation like clockwork.

As the chopper lands, I lead the way to the open side door, head down to avoid the worst of the downdraught. Inside, the cabin is filled with seats and a strong smell of aviation fuel. I head up to the pilot.

"Hello," he shouts over the sound of the engine and rotors. He has a beaming smile.

All in a day's work.

"Thank you, thank you." I shake his hand. I must look a wreck, but I don't care. We've nearly out of here.

With everyone on board, the side door slams shut and the pilot pulls back on the throttle. The helicopter's engines roar. The rotor blades respond, slowly at first, then biting the air with increasing frequency, a deep throb filling the cabin. We take off. Pivoting on my seat, I manage to find a small porthole and press my face against the cold Plexiglas as the view unfolds. The *Shokalskiy* appears so small, set among icebergs that are far too close for comfort. She appears almost defiant, as if challenging the Antarctic to do its worst. It almost did. The scale of what lies below is breathtaking. The entire icescape is a battleground of white; floes of all sizes jostle for position in a mind-bending jigsaw. Even at several hundred feet, I can't see the end of it—the jumble of rafted ice stretches all the way to the horizon. No wonder the *Shokalskiy* failed to escape; she never stood a chance of getting out.

I can't help but think of Igor and the crew.

Poor bastards. I wish we were all getting out of this together.

I look back down and find I've lost sight of the vessel among the chaotic scene. It's as if the *Shokalskiy* had never been.

We fly on. Few words are spoken, the enormity of all that's happened striking home now it's nearly over. How it could have been so much worse.

Moments later we pass over the red-hulled *Xue Long*. The Chinese vessel is surrounded by ice, immobile but majestic, the nearest bergs aft of the ship. On the deck, I see waving figures. The Chinese have been amazing. So many have worked so hard to help us, but without the Chinese we wouldn't be getting out at all. And now they look like they're stuck. I can only hope they get out soon . . . and safely.

The pilot pushes on. The shattered icy surface passing underneath, seemingly without end. Slowly, the bright red *Aurora Australis* appears on the horizon, a deep trench carved out of the pack behind her. The sea ice here looks like it's several feet thick.

Heaven knows how the Australians have managed to get in so far.

The pitch of the engine changes as the helicopter turns and gently comes in to land beside the icebreaker.

We touch down. The rotors slow and the side door is flung wide open. Light pours into the cabin. The rotors whip the surface snow into a frenzy. Through the wild drift, a smiling, bearded face emerges at the entrance.

"Welcome home!" he proclaims.

We've been in a cocoon for four weeks, with no new faces. Suddenly there's a familiar accent and a warm smile. It catches me off guard.

I stagger off the helicopter. People come forward to help us toward the waiting ship. Five storeys high and four times the size of the *Shokalskiy*, the *Aurora Australis* towers above us. I look at my watch. Amazingly, the call to leave our vessel was only made two hours ago. Things have moved bloody quickly. No wonder I feel so disoriented.

I almost run across the snow and ice toward the ship, leading the charge to get on board. I need to see the family, to know for sure they're okay.

A sea of faces look down from the decks above. They may be

strangers, but they're smiling, waving. I'm starting to feel emotional—the worries and stress of the last ten days have taken their toll.

I'm gently guided onto a lifeboat waiting by the side of the Australian vessel. Minutes later, the side arm of the *Aurora Australis* has lifted us up onto the main deck, and we're guided into a warm canteen filled with people. The team are hugging all around me. Cheers and slaps on the back fill the room. I feel numb, uncomprehending of what's happening around me. There are only three people I want to be with right now. I search the crowd desperately, seeking the ones I love.

Suddenly, through the throng I make out the smiling, weary faces of Annette, Cara, and Robert across the room. The relief almost overwhelms me.

Everyone is safe.

EPILOGUE

The lights sparkle in the darkness. It's warm, very warm.
I'm looking out from the top deck of the *Aurora Australis*
as the Australian icebreaker makes its way slowly up the dark
gray waters of the River Derwent in Tasmania. We should be at
Hobart within the hour.

It's four o'clock in the morning, and a small group of us have
gathered quietly on the top deck to watch the city's approach.
Only the lapping of the waves and the dull rumble of the engine
vents break the silence. I catch a waft of eucalypt from the val-
ley side. It's the first time I've smelled a tree in over six weeks.

Annette stands beside me. I reach out for her hand and she
turns to me.

"Nearly home," I whisper.

"I can't wait," she says, her eyes full of emotion.

Nearby, Cara and Robert lean on the railings, pointing out
features to one another as the ship moves up the channel.

Together we've had an extraordinary journey.

After our rescue, the *Aurora Australis* returned to Casey to
finish the Antarctic base resupply before heading to Hobart.
While at Casey, we learned the westerly winds Igor had been so

adamant about finally arrived, releasing both the MV *Akademik Shokalskiy* and the *Xue Long* from their icy prisons. We roared and cheered when we received the news. I'm relieved to say the icebergs kept a healthy distance from both vessels during their escape.

During the three weeks we've been on the *Aurora Australis* I've rested and reflected on all that's happened. There's been a lot to process. The Australasian Antarctic Expedition 2013–2014 achieved so much. The team gathered a trove of data on many scientific fronts that promise new insights into how our planet works. Several major research papers have already been planned. The trees on Campbell Island and the Auckland Islands look like they will lead to the first century-long record of westerly winds in the southwest Pacific, while our survey of life on the New Zealand subantarctic sea floor will help future monitoring efforts of these precious archipelagos. From the Southern Ocean, we have some of the first measurements of ocean-mixing across the Antarctic Convergence, helping us understand the importance of this front in ocean circulation and global climate. Farther south, we have a greater knowledge of the impact of giant iceberg B09B on Antarctic Bottom Water formation and life in and around Commonwealth Bay. Excitingly, the rock samples taken across Cape Denison will provide the first direct age control on the changing shape of the East Antarctic Ice Sheet along a 1,500-mile stretch of coastline. These are just some of the many important research projects members of the expedition undertook while we were away. The next few years will be a busy time working it all up for publication.

I feel fiercely proud of all we've achieved. There have been challenges, for sure, but I remain firm in my belief that engaging with the public, exciting people with all that we do, is critical for creating a modern, scientifically literate society. As scientists, we can do so much more to get everyone involved. Making discoveries is one of the most exhilarating of all experiences in life, but one we all too rarely share with others. Thanks to modern satellite technology, the Australasian Antarctic Expedition 2013–2014 broadcast its science from the very edge of the world, sharing our work and findings in the spirit of the first expeditions south. The response has been positively overwhelming. If you're a scientist, I can't encourage you enough to tell your story and see where it takes you. I suspect you'll be pleasantly surprised just how interested people are to learn more.

Importantly, this expedition has also reminded me of things I've taken for granted in recent years. It's shown me what teamwork can achieve. When all's said and done, teamwork made it all possible. Operating in the Antarctic carries inherent risks, and we faced them together. Shackleton and the remarkable men on the *Endurance* inspired me tremendously in this. Their hard-won experiences remain as true today as a century ago, whether at sea, on the ice, or at home. Our expedition did not face nearly the same dangers—something for which I will be eternally grateful—but it was truly a team effort, and one in which I am honored to have played just a small part. Many of us were strangers at the start of the Australasian Antarctic Expedition 2013–2014. Now, lifelong friendships have been forged.

If I'm honest, though, the greatest lesson of all has come from my family. I've realized one unassailable fact: Without them I'm nothing.

I'm never letting you go.

I believe it is in our nature to explore, to reach out into the unknown. The only true failure would be not to explore at all.
—SIR ERNEST SHACKLETON (1874–1922)

ACKNOWLEDGMENTS

I owe a tremendous debt to friends and mentors involved in the expedition. First and foremost, I am inexpressibly grateful to the fantastic team on the Australasian Antarctic Expedition 2013–2014, and I must include here the Heritage staff of Nikki, Nicola, and Brad. We were incredibly fortunate to have such an amazing group of people on board. Few were what you'd describe as expeditioners when we set out, but they braved an intense experience with a level of courage and professionalism that I am in awe of. When everyone returned home, they spoke passionately about the pristine nature of the icescape, the wildlife, the remoteness. They're true ambassadors for Antarctica in the very best sense of the word, testament to the power of the southern continent. It has been a privilege to be part of such a wonderful group of people.

To Chris Fogwill, my co-leader—without your friendship, brilliant scientific insights, constant encouragement and support, and remarkable planning, I know we would never have made it to Cape Denison and through the other side.

To Greg Mortimer for all your help and guidance during preparations and on the expedition—your years of experience helped steady all our nerves.

To the indomitable crew of the MV *Akademik Shokalskiy*,

particularly Captain Igor Kiselev, who were extraordinary in an extraordinary situation. You were astounding.

To the wonderful crews of the *Xue Long*, the *Aurora Australis*, the *Astrolabe,* and the Australian Rescue Coordination Centre, who worked so selflessly to take us to safety, a huge, massive thank you. A big thanks also to the crews of the *Polar Star* and the *Fedorov* for agreeing to make the attempt if all else failed!

The strong team spirit on the MV *Akademik Shokalskiy* would not have been possible without all our family, friends, team members, and sponsors at home. You'll never know just how much all your reassurances helped those on board.

I would like to express a huge debt of gratitude to my Dean, Professor Merlin Crossley, and Head of School, Associate-Professor David Cohen, at the University of New South Wales, for what they did, both publicly and behind the scenes. It made a world of difference. Chris and I were extremely fortunate when the university found a salary for Jonathan Pritchard to help with planning and administration. "Jono," as his friends know him, was someone we relied on . . . a lot. How he dealt with the avalanche of forms, quotes, and payments I'll never know. You're the best, Jono!

A heap of thanks to Leticia and Google Australia for supporting the idea of an Antarctic expedition prize for the Doodle4Google competition and helping us reach out to schools across Australia and New Zealand. To the Commonwealth Bank of Australia for sponsoring the competition prize. And to the National Film and Sound Archive (or NFSA for short) for reaching out during preparations and arranging for me to speak to thousands of school children across the country—you're truly a marvelous institution.

Alvin, you kept me sane managing all the media interest during those intense ten days; thanks to you, I still had time to do my day job on the ship. And you handled it all without hesitation or complaint during the Christmas–New Year holiday period. It was beyond the call of duty!

Anthony Ditton kindly agreed to join us on the first leg. An outdoors enthusiast with awesome technology skills, he helped keep us connected when the equipment threatened to give up. With Ewan and Bec Horsburgh, he developed the brilliant website for the expedition (spiritofmawson.com) and kept it updated during our time in the Antarctic. Thanks, guys!

An enormous thanks to Tim Shadbolt, the Mayor of Invercargill. Irrepressibly good-humored, Tim convinced us to make Bluff the departure point of the expedition. Invercargill is a wonderfully friendly, welcoming city. I can't recommend it enough.

Many thanks to Brent Bevan and his team at the Invercargill office of the New Zealand Department of Conservation. They helped us navigate the application forms to work on the New Zealand subantarctic islands. No question was too daft, no opportunity turned down. It was a breath of fresh air during preparations for the expedition. To Ed Butler, who was at Antarctica New Zealand and kindly provided the Field Operations Guides and First Aid documentation; it was all incredibly useful. I would also like to thank the Australian Antarctic Division for turning around the mountain of permits we submitted for the expedition in a timely and efficient manner, and for the daily weather and weekly sea-ice reports they sent before and during the expedition; they were a tremendous help. Thanks also to Rob Easther for the months of liaison with the Australian Antarctic Division over field operations and permitting; it helped a huge amount, and I know it kept Chris sane!

Our sponsors made a big difference. We had support from the wonderful people at meteoexploration.com, Argo Australia, Macpac, Skycom, Labwarehouse, Ultimate Positioning, Newton Microscopes, and Inmarsat. A large part of the oceanographic program wouldn't have been possible without the U.S. National Oceanic and Atmospheric Administration (NOAA).

The universities of Wisconsin, Exeter, Waikato, and Landcare Research all provided much-needed equipment and ideas. Without you, the science program just wouldn't have happened.

The writing of this book was far from the cathartic experience I had hoped it would be. I'm incredibly grateful to all those who read early drafts and made invaluable comments and suggestions, particularly Chris, Eleanor, and Annette, for whom the return journey was far from easy. My agent Peter McGuigan, the team at Foundry Literary + Media, and Bret Witter helped make this book immeasurably better, giving essential advice and guidance from the start. Without your fantastic support, I'm not sure I would have ever written it. To Michaela Hamilton, Chris Fortunato, and all the lovely people at Kensington Books in New York; Caspian Dennis at Abner Stein in London; Ben Ball, Jeremy Sherlock, and Beth Patch at Penguin Australia, and editor Hilary Reynolds, for their support and insightful, sensitive input—it made a world of difference. Any mistakes of course remain wholly mine.

And last but not least, to my beautiful wife Annette and my wonderful children Cara and Robert, thank you for being by my side through everything. We shared an incredible adventure together and made it back safe, stronger than ever. I'm so sorry it was more exciting than we'd planned, but I really couldn't have done it without you. I love you all so very much.

SOURCES

Expedition Papers and Associated Articles

Clark, G., Marzinelli, E., Fogwill, C.J., Turney, C.S.M., Johnston, E., 2015. Effects of sea-ice cover on marine benthic communities: a natural experiment in Commonwealth Bay, East Antarctica. *Polar Biology* **38**, 1213–1222.

Fogwill, C.J., van Sebille, E., Cougnon, E.A., Turney, C.S.M., Rintoul, S.R., Galton-Fenzi, B.K., Clark, G.F., Marzinelli, E.M., Rainsley, E.B., Carter, L. 2016. Impacts of a developing polynya off Commonwealth Bay, East Antarctica, triggered by grounding of iceberg B09B. *The Cryosphere* **10**, 2603-2609.

Palmer, J.G., Turney, C.S.M., Fogwill, C., Fenwick, P., Thomas, Z., Lipson, M., Jones, R.T., Beavan, B., Richardson, S., Wilmshurst, J. 2017. Growth response of an invasive alien species to climate variations on subantarctic Campbell Island. *New Zealand Journal of Ecology*.

Phipps, S.J., Fogwill, C.J., Turney, C.S.M. 2016. Impacts of marine instability across the East Antarctic Ice Sheet on Southern Ocean dynamics. *The Cryosphere* **10**, 2317-2328.

Rainsley, E., Turney, C.S.M., Golledge, N.R., Wilmshurst, J.M., McGlone, M.S., Hogg, A.G., Thomas, Z.A., Flett, V., Palmer, J.G., Jones, R.T., de Wet, G., Hutchinson, D.K., Lipson,

M.J., Fenwick, P., Hines, B.R., Binetti, U., Fogwill, C.J. In review. Late Pleistocene glacial history of the New Zealand subantarctic islands. *Quaternary Research*.

Turney, C. 2014. This was no Antarctic pleasure cruise. *Nature* **505**, 133.

Turney, C., Fogwill, C., Palmer, J., van Sebille, E., Thomas, Z., McGlone, M., Richardson, S., Wilmshurst, J., Fenwick, P., Zunz, V., Goosse, H., Wilson, K.-J., Carter, L., Lipson, M., Jones, R., Harsch, M., Clark, G., Marzinelli, E., Rogers, T., Rainsley, E., Ciasto, L., Waterman, S., Thomas, E.R. and Visbeck, M. 2017. Tropical forcing of increased Southern Ocean climate variability revealed by a 140-year subantarctic temperature reconstruction. *Climate of the Past* **13**, 231-248, doi: 10.5194/cp-13-231-2017.

Turney, C.S.M., Klekociuk, A., Fogwill, C.J., Zunz, V., Goosse, H., Parkinson, C.L., Compo, G.P., Lazzara, M., Keller, L., Allan, R., Palmer, J.G., Clark, G. and Marzinelli, E. In review. Changing mid-twentieth century Antarctic sea ice variability linked to tropical forcing. *The Cryosphere Discussions*.

Turney, C.S.M., McGlone, M., Palmer, J., Fogwill, C., Hogg, A., Lipson, M., Thomas, Z., Wilmshurst, J., Fenwick, P., Jones, R., Hones, B. and Clark, G. 2016. Intensification of Southern Hemisphere westerly winds 2000 to 1000 years ago: Evidence from the subantarctic Auckland and Campbell Islands (50–52°S). *Journal of Quaternary Science* **31**, 12–19.

Turney, C.S.M., Palmer, J., Hogg, A., Fogwill, C.J., Jones, R., Ramsey, C., Fenwick, P., Grierson, P., Wilmshurst, J., O'Donnell, A., Thomas, Z., and Lipson, M. 2016. Multi-decadal variations in Southern Hemisphere atmospheric ^{14}C: Evidence against a Southern Ocean sink during the Little Ice Age CO_2 anomaly. *Global Biogeochemical Cycles* **30**, doi: 10.1002/2015GB005257.

Tynan, E., 2016. Oceanography: Changing icescapes. *Nature Geoscience* **9**, 869-869.

van Sebille, E., Waterman, S., Barthel, A., Lumpkin, R., Keating, S.R., Fogwill, C. and Turney, C. 2015. Pairwise surface drifter dispersion in the western Pacific Sector of the Southern Ocean. *Journal of Geophysical Research—Oceans* **120**, 6769-6781, doi: 10.1002/2015JC010972.

Wilmshurst, J.M., McGlone, M.S. and Turney, C.S.M. 2015. Integrating pollen and historical records to trace the invasion of a tree daisy (*Olearia lyallii*) on subantarctic Auckland Islands. *Annals of Botany Plants* **7**, doi: 10.1093/aobpla/plv104.

Wilson, K.-J., Barthel, A., Lipson, M., Fogwill, C. and Turney, C. In review. New breeding records and other observations of seabirds on Auckland Islands, Campbell Island and The Snares. *Ornithological Society of New Zealand.*

Wilson, K.-J., Turney, C., Fogwill, C., Blair, E. and Hunter, J. 2016. The impact of the giant iceberg B09B on population size and breeding success of Adélie penguins in Commonwealth Bay, Antarctica. *Antarctic Science*, doi: 10.1017/S0954102015000644.

Wilson, K.-J., Turney, C., Fogwill, C. and Hunter, J. 2015. Low numbers and apparent long-term stability of south polar skuas *Stercorarius maccormicki* at Commonwealth Bay, Antarctica. *Marine Ornithology* **43**, 103–106.

Wood, J.R., Wilmshurst, J.M., Turney, C.S.M. and Fogwill, C. 2016. Palaeoecological signatures of vegetation change induced by herbivory regime shifts on subantarctic Enderby Island. *Quaternary Science Reviews* **134**, 51–58.

Web Resources

If you would like to learn more about the Australasian Antarctic Expedition 2013–2014, including updates on our scientific findings, please visit spiritofmawson.com. Movie footage from the expedition, including the live broadcast of the orca hunt on the edge of Commonwealth Bay, can be found on the Intrepid Science YouTube Channel at youtube.com/intrepid-science. *The Guardian*'s award-winning documentary *Fast Ice:*

Rescue from Antarctica, with interviews of team members, can be viewed at youtube.com/watch?v=TSKEG12UtfA. You can learn more about my research, including how to follow the team on future expeditions, at christurney.com and intrepidscience.com.

Other Reading

Anderson, A., 2005. Subpolar settlement in South Polynesia. *Antiquity* **79**, 791-800.

Bintanja, R., van Oldenborgh, G.J., Drijfhout, S.S., Wouters, B., Katsman, C.A. 2013. Important role for ocean warming and increased ice-shelf melt in Antarctic sea-ice expansion. *Nature Geoscience* **6**, 376–379.

Bromwich, D.H., Steinhoff, D.F., Simmonds, I.A.N., Keay, K., Fogt, R.L. 2011. Climatological aspects of cyclogenesis near Adélie Land Antarctica. *Tellus A* **63**, 921–938.

Childerhouse, S., Michael, S., Adams, L., Burns, T., Cockburn, S., Hamer, D., Maloney, A., Pugsley, C. 2015. *New Zealand sea lion research at the Auckland Islands 2014/15*. Blue Planet Marine, p. 50.

Clark, G.F., Stark, J.S., Johnston, E.L., Runcie, J.W., Goldsworthy, P.M., Raymond, B., Riddle, M.J. 2013. Light-driven tipping points in polar ecosystems. *Global Change Biology* **19**, 3749–3761.

Dingwall, P.R., Jones, K.L., Egerton, R. 2009. *In care of the Southern Ocean: An archaeological and historical survey of the Auckland Islands*. New Zealand Archaeological Association Monograph 27, Auckland.

Fogwill, C.J., Turney, C.S.M., Golledge, N.R., Etheridge, D.M., Rubino, M., Thornton, D.P., Baker, A., Woodward, J., Winter, K., van Ommen, T.D., Moy, A.D., Curran, M.A.J., Davies, S.M., Weber, M.E., Bird, M.I., Munksgaard, N.C., Menviel, L., Rootes, C.M., Ellis, B., Millman, H., Vohra, J., Rivera, A., Cooper, A. 2017. Antarctic ice sheet discharge driven by atmosphere-ocean feedbacks at the Last Glacial Termination. *Scientific Reports* **7**, 39979.

Fogwill, C.J., Phipps, S.J., Turney, C.S.M., Golledge, N.R. 2015. Sensitivity of the Southern Ocean to enhanced regional Antarctic ice sheet meltwater input. *Earth's Future* **3**, doi: 10.1002/2015EF000306.

Fogwill, C.J., Turney, C.S.M., Golledge, N.R., Rood, D.H., Hippe, K., Wacker, L., Wieler, R., Rainsley, E.B., Jones, R.S. 2014a. Drivers of abrupt Holocene shifts in West Antarctic ice stream direction determined from combined ice sheet modelling and geologic signatures. *Antarctic Science* **26**, 674–686.

Fogwill, C.J., Turney, C.S.M., Meissner, K.J., Golledge, N.R., Spence, P., Roberts, J.L., England, M.H., Jones, R.T., Carter, L. 2014b. Testing the sensitivity of the East Antarctic Ice Sheet to Southern Ocean dynamics: past changes and future implications. *Journal of Quaternary Science* **29**, 91–98.

Gille, S.T. 2002. Warming of the Southern Ocean since the 1950s. *Science* **295**, 1275–1277.

Golledge, N.R., Kowalewski, D.E., Naish, T.R., Levy, R.H., Fogwill, C.J., Gasson, E.G.W. 2015. The multi-millennial Antarctic commitment to future sea-level rise. *Nature* **526**, 421–425.

Hall-Aspland, S.A., Rogers, T.L., Canfield, R.B. 2005. Stable carbon and nitrogen isotope analysis reveals seasonal variation in the diet of leopard seals. *Marine Ecology Progress Series* **305**, 249-259.

Herbert, W., 1969. *Across the Top of the World: The British Trans-Arctic Expedition*. Longmans, London.

Holland, P.R., Kwok, R. 2012. Wind-driven trends in Antarctic sea-ice drift. *Nature Geoscience* **5**, 872–875.

Jones, R.T., Turney, C.S.M., Lang, B., Brooks, S.J., Rundgren, M., Hammarlund, D., Björck, S., Fogwill, C.J. 2017. Delayed maximum northern European summer temperatures during the Last Interglacial as a result of Greenland Ice Sheet melt. *Geology* **45**, 23-26.

Kusahara, K., Hasumi, H., Williams, G.D. 2011. Impact of the Mertz Glacier Tongue calving on dense water formation and export. *Nature Communications* **2**, 159, doi: 110.1038/ncomms1156.

Maddison, B. 2015. *Class and Colonialism in Antarctic Exploration, 1750–1920*. Routledge, London.

McGlone, M.S. 2002. The late Quaternary peat, vegetation and climate history of the southern oceanic islands of New Zealand. *Quaternary Science Reviews* **21**, 683–707.

McGlone, M.S., Turney, C.S.M., Wilmshurst, J.M., Pahnke, K. 2010. Divergent trends in land and ocean temperature in the Southern Ocean over the past 18,000 years. *Nature Geoscience* **3**, 622-626.

McGonigal, D., Woodworth, L., 2001. *Antarctica: The Complete Story*. Frances Lincoln Ltd, London.

Mengel, M., Levermann, A. 2014. Ice plug prevents irreversible discharge from East Antarctica. *Nature Climate Change* **4**, 451–455.

Metcalf, J.L., Turney, C., Barnett, R., Martin, F., Bray, S.C., Vilstrup, J.T., Orlando, L., Salas-Gismondi, R., Loponte, D., Medina, M., De Nigris, M., Civalero, T., Fernández, P.M., Gasco, A., Duran, V., Seymour, K.L., Otaola, C., Gil, A., Paunero, R., Prevosti, F.J., Bradshaw, C.J.A., Wheeler, J.C., Borrero, L., Austin, J.J., Cooper, A. 2016. Synergistic roles of climate warming and human occupation in Patagonian megafaunal extinctions during the Last Deglaciation. *Science Advances* **2**, doi: 10.1126/sciadv.1501682.

Miles, B.W.J., Stokes, C.R., Vieli, A., Cox, N.J. 2013. Rapid, climate-driven changes in outlet glaciers on the Pacific coast of East Antarctica. *Nature* **500**, 563–566.

Morrison, K.W., Battley, P.F., Sagar, P.M., Thompson, D.R. 2015. Population dynamics of Eastern Rockhopper Penguins on Campbell Island in relation to sea surface temperature 1942–2012: current warming hiatus pauses a long-term decline. *Polar Biology* **38**, 163–177.

Parish, T.R., Walker, R. 2006. A re-examination of the winds of Adélie Land, Antarctica. *Australian Meteorological Magazine* **55**, 105–117.

Rignot, E., Bamber, J.L., van den Broeke, M.R., Davis, C., Li, Y., van de Berg, W., van Meijaard, E. 2008. Recent Antarctic ice mass loss from radar interferometry and regional climate modelling. *Nature Geoscience* **1**, 106–110.

Rintoul, S.R. 2007. Rapid freshening of Antarctic Bottom Water formed in the Indian and Pacific oceans. *Geophysical Research Letters* **34**, L06606.

Rogers, T.L., Ciaglia, M.B., Klinck, H., Southwell, C. 2013. Density can be misleading for low-density species: benefits of passive acoustic monitoring. *PloS One* **8**, e52542.

Shadwick, E.H., Rintoul, S.R., Tilbrook, B., Williams, G.D., Young, N., Fraser, A.D., Marchant, H., Smith, H., Tamura, T. 2013. Glacier tongue calving reduced dense water formation and enhanced carbon uptake. *Geophysical Research Letters* **40**, 904–909.

Tamura, T., Williams, G.D., Fraser, A.D., Ohshima, K.I. 2012. Potential regime shift in decreased sea ice production after the Mertz Glacier calving. *Nature Communications* **3**, 826.

Thompson, D.W.J., Solomon, S. 2002. Interpretation of recent Southern Hemisphere climate change. *Science* **296**, 895–899.

Trathan, P.N., Forcada, J., Murphy, E.J. 2007. Environmental forcing and Southern Ocean marine predator populations: Effects of climate change and variability. *Philosophical Transactions of the Royal Society B: Biological Sciences* **362**, 2351–2365.

Turney, C.S.M., Kershaw, A.P., Clemens, S.C., Branch, N., Moss, P.T., Fifield, L.K. 2004. Millennial and orbital variations of El Niño/Southern Oscillation and high-latitude climate in the last glacial period. *Nature* **428**, 306–310.

Turney, C.S.M., Jones, R.T. 2010. Does the Agulhas Current

amplify global temperatures during super-interglacials? *Journal of Quaternary Science* **25**, 839–843.

Turney, C., Fogwill, C., Van Ommen, T.D., Moy, A.D., Etheridge, D., Rubino, M., Curran, M.A.J., Rivera, A. 2013. Late Pleistocene and early Holocene change in the Weddell Sea: a new climate record from the Patriot Hills, Ellsworth Mountains, West Antarctica. *Journal of Quaternary Science* **28**, 697–704.

Turney, C.S.M., Fogwill, C.J., Klekociuk, A.R., van Ommen, T.D., Curran, M.A.J., Moy, A.D., Palmer, J.G. 2015. Tropical and mid-latitude forcing of continental Antarctic temperatures. *The Cryosphere* **9**, 2405–2415.

Turney, C.S.M., Jones, R.T., Fogwill, C., Hatton, J., Williams, A.N., Hogg, A., Thomas, Z.A., Palmer, J., Mooney, S., Reimer, R.W. 2016. A 250-year periodicity in Southern Hemisphere westerly winds over the last 2600 years. *Climate of the Past* **12**, 189–200.

Turney, C.S.M., Palmer, J., Bronk Ramsey, C., Adolphi, F., Muscheler, R., Hughen, K.A., Staff, R.A., Jones, R.T., Thomas, Z.A., Fogwill, C.J., Hogg, A. 2016. High-precision dating and correlation of ice, marine and terrestrial sequences spanning Heinrich Event 3: Testing mechanisms of interhemispheric change using New Zealand ancient kauri (*Agathis australis*). *Quaternary Science Reviews* **137**, 126–134.

Warner, R.C., Budd, W.K. 1998. Modelling the long-term response of the Antarctic ice sheet to global warming. *Annals of Glaciology* **27**, 161–168.

Williams, G.D., Bindoff, N.L. 2003. Wintertime oceanography of the Adélie Depression. *Deep Sea Research Part II: Topical Studies in Oceanography* **50**, 1373–1392.

Wilson, K.-J. 1990. Fluctuations in populations of Adélie penguins at Cape Bird, Antarctica. *Polar Record* **26**, 305-308.

Ernest Shackleton and the Imperial Trans-Antarctic Expedition (1914–1916)

Huntford, R. 1996. *Shackleton*. Abacus, London.

Hurley, F. 1914–1916. *The Imperial Tran-Antarctic Expedition Diaries* can be viewed online at http://www.sl.nsw.gov.au/frank-hurleys-diaries. Mitchell Library, State Library of New South Wales.

———1925. *Argonauts of the South*. G.P. Putnam's Sons, New York.

———2001. *South with Endurance: Shackleton's Antarctic Expedition 1914–1917*. Viking, Camberwell, Australia.

———2011. *The Diaries of Frank Hurley 1912–1941*. Anthem Press, London.

Hussey, L.D.A. 1949. *South with Shackleton*. Sampson Low, London.

Mill, H.R. 1923. *The Life of Sir Ernest Shackleton*. William Heinemann Ltd, London.

Morrell, M., Capparell, S. 2003. *Shackleton's Way: Leadership Lessons from the Great Antarctic Explorer*. Nicholas Brealey Publishing, London.

Shackleton, E. 2002. *South: The Endurance Expedition to Antarctic*a (1919). The Text Publishing Company, Melbourne.

Shackleton, E. 1912. The future of exploration. *The North American Review* **195**, 414–424.

Thomson, J. 2003. *Elephant Island and Beyond: The Life and Diaries of Thomas Orde-Lees*. Bluntisham Books and The Erskine Press, Norwich.

Worsley, F.A. 1931. *Endurance: An Epic of Polar Adventure*. Jonathan Cape and Harrison Smith, New York.

Douglas Mawson and the Australasian Antarctic Expedition (1911–1914)

Turney, C. 2012. *1912: The Year the World Discovered Antarctica*. Text Publishing, Melbourne.

Bickel, L. 2000. *Mawson's Will: The Greatest Polar Survival Story Ever Written*. Steerforth Press, Hanover, NH.

Flannery, N.R. 2005. *This Everlasting Silence: The Love Letters of Paquita Delprat and Douglas Mawson 1911–1914*. Melbourne University Press, Melbourne.

Jacka, F., Jacka, E. 1988. *Mawson's Antarctic Diaries*. Allen and Unwin, London.

Madigan, C.T. 2012. *Madigan's Account: The Mawson Expedition*. Wellington Bridge Press, Hobart.

Mawson, D. 1915. *The Home of the Blizzard: Being the Story of the Australasian Antarctic Expedition, 1911–1914*. William Heinemann, London.

Mawson, P., 1964. *Mawson of the Antarctic*. Longmans, Green and Co Ltd, London.

INDEX

ABOUT THE AUTHOR

Earth scientist CHRIS TURNEY is the author of *1912: The Year the World Discovered Antarctica, Bones, Rocks and Stars: The Science of When Things Happened*, and *Ice, Mud and Blood: Lessons from Climates Past*. His numerous awards include the Sir Nicholas Shackleton Medal for pioneering research into climate change (2007). He is currently Professor of Climate Change and Earth Sciences at the University of New South Wales, Australia. You can learn more about Chris's research and expeditions at www.christurney.com and www.intrepidscience.com.